MEDIA
FOR
MANAGERS

FRANK M. CORRADO

Adjunct Associate Professor
J. L. Kellogg Graduate School of Management
Northwestern University

PRENTICE-HALL, INC., *Englewood Cliffs, NJ 07632*

Library of Congress Cataloging in Publication Data

CORRADO, FRANK M. (date)
  Media for managers.

  Includes bibliographical references and index.
  1. Public relations.   2. Communication in management.
I. Title.
HD59.C64   1984   658.4'5   83-8705
ISBN   0-13-572446-5

Editorial/production supervision and interior design: Maureen Wilson
Cover design: Christine Gehring-Wolf
Manufacturing buyer: Ed O'Dougherty

Printed in the United States of America

10 9 8 7 6 5 4 3 2 1

ISBN 0-13-572446-5

PRENTICE-HALL INTERNATIONAL, INC., *London*
PRENTICE-HALL OF AUSTRALIA PTY. LIMITED, *Sydney*
EDITORA PRENTICE-HALL DO BRASIL, LTDA., *Rio de Janeiro*
PRENTICE-HALL CANADA INC., *Toronto*
PRENTICE-HALL OF INDIA PRIVATE LIMITED, *New Delhi*
PRENTICE-HALL OF JAPAN, INC., *Tokyo*
PRENTICE-HALL OF SOUTHEAST ASIA PTE. LTD., *Singapore*
WHITEHALL BOOKS LIMITED, *Wellington, New Zealand*

To the long grey line of ghosts who taught me what it means to be a reporter and good PR person . . . but especially to Rick Rowden, who showed me how to apply the seat of the pants to the seat of the chair, and Dick Sullivan, who will always be there when the circus comes to town

and

To Valdas Adamkus, who opened all the doors

Contents

Foreword

The story goes that the chief executive of a drill bit producing company was interviewing a variety of candidates for the job of chief engineer. Of each successive candidate, the executive asked, "What does our company do?" With predictable regularity the answer came back, "This company makes drill bits."

Finally, one candidate showed the spark the chief executive was looking for. To the standard question, "What does this company do?" the successful candidate answered, "This company helps its customers make holes in surfaces." By defining the company more widely and more adequately, the successful candidate demonstrated a capacity to remain open to new engineering and marketing possibilities.

As this story shows, nothing is so important to the success of a company as an adequate understanding of its nature, particularly on the part of its officers and managers. The theme of this important book by Frank M. Corrado deals directly with the question of how a corporation should be defined. His argument—an argument to which I wholeheartedly subscribe—is that, increasingly, American corporations must be understood more broadly than as simple economic entities.

Of course, the corporation must seek a profit in order to exist. But it is allowed to pursue that goal—it is allowed to *exist*—only to the degree that it is seen to be satisfactorily meeting some of society's needs. It is, after all, society that sanctions the corporation, and it is from society that corporations must continuously earn their right to operate.

Society is not an undifferentiated mass. From the point of view of the corporation, society is usefully seen as a variety of different stakeholders, or constituents—that is, those groups whose interests are affected by the operations of the corporation. The roster of such groups includes the stockholders, of course, but it also includes the employees, annuitants, customers, the local communities, governmental bodies, and, in the case of the multinational enterprise, the home and the host countries.

With rare exceptions, it is not possible to fully satisfy all these constituencies simultaneously. But to only partially satisfy all of them is to partially *dissatisfy* all of them. In fact, the critics of the corporation are often just dissatisfied constituents.

What has recently been called an increasing chorus of criticism of corporations is simply a consequence of the increasing public interest, awareness, and concern with corporations—a concern that business give an accounting of its actions to the public, and that it maintain open communication with its constituents.

Without question, these new demands pose new burdens and new tasks on businesses which are more accustomed to operating outside the glare of public scrutiny.

But there's no turning back the clock. Nor, I think, should we want to. This same spirit of public questioning, debate, and criticism both inspires our free enterprise system and undergirds our political liberties. In fact the two are closely bound together. It's no mere accident that we talk of the "marketplace of ideas."

In this new atmosphere, the responsibility for fulfilling the public expectations of the corporation for openness and responsiveness falls on all of its officers and managers. Put simply, just as war is too important to be left solely to the generals, corporate communications are too important to be left entirely to the communications professionals.

This book is designed for all managers wise enough to recognize their responsibilities in the public realm. It will richly reward their efforts to master its lessons.

JAMES E. LEE

Chairman, President, and
Chief Executive Officer
Gulf Oil Corporation

Preface

In the last decade, American business people have learned a hard lesson: there is competition beyond the marketplace. That new competition is for the hearts and minds of people in our society, in the marketplace of social and political values.

It no longer is enough to just be "for prosperity." Business has learned it has to support new societal goals as well: a safe workplace, clean air, products that perform as advertised. Business has learned that it is important to take time to understand that the public interest group crusades aligned to those issues have really been a manifestation of a deeper change in society. Society has begun to look at business in a broader context than purely "economic." Society sees business now as an "institution" with attendant public responsibilities, as well as private ones.

And while the eighties have brought in a period of less restrictive government policies towards business, the performance expectations of the public for business have remained high, especially since the deep economic recession began to bring about a fundamental restructuring of American industry.

In this period of significant change, a major imperative that has come forward has been the need for business to communicate more effectively with its constituencies, especially employees and investors. Going into the eighties, the current generation of managers was faced with the need to learn how to deal with more nonmanagerial issues, and began spending an increasing amount of time making speeches, presenting testimony, and dealing with interest groups and the media. A study by the Conference Board in 1981 concluded that managerial competence in public affairs is already considered by many senior managers to be an "essential managerial attitude."

Managers have learned that in the new marketplace of ideas, it is incumbent upon them to develop a perspective, a way of thinking that provides them with a facility in dealing with constituencies, arguing proactively and aggressively the corporate vision expressed by the board. Now, with a major information/

communications revolution underway in American society, corporate communications is about to assume a major role in corporate governance.

Already in many firms the communications function has been elevated in status from the director level to a vice presidential one. At the same time, companies are beginning to look at new organizational schemes that will help them manage an environment that is undergoing dramatic technological upheaval. The new technologies may fundamentally change both the organization itself and the way management is practiced. The eighties, as John Naisbitt has said in his book, *Megatrends*, are a time of "parenthesis," where we are sorting out the future and its relation to our past. Communications and information are the major change agents of this period.

More practically, in the current environment effective communications strategy and tactics can make important, specific contributions:

- in helping value the firm correctly in the marketplace so as to maximize shareholder value and lessen chances of unfriendly takeover.
- in building employee morale and effectiveness in difficult economic times, thus increasing productivity and profitability.
- in improving the marketing of products by lending credibility to their efficacy and value.
- in managing crisis.

Traditionally, managers have had difficulty in developing either a perspective or a competence in communications. This is due in part to a lack of emphasis placed on it in our major business schools. Also, there are few books available that look at communications from the *manager's* perspective. *Media for Managers* is an attempt to present in one book most of the major communications issues facing managers in the eighties. The book is not limited to "public relations" or "public affairs" or "communications," nor does it specifically deal with communications from an organizational behaviorist's point of view, but rather it attempts to provide a broad overview for managers.

The book is divided into three major sections. The first covers generally the principles of communications management: how a corporate vision is established and iterated in policy, how the staff function is addressed organizationally, and its internal and external components. The second section looks at the practice of communications management, with special attention to news media dealings, crisis communications, and financial relations. A third section of the book addresses the new communications and information technologies and how they will impact business and society. A final chapter summarizes the main points of the book and offers a series of questions that managers may find useful in helping evaluate their companies. In addition, there are several appendices that cover credibility and crisis planning, with a special section on communications issues for public and nonprofit organizations.

If the seventies showed us that the economic performance of a company can be impacted by noneconomic events, the eighties are showing us that communications directly impacts profits, effectiveness, and productivity in a global marketplace. The nineties will show us a world of communications and information beyond our dreams. Information in our society will be both the "power" and the "capital" of that era. No company can expect to survive this coming age unless it understands this. Communications competency for managers is no longer optional.

Nobody writes a book by themselves and I must acknowledge many people who helped out during the last two years. I am especially indebted to my students at the J. L. Kellogg Graduate School of Management at Northwestern University who aided me in developing the ideas that became this book and refining initial thoughts into specific words. Two of those students, Allison Fielding Zepp and Barbara Goodman, provided research help for Chapters One and Nine. I am also very grateful to my colleagues at Northwestern who gave me the time and encouragement to pursue this effort, including Donald Haider, Hervey Juris, and Elliot Zashin. Also, a number of professionals in the news and public relations business gave assistance at key points: Harlan Draeger of the *Chicago Sun Times*, William Farrell of *The New York Times*, Leonard Thebergé of The Media Institute, Jim Horton of Robert Marsten & Associates, Ray Ewing of Allstate Insurance Co., and Nan Kilearry of Montgomery Ward and Co. Richard Hyde of Hill and Knowlton was instrumental at many key points in the development of this book, especially with the chapter on crisis communications. Larry Newman of Manning, Selvage & Lee provided me with a good understanding of strategy and tactics; and my old boss, Bill Ruckelshaus, and his associate Bill Oliver from The Weyerhauser Company gave me some excellent insights on profits and communications.

As a first time author I am especially grateful to the staff of Prentice-Hall, including Jayne Maerker, Maureen Wilson, Paul Misselwitz, and their associates, but most of all to Frank Enenbach who provided the encouragement that made all this happen. My editor Jennifer Alter and typists Dorothy Dersch and Suzanne Daleen nursed me through to a final draft. Ann Kaseberg, our departmental assistant at Kellogg cheered me up through a tough summer and I am grateful to her as well as to my family—Karen, Kelli, Mike, and Joe, and my parents and brother, who have had so much to do with everything.

The New Marketplace

1

A PERFECT OPPORTUNITY

Study the excellent companies and you find that invariably good profits go together with good working conditions and open communications. You almost can't have one without the other.

—James Beré, CEO
Borg-Warner

Public expectations for business began increasing in the mid-seventies. A 1974 poll by Opinion Research Corporation showed that 70 percent of the American public felt business had a moral obligation to help other institutions achieve social progress. More recent polls continue to confirm these expectations.[1]

The environment following the 1980 Presidential election has seemed opportune for American business to prove its oft-stated contention that it can outperform government in protecting consumer, worker, and citizen and provide services and goods in an efficient manner. Said the White House consumer affairs adviser, "This will be a golden opportunity for the business world to prove what they have been claiming for so long, that they can protect the consumer better than government."[2]

Looking at the 1980 election historically, it was the third time in this century that business had been given that golden opportunity to provide national leadership. In each of the two previous instances, that leadership when presented an opportunity had failed to meet public expectations. In the early 1900s, there were attacks by muckrakers, populists, social gospel advocates, and trade unionists united under the banner of "progressivism" against the abuses of Social Darwinism and absolute free enterprise. Antitrust legislation and federal and state laws regulating employment, food, drugs, and interstate commerce resulted. These statutes set the boundaries of the modern free-enterprise system.

1

From around 1916 to 1930 business was given its second opportunity to provide leadership. At the start of the Great Depression, however, government again intervened to provide a minimal economic base for citizens and to more closely regulate the exchange of securities. Social security, health and education support, and economic-development services were the outgrowth of this period of strong government presence in the marketplace.

The period following World War II provided an environment for significant business growth as a nation, starved by war, began to regain its balance and satisfy its hunger for consumer goods. But with prosperity, a new generation, unfamiliar with war and depression, began to look for a quality of life beyond corporate bounds. That search for a quality of life beyond the satisfaction of economic need resulted in the interest-group attacks of the seventies and the growth of strong expectations for business participation in solving societal problems.

BLURRED TURF LINES

The start of the eighties, with a new probusiness attitude in government and greater tolerance by the public, might induce some managers to forget the hard lessons of American twentieth-century history. The changing times could tempt business leadership to turn its back on the external environment and "tend to business." Enticing as such a strategy might be, it would be careless and unmindful of history. Should business fail to measure up to the expectations now established for it by the present political leadership, public confidence and approval will be ephemeral at best and a turn toward national economic planning may emerge.

It would be a serious mistake for managers to misread the political environment of the eighties. The new freedom to act with less government regulation is tied to execution of an implicit performance contract. "The public agenda of private companies will have to be rethought if the assertion of its new role is to carry a moral, economic, or even a political legitimacy," cautions one observer.[3]

With a deepening recession and rising unemployment, corporate America's image suffered throughout 1982 as poll after poll showed increasing hostility toward American business.

Much of that anger seemed to be pointed toward senior corporate managers who in many publicized instances were perceived to have spent enormous sums to acquire other companies or to protect themselves with "golden parachutes," who closed down plants that might have been left open, or who had shown great insensitivity to their employees. "Are such managers tarred and feathered and ridden out of town on a rail?" asked one observer. "Not today, not in this nonaccountable corporate culture, where great corporations are terminally mismanaged until they shudder and crash, obliterating the aspirations, dreams, and personal economies of workers, investors, and communities, while movers and shakers who brought them to this pass withdraw like ghosts to the cosseted limbos of the old-boy network, conveyed from the smoking ruins in limousines with tinted windows."[4] Some of the negative business stories of 1982 supporting these contentions include the Bendix takeover fight for Martin Marietta, the fall of DeLorean motors, the Penn Square Bank collapse, the Christmas shutdown of the Lackawana, New York, steel plant, and the debacle at International Harvester.

Business news was front page news in the early 1980s and management more than ever was on display. The old business school creeds of short-term maximization of profits no longer were playing on a stage that had developed a Kabuki flavor to it, as Japan showed the world that long-term, economic vision and a society-oriented culture was the new name of the game.

What this means for the manager is that the turf lines between what is strictly "public" and what is "private" are now unclear. Managers are traditionally taught to concern themselves with the marketplace, but they can see that outside forces have been increasingly affecting their economic activity. As Professor George Cabot Lodge of Harvard University has been saying for some years now, traditional business ideology—individualism, property rights, competition, the limited state, and specialization—are being modified to conform with a new reality of community primacy, the rights and duties of membership, and business-government partnership.[5]

Today's postindustrial society, says Lodge, is pluralist and demands from its institutions that they take responsibility beyond their own specific mission. Profitability and shareholder responsibility are no longer the only criteria of the business creed. When GM acts, for example, it affects many Americans who are not necessarily its consumers, employees, or stockholders. Whole regions are affected, whole groups of people not immediately a part of the megacorporation.

In this new environment managers find themselves exercising a "political" function in responding to demands from affected individuals and groups. Business managers no longer find it possible to say, "We will stick to doing what we do best and ignore the demands of all constituencies other than stockholders." Managers, says author and consultant Peter Drucker, "will have to learn to operate in a political environment." He adds, "Managers will find increasingly that in turbulent times they have to be leaders and integrators in a pluralist society, in addition to managing their institutions."[6]

THE NEW CONSTITUENCIES

Among lessons of the seventies is one that clearly shows managers must go beyond the economic milieu, that constituencies of the firm include not only stockholders, employees, and customers but government agencies, legislatures, communities, special-interest groups, the press, and even the general public.

By nature, managers are directed inwards in their thinking, toward the firm.

They prefer the structured, authoritarian, quantitatively organized world they were trained for. "The business of business is business," says Nobel Prize-winning economist Milton Friedman. But in fact, top corporate managers have found it necessary to spend more and more of their time dealing with the noneconomic environment.

Companies have opened offices in state capitals and in Washington. They have met with public-interest groups; they have initiated programs to track public issues. They have become more accessible to the press. They are appearing more frequently before public groups. They have become more involved with trade associations and political-action committees in order to establish countervailing forces to activist public-interest and consumer groups.

Two hundred chief-executive officers interviewed in 1976 and again in 1979 reported spending more than half their time on public issues in 1979 as compared to 20 percent in 1976. A 1981 study by the Conference Board noted that experience in dealing with public issues was becoming requisite for advancement to senior management. In the past, reminisced E. I. Du Pont's former chairman, Irving Shapiro, "You could get by in business by following four rules: stick to business, stay out of trouble, join the right clubs, and don't talk to reporters."[7]

Today, however, failure to be aware of the external environment and to plan for arguing the company's case can often result in unfriendly takeovers, delays in construction, consumer boycotts, government intrusion, and other impediments to conducting business. Policies that implement a strategy for dealing with multiple constituencies must be developed. A corporate official notes, "Companies like ours are a public institution with several publics to account to, not just shareholders. . . . Part of my job is to be a public figure and to take positions on public issues, not just company activities."[8]

THE NEED FOR A
CREDIBLE VISION

Whose job is it to develop the firm's strategy for arguing its case with constituencies? Whose job is it to establish the company's image in both an economic and a noneconomic context? The chief executive and his senior staff? Division managers? The communications department?

William C. Norris, chairman of Control Data Corporation, which has positioned itself as a business that hopes to profit by tackling societal problems in health, education, and medicine, firmly insists that responsibility for involvement in the new marketplace rests with the board of directors.

"Directors must foster the creation of a new business culture," he states. "Indeed, in many companies only in the board room can the necessary actions take place . . . to create a new climate where business and government work together to deal with the problems of society."[9]

A *corporate vision*, developed by the board and communicated to its various internal and external publics, positions that company in both the economic and the noneconomic marketplaces. If that vision is consistently applied and explained in terms of its impacts on economic and noneconomic constituencies, credible positions can be taken on many issues. A company that speaks out only to be heard rather than from a credible vision will never be as successful in the public marketplace.

The vision of the board of directors is the single most important corporate document. It establishes the economic mission of the firm and at the same time, if properly developed, acknowledges the firm's responsibility as an institution committed to the betterment of society.

A clear corporate vision is necessary not only for public consumption. As William G. Ouchi points out in his popular book, *Theory Z*, a clear corporate vision or philosophy is at the very heart of the new and very successful Japanese-style management approaches. "The statement of objectives," he writes, "should include more than financial objectives such as the rate of growth and of profitability. It should also include less tangible objectives such as the rate of technological advance and the quality of service to customers."

He emphasizes that the philosophy of firms "must relate the organization to its wider environment." Ouchi shows how a number of companies—Hewlett-Packard, Dayton-Hudson, Rockwell, Eli Lilly, and Intel, among others,—have moved in this direction. In the Dayton-Hudson Co. statement of corporate philosophy, for example, Ouchi notes that the corporate vision specifies how the company "can serve each constituency," with details on such topics as "observing the highest legal, ethical, and moral standard" and a promise to "contribute annually 5 percent of taxable income to improve the communities of which the company is a part."

He sees the benefits of such an approach from a practical business viewpoint, noting that a well-articulated philosophy gives everybody in the company a sense of purpose and uniqueness and brings about a certain "efficiency in planning and coordination between people who share in this common culture."[10]

COMMUNICATING THE NEED FOR CHANGE

Not only is there a need for strong corporation vision, but there is developing a need for better communication of that vision to the organization's constituencies, especially employees. In many organizations, a new vision means an overhaul of the company's culture—the history, the mythology, the traditions, the way things are done—that determines its successes or failure. The great economic shakeout of the early 1980s has forced many firms to redefine that vision—What business are they really in? What business should they be in? Many old-line manufacturing companies, especially in the frost belt, are realizing that they must reorient themselves to the new information/communication society that is emerging. They realize they must start changing the way their companies are run. Their culture is moving from a production orientation to a marketing orientation and from regulated to deregulated business environments. Already, large corporations like Pepsi, Sears, and AT&T have undertaken this process. This does not happen overnight (although AT&T is trying to accomplish just that). Usually it takes years of continuous management communication and emphasis to install such a culture. It took Pepsi fifteen years to go from a comfortable second to an aggressive competitor. Seven years of emphasis by the chairman on a credo of service to customers paid off brilliantly for Johnson & Johnson when the Tylenol crisis hit in 1982.

Credibility is what makes the corporate vision hard and durable, like steel. Credibility is the *value* that is given to words or actions. It relates to their worth or trustworthiness. Many companies produce goods of one kind or another and assign to those goods a value. But the real value of the product comes in the marketplace, where it is judged and valued against all others. This analogy transfers readily to credibility. Companies can communicate whatever message they want to at whatever volume they can afford. But the message will be given its value in the marketplace of ideas, just as goods are given their value in the marketplace. If a firm's message engenders believability, it will be more highly valued. (See Appendix 1.)

Since business has suffered credibility problems on several occasions throughout this century, people continue to distrust it as an institution committed to societal improvement. On the other hand, business is the sum of many parts, and some of the parts are good and some are bad. In the long run, companies are evaluated like people: If they don't speak and act consistently, it will eventually become obvious, and any attempts to create an "image" will not be lasting. A positive corporate image is never a product, it is a byproduct of credibility.

The actual development and statement of a *credible* corporate vision begins in the board room. If the board's vision is limited to "We are in business to maximize profits to our shareholders," then it would appear the company has little or no mandate to defend itself in the noneconomic environment. Over the years there has been litigation to attempt to define to what lengths a company can go in expending funds to protect itself from noneconomic attacks. In 1978 the Supreme Court ruled that corporations have the right to get involved in strictly noneconomic events such as state referenda. In *First National Bank of Boston v. Belotti*, the court said that free speech rights of corporations were protected.

THE GENERIC IMAGE
PROBLEM

The emphasis of this book is on managing communications at the *micro* level, at the manager's level. Nevertheless, it is important to touch at least briefly on the *macro* problem of the generally negative image society maintains of business.

Public-opinion polls throughout this century have shown a general public distrust of business. That image continues to be reinforced in the present environment through the mass media, especially television.

In the spring of 1981 the Media Institute, a corporate-financed Washington research organization, which keeps track of media coverage of business, issued a report showing that business people are portrayed as "crooks, conmen, or clowns" in two-thirds of all television programming.[11] More than half these shows portray businessmen engaged in some criminal activity, the report states. It confirms the conclusions of a 1979 book, *The View from Sunset Boulevard*, in which author Ben Stein wrote: "One of the clearest messages of television is that businessmen are bad, evil people." They are portrayed, said Stein, as fools, bullies, conmen, fat and sleazy, hard-hearted, cruel, conniving, and often with underworld connections. This perception reflects the opinions of the writers and producers of these shows, Stein contends.[12]

Television is not the only medium that has been unkind to business over the years. Movies and publishing have contributed to the negative image as well. *Network, The China Syndrome, The Formula, Body Heat,* and *Norma Rae* have perpetuated the negative image. In publishing, books such as Paul Erdman's *The Crash of '79,* John DeLorean's *On A Clear Day You Can Almost See General Motors,* and numerous popular novels keep up the perception.

Overcoming these images will take time and concerted effort. It is ironic that large corporate television advertisers who have shown themselves concerned over sex and violence on TV, and who have been responsive to criticism from groups protesting their sponsorship of such shows, have not been effective in influencing their own depiction. This problem of generic credibility must be treated as a separate subject, but at some point it must be addressed if American business is to move to a stronger arguing position in the marketplace of ideas.

SUMMARY   1. Business leadership in the eighties has a new opportunity to increase credibility and exert public leadership.

2. Business is operating in a new environment where the lines between what is public and what is private have blurred.

3. The firm through its board of directors must establish a credible vision that responds to both shareholder and public expectations.

4. Communications is becoming more important to the economic mission of the firm.

5. Business must overcome a negative generic image.

NOTES

1. Florence Skelley, executive vice president, Yankelovich, Skelley and White, remarks before the Chicago chapter, Public Relations Society of America, February 27, 1981. Ms. Skelley suggests that people in the eighties are asking business to solve numerous social issues not because they feel business is more responsible than government but because they feel business has a talent for solving problems.

2. *New York Times*, April 4, 1980.

3. Donald Haider, "Change Partners, Government Is Out, Business Is In," *Chicago Tribune*, August 2, 1981.

4. Michael M. Thomas, "Peanuts," *The New York Times*, October 22, 1982, p. 29.

5. George Cabot Lodge, "Top Priority: Renovating Our Ideology," in Frederick S. Lane, *Current Issues in Public Administration* (New York: St. Martin's Press, 1978), p. 437.

6. Peter F. Drucker, *Managing in Turbulent Times*, (New York: Harper & Row, 1980), pp. 220–21.

7. Quoted in James W. Singer, "Behind the New Aggressiveness," *National Journal*, August 16, 1980, p. 1367.

8. See "PR to the Rescue," *BusinessWeek*, January 22, 1979, p. 50.

9. William C. Norris, "Corporate Policies for Creating a New Business Culture," remarks for delivery at Northwestern University, November 5, 1980.

10. William G. Ouchi, *Theory Z* (New York: Avon Books, 1981), pp. 111–27.

11. "Crooks, Conmen, and Clowns" (Washington, D.C.: Media Institute, 1981).

12. Ben Stein, *The View from Sunset Boulevard* (New York: Basic Books, 1979), p. 15.

Communications Management

2

A NEW PRIORITY FOR
THE EIGHTIES

The process of stating a clear corporate vision cannot be minimized but neither can the process of communicating that vision effectively both within and without the organization. In this decade CEOs are learning the importance of not only developing a strategic message through their board and senior managers, but also learning the importance of taking that message to constituencies, especially employees and shareholders. In banks, in newly merged companies, in hospitals facing cost containment, in old-line industries trying to compete in a changed environment, CEOs are learning the value of "preaching." Many times the message is quite simple: "We have a good company, we are profitable, but the environment is changing and, therefore, we must change." These are strategic messages. They don't necessarily spell out specific action, but they do point employees in a direction for the future.

These strategic messages deal with three subjects: (1) employees and other constituencies, (2) markets, and (3) products. Concerning employees and other constituencies, PR professional Jim Horton notes, "Organizations with a true and credible message about people usually have strong top management concern with employees and dedication to personnel development and training."[1] These same corporations make strong commitments to customers and make sure their employees believe in and service those customers. Finally, organizations like Procter & Gamble, Kodak, Sears, and others work to develop the best products possible. But inculcating the organization with these messages usually takes decades, not days, and flies in the face of today's results-oriented MBA thinking.

In delivering these messages CEOs are also faced with the problem of messages being diluted as they go down the chain. It has been estimated that each time a message is communicated in an organization, fifty percent of its meaning is lost. Nevertheless, CEOs must work to surmount these problems, for a clear corporate vision is essential to corporate survival in this decade.

THE ELEVATED FUNCTION

Just as competence in finance, accounting, and marketing has always been considered requisite for entry into middle management, a clear understanding of communications principles and the skills for applying those principles is now becoming requisite as well.

A survey of eighteen Chicago-based corporations by students at the J. L. Kellogg Graduate School of Management showed that thirteen had elevated the corporate communications function to the vice-presidential level. A study during that same period by the Conference Board reported that in more than half of those surveyed "a great deal of weight" would be attached to public-affairs competence in the selection of the next chief executive and also in filling other senior posts.[2] While the Conference Board report emphasized communications competence in public affairs, it indicated a movement toward general communications competence. To serve the company's interests successfully, the manager must be literate in both *external*-affairs issues (not directly related to the economic mission) and also in *internal*-communications activities (related to the economic mission of the firm), i.e., financial communications, employee relations, and PR.

"There may be a continuing discrepancy," a company planner told the Conference Board, "between what it takes to get to the chief-executive position and what it takes to perform well in it."[3] Getting to the top for managers requires a strong emphasis on mastering the [internal activities] of the corporation. Involvement in communications is chancy. There are external powers that cannot be directly controlled, there is a "us-versus-them" attitude in the corporation, a bunker mentality. There is normally little reward for communications ability.

Once in senior management, the situation can change drastically. A 1976 Conference Board poll showed that 89 percent of the chief-executive officers surveyed believed the public's perception of the firm is critical to its success. That same study noted that well more than half of the top executives were spending a quarter of their time on communications issues, and 92 percent were spending more time than they had spent three to five years earlier.[4]

It is vital for a chief executive to be actively involved in communications and to set up his participation as an example for others. The Conference Board study stated that the philosophy and perceptions of the chief executive are the key to the company's communications program and that the "feeling" for communications cannot be foisted upon the chief executive by the staff. Rather, "It must come from personal commitment."[5] As the principal representative of

> There is obviously a need then to close the gap between the perceptions of middle management and the reality of senior management. Some companies have begun to make changes to address this problem. They include:
>
> - Rotating young "fast-trackers" through the public-affairs department
> - Defining competence in communications and rewarding it
> - Encouraging managers to become involved in community affairs
> - Improving managerial recruitment criteria
> - Providing in-house training in communications

the company, the chief executive represents the company before major constituencies. This is a leadership role, very similar to that exercised by a political leader—representing the organization at the highest levels of government as well as with the community, top stockholders, regulators, the major customers, and employees.

COMMUNICATIONS' EXPANDING ROLE

In the past the communications program of the firm was more *functional* than *managerial*, more tactical than strategic. There were no goals or strategies, no plans, policies, or programs. Rather, there was a position that was reactive in nature and included a number of assorted tasks such as shielding officials from the press, producing the required annual report, writing an occasional speech, and putting out the monthly employee newsletter. The function was known in most companies as "public relations" and was relatively unimportant from a management perspective.

Also, PR people suffered from the centuries-old prejudice against the messenger of bad tidings. The PR department was the link to the outside world. If the PR chief was doing his job, he would tell things "straight" to management, and often he was blamed for the problem. The PR person also was perceived as a "fixer" who could perform magic with the press, turning around a bad image or making an ordinary chief executive into a *wunderkind*.

But the seventies changed that. Bechtel Corporation, for example, which traditionally had had a low profile, found that its multibillion-dollar construction business was attracting considerable public attention because of delays and cost overruns on its Alyeska oil pipeline and the San Francisco BART subway project, as well as on nuclear safety issues, the company's involvement in the Arab oil boycott, and some alleged connections with the CIA.[6] Paper and steel companies felt the heat of environmental furor; auto makers found Ralph Nader at their annual meetings or attacking them in the press; labor unions pressed for safer working conditions.

Companies that had never had much concern with public image were taking a beating in the media from special-interest groups and government agencies and found it necessary to become aggressive not only in defending their reputation, but in minimizing the impact of regulatory assaults that were substantially affecting the bottom line.

Chief executives surveyed in the late seventies indicated that only half felt their corporate communications programs were satisfactory. One study showed that 60 percent of those questioned said they had no confidence in their PR chiefs.[7] A study of the field of PR headed by Philip Lesly reported that on a scale of 0 to 10, top executives and opinion leaders rated the PR people they knew at 5.8, only a bit above average.

The consensus among executives was that new strategies had to be developed to address the interests and concerns of a company's multiple publics. Chief executives felt efforts were needed in five major areas:

1. Development of new communications skills
2. Emphasis on economic-education programs
3. Strengthening of government relations
4. Widening of community participation
5. Improved research methods.[8]

Many types of response strategies began developing as the *function* of PR came under *management* scrutiny. At Bechtel the strategy changed from reactive to proactive. The company began running institutional ads in the national press, got involved in political-action committees to support friendly politicians, made its executives available to the media, and built up a staff of Washington lobbyists.

MANAGERIAL ISSUES

A new generation of managers is beginning to look at the corporate communications function from a different perspective. The old perception of PR as "black magic" is giving way to MBA thinking, which stresses the importance of evaluative technique in PR activities and the introduction of methods for costing out communications services to organizational components. Along with this comes organization and definition. Key managerial issues that should now be given serious thought include:

- *Management perceptions*—how the firm views the communications function, how the function fits into the corporate structure
- *Communications strategy*—plans for delivering corporate messages
- *Communications policy*—the statement of the firm's communications philosophy in relation to corporate goals
- *Program management*—where the function should be located, what size it should be, how it should be financed, personnel considerations, and evaluations of activities.

MANAGEMENT PERCEPTIONS

Much of the literature concerning PR in the corporate setting stresses the importance of a strong link between the communications staff and top management. In each organization there is a definite philosophy or attitude toward the function.

Many communications managers believe the single most important factor leading to the success of their programs has been strong support from the chief executive and other executives. For example, it is difficult to build a credible media relations program if senior management won't make itself available to the press. The same is true with employee communications, especially in these days when access to information is so easy. If a special-interest group attacks the firm, the employee wants to "see" and "hear" management's response. Employees are media wise. If their boss ducks an issue, they know right away.

If the management approach is "let's ride this out" or "maybe it'll just go away," the communications approach will reflect it. The old saw that you can't make a silk purse out of a sow's ear applies. No amount of fancy footwork by a PR program will be able to create an image that just isn't there to begin with or make a hero out of a chief executive who is hiding under his or her desk.

Without the blessings of senior management, a corporate communications program has little real chance of success. If there is an instinct to "surround the wagons" or "hide behind the bunker," a communications program will never be able to overcome it, no matter what lip service is paid. "No PR staff program is going anywhere," one staffer told the Conference Board, "without the blessings of the brass and the funds to make it work."

Convincing top management of the importance of communications is easier now than it used to be. Business has gone through periods when production was important, then marketing, then law. "Today," said a veteran media observer, "public relations skills are what's called for, and public relations is achieving a status in the corporate world comparable to production, marketing, finance, and law."[9]

COMMUNICATIONS STRATEGY

Communications strategy is the game plan for achieving business goals. As noted in the beginning of this chapter, the strategic communications of a company represents its vision of the future and is iterated in messages to employees, to the marketplace, and to those who buy its products.

If a corporation's objectives include maintaining market share in a durable goods area such as washing machines, the communications strategy will differ dramatically from those of a highly visible auto manufacturer. Differences in size, impact on customer, labor concerns, environmental impact, foreign trade problems, and other factors will dictate different communications strategies for different constituencies.

In the present environment, the washing machine company's communications strategy might be to emphasize product publicity (cost and energy savings, for example), while the auto company's strategy might be to build stronger relations on Capitol Hill. The business itself often determines the strategy. An insurance company or a drug company has to be more communications-oriented than an electric motor company or a food wholesaler.

Communications strategy comes easily—when a company knows where it is going. The new owner of an old-line metal fabricating company found that he had a good product and good profit potential, but runaway costs and a sluggish market. He decided that his job was to reorient the company to the new business environment by emphasizing cost-cutting and marketing.

In looking at what he had inherited, he found a management staff wedded to tradition, workers who feared the company was unstable and who were tired of constant management changes, customers now more concerned with price than reputation, and a demoralized sales force.

With the help of a consultant, the company president formulated a simple message: "We are a solid company, we can be profitable, but the marketplace is changing and therefore, we must change." He put together a little slideshow making these points. First he delivered the message to his sales force and top managers at a get-acquainted dinner. Then, using his consultant as a facilitator, he got the managers involved in marketing and cost-cutting task forces.

His next priority was to get the message to the lower-level employees. He took out some of the technical material from the slideshow, then went around to each plant to hold informal "stand-to's" with employees, answering questions, talking one-on-one, and announcing a cost-cutting suggestion campaign to run sixty days in length. This was a means to get employees to buy into the new culture of the organization. Finally, he started an advertising program that emphasized new messages: We are improving quality and cutting costs at the same time. We are competitive.

Like a politician, then, the new owner had put together a platform based on a single theme, then adapted it for different audiences. And he personally got involved in communicating the message. This is strategic communications in a nutshell: a vision clearly stated and communicated to appropriate constituencies within and without the firm. For real success, the CEO will have to drive home this new policy for years to come, until it is well ingrained.

Sound management of the communications function requires that specific objectives be established and reviewed often. The strategic communications process can be broken down into five phases:

1. *Determination of corporate goals or objectives.* One large insurance company, for example, has for its goal the offering of a variety of competitive insurance products enabling it to meet all the needs of every account efficiently and economically. Emphasis is on provision of new or improved products for its agents to sell, constant communication with its sales force, and strengthening of its distribution channel.

2. *Development of communications strategies designed to achieve corporate objectives.*

In helping to achieve the insurance company's strategy, its communications department puts together plans to improve marketing through product publicity, increase employee satisfaction and commitment, and work with customers to meet corporate goals.

3. *Selection of key audiences.* In the aligning of communications objectives with corporate goals, it is necessary to determine which individuals, groups, or interests must be communicated with and what messages will be delivered. Important audiences for the insurance company will be its agents, its customers—current or potential—news editors, and shareholders.

4. *Setting achievable communications objectives.* The tactics used to implement communications strategies must be achievable in terms of delivering specific messages and achieving a potentially measurable change in attitude. If one tactic is to sponsor legislation to cut highway deaths by cracking down on drunk drivers, the effectiveness of that tactic in improving the company's image of being consumer oriented should be measurable.

5. *Reassessment of the above steps.* Once the message is communicated, the impact must be measured and corrections and adjustments in the strategy undertaken.[10]

Christopher P. A. Komisarjevsky of Hill and Knowlton, writing in the *Journal of Business Strategy*, has outlined a communications matrix (see Figure 2-1), which visualizes communications as a management function and attempts to demonstrate how communications is factored into corporate decision making.

COMMUNICATIONS POLICY

The firm's communications policy is reflective of its overall vision and directed toward achievement of its goals. If the firm's goals include improved valuation of the firm, then communications policy should emphasize improved relations with shareholders, both large and small, a proactive approach to the financial press, and accessibility of top officials to financial audiences. If the firm is seeking to improve its valuation but its philosophy is not proactive, it may have a difficult time achieving results.

Policies that restrict and tightly control press access to corporate officials may be more favored than those allowing the press to talk to anyone about their area of competence but also may be reflective of a defensive corporate philosophy.

Policymaking is important in that it establishes the ground rules for developing corporate communications plans to achieve stated goals. Policies delineate how communications are to be handled, when a new level of decision maker must be brought in, when and how the logo is to be used, what amount of discretion the division or field manager has in communications decision making, what type of information is off limits, and more.

The establishment of these rules is a managerial effort, but the process should be open to input from the functional program. Most senior managers consider their role in communications to be policymaking, rather than functional. They attempt to establish a clear line that separates management from

Information sharing before, during, and after decision making

Corporate Decisions	Chief Executive Officer	Strategic Planner	Financial Officer	Legal Counsel	Division/Product Manager	Government and/or Public Affairs Mgr.	Corporate Communications Mgr.	Internal Communications Specialist	Media Specialist	Marketing Specialist	Public Policy/Issues Specialist	Advantages of Coordinated Corporate Communications
Financial disclosure	•	•	•				•	•				Enhances investor relations and meaningful communications with the financial community.
Corporate press relations	•	•					•	•	•			Creates public climate within which corporate actions can be fairly evaluated.
Strategic planning	•	•	•	•		•	•					Provides opportunity for corporation to anticipate and speak out on critical issues.
Government affairs			•		•	•	•	•		•		Underscores corporate commitment among select leaders, e.g., Washington Thought-Leaders.
Product marketing				•		•	•	•	•	•		Complements and leverages product advertising with third-party endorsement and opinion leaders.
Community affairs					•	•	•					Demonstrates commitment to neighborhood from which corporation draws employees and other support services.
Corporate contributions					•	•	•	•		•		Demonstrates interest in and support for educational, cultural, and social needs.
Investor relations	•					•	•					Makes more effective existing efforts.
Internal relations	•					•	•	•		•		Increases understanding of corporation among employees, building morale and productivity.
Customer relations						•	•		•	•		Supports product marketing by enhancing support for trade, retailers, and wholesalers.

Corporate Staff and Line Management — Communications Staff and/or Outside Counsel

FIGURE 2-1 Communications Matrix

SOURCE: *The Journal of Business Strategy*, Winter 1982. Copyright 1982 by Christopher P. A. Komisarjevsky, senior vice president, Hill and Knowlton, Inc., and reprinted with permission of the authors.

function. Of course, that line does not really exist. A chief executive talking to a reporter is just as much involved in function as a PR person is. Functional PR persons, whether chief executives or PR officers, should have input into the policy process because it is their experience that draws attention to the need for policy. Policies should also be reviewed regularly. People change over time and so do companies. A policy that routes all calls through PR might have been beneficial and practical at one point but may no longer be necessary because managers have become more media smart. Figure 2–2 illustrates a well-defined corporate communications policy for employee communications.

Weyerhaeuser Company recognizes the need for employees to hear and be heard on issues that affect them, and believes that its business and other corporate interests are served by effective, two-way communication with employees.

Toward these ends, the company has the responsibility to create an atmosphere conducive to good communications through the affirmative use of internal communication systems, as well as management procedures that promote the unencumbered exchange of ideas and information among appropriate individuals and groups at all levels and in all locations.

All levels of management have a responsibility to provide employees with the information they need to do their jobs properly, and to assure that management-to-employee communication is timely, clear, relevant, accurate, and consistent. Management style and attitudes are expected to contribute to an atmosphere in which employees feel free to express their views and to question company policies and practices.

At the same time, management recognizes that for competitive, legal, confidential, or other legitimate business reasons, we must sometimes restrict communication on certain matters. It should equally be recognized, however, that these instances should be the exception and not the rule.

SOURCE: The Weyerhaeuser Company, Tacoma, Washington, 1981.

FIGURE 2-2   Weyerhaeuser Communications Policy

PROGRAM MANAGEMENT

The communications-program manager has three major responsibilities: (1) consultation, (2) assistance, and (3) management. Above all else, he is a consultant to top management. Questions like "How are we going to handle this takeover attempt?" or "How do we break this news to the employees?" or "How can we deal with this bad press?" are presented to the program manager, and solutions are developed.

The same program manager provides *tactical* assistance in implementing strategy coordinating the annual report, developing speeches for senior managers, drawing up product-support publicity campaigns, and the like.

Finally, the *management* responsibility of the program executive is to execute and staff a communications program, evaluate its effectiveness, and come up with suggestions for improving its future impact.

Backup for the communications programs often is provided by outside PR counsel. These organizations offer help in such areas as public-opinion sampling, grassroots campaigns, and contact with key legislative or interest-group leaders. Some PR companies have specialties in certain areas, such as product publicity (Burson-Marsteller), financial (Doremus), or crises management and takeover defense (Hill and Knowlton). (See Figure 2–3.)

	1982 Net Fee Income	Employees as of Oct. 15, 1982	%Change from 1981 Income
1. Hill and Knowlton*	$54,000,000	1,050	+14.8
2. Burson-Marsteller*	50,550,000	1,060	+23.0
3. Carl Byoir & Associates* [1]	21,887,000	480	+ 4.9
4. Ruder Finn & Rotman	16,300,000	400	+ 7.2
5. Daniel J. Edelman	8,500,000	176	+ 4.8
6. Doremus & Company* [2]	8,315,014	159	+24.2
7. Manning, Selvage & Lee*	8,304,000	142	+15.5
8. Ketchum PR*	7,802,484	118	+31.2
9. The Rowland Company	7,480,629	123	+ 3.4
10. Ogilvy & Mather PR* [3]	7,432,000	133	+ 8.3
11. Fleishman-Hillard	6,191,000	104	+45.6
12. Rogers & Cowan	6,054,000	121	+13.1
13. Gray and Company	—	107	—
14. Robert Marston and Associates	5,251,000	70	+21.6
15. Booke Communications Incorporated Group	5,239,000	78	+ 8.9
16. Creamer Dickson Basford*	4,810,000	100	+ 3.2
17. Bozell & Jacobs PR *	4,460,000	89	− 4.3
18. Baron/Canning and Company	3,782,000	49	+16.6
19. Dudley-Anderson-Yutzy PR	3,449,000	65	+ 9.2
20. Ayer Public Relations Services*	3,446,500	45	+ 5.6
21. Golin/Harris Communications	3,368,725	64	+17.4
22. Regis McKenna	3,010,269	50	+34.9
23. Kanan, Corbin, Schupak & Aronow	2,617,652	36	+18.5
24. Aaron D. Cushman and Associates	2,601,350	52	+ 2.3
25. Financial Relations Board	2,585,868	59	+ 6.8
26. The Strayton Corporation	2,410,000	36	+28.5
27. Porter, Novelli and Associates*	2,235,000	43	+31.3
28. Hank Meyer Associates	2,159,074	22	− 7.6
29. The Rockey Company	2,145,000	43	+16.6
30. The Hannaford Company	2,103,337	35	+17.6
31. Dorf/MJH	2,032,817	51	+72.2
32. Anthony M. Franco	2,000,000	42	+24.6
33. Richard Weiner	1,950,000	43	+37.9
34. Gibbs & Soell	1,877,660	38	− 4.9
35. Padilla and Speer	1,862,071	29	+19.4
36. Geltzer & Company	1,800,300	30	+ 2.2
37. Lobsenz-Stevens	1,735,000	33	+ 8.5
38. Public Relations Board	1,628,556	48	+ 2.3
39. ICPR	1,511,000	32	−11.3
40. John Adams Associates, Inc.	1,476,736	27	+97.3
41. Charles Ryan Associates	1,378,444	23	+14.4
42. Porter, LeVay & Rose	1,339,425	24	+50.4
43. Cohn & Wolfe	1,317,000	40	+81.5
44. Simon/Public Relations Inc.	1,290,000	23	+45.7
45. Gross and Associates/PR	1,247,308	26	−18.1
46. Woody Kepner Associates	1,221,000	18	+21.6
47. Edward Howard & Co.	1,214,363	21	−17.3
48. Mallory Factor Associates	1,214,000	20	+29.7
49. Smith & Harroff	1,190,000	13	+ 1.8
50. Public Communications, Inc.	1,180,000	24	−17.0

[1] Acquired Newsome & Company, Inc. Nov. 1, 1982.
[2] Includes all wholly owned BBDO International PR Units.
[3] Includes AAB Assessoria Administrativa Ltda. acquired Feb. 1, 1982.

FIGURE 2-3   Fifty Largest U.S. Public Relations Operations, Independent and Ad Agency Affiliated, for Year Ended December 31, 1982

*Denotes advertising agency subsidiary.

SOURCE: Reprinted from *1983 O'Dwyer's Directory of PR Firms*. Copyright 1983 by J. R. O'Dwyer Co. Inc.

STAFFING

The communications function in a corporation is determined by size and mission. One or two people, or even an outside agency, can adequately handle a small company, while a Fortune 500 company might need a hundred people plus multiple outside agencies. A "wrong fit"—too few people—will result in an office that can only do "firefighting," that is, react to press calls, speech needs, publications orders.

In most companies, the communications program is centralized at the vice-presidential level, and overall policy direction is usually located at corporate headquarters. Sometimes, however, function and personnel are decentralized. Some remain at headquarters, others go to operating divisions in the field, and some are retained in overseas offices. Some personnel may also be assigned to marketing operations, others may be stationed in New York near the financial and communications media, and usually there is a separate Washington office.

Many executives feel that control of corporate communications must be centralized. They believe that as a central unit corporate communications can uniformly keep track of related activities at middle and lower management. When General Electric closed its corporate communications office in the fall of 1980 and detailed the staff to specialized areas, it said the purpose of the move was to make PR less visible and more accountable on the bottom line.

There are no hard and fast rules pertaining to either size or location of communications programs. Some industries, like insurance, because of the nature of their business, have needs for large centralized staffs, with budgets in excess of a half million dollars. While corporate communications departments have been expanded significantly in the last decade, there are obvious limitations: size of organization, expected return on PR investment, type of company. In companies such as Mobil at one time it appeared that the sky was the limit. The major recession of the early 1980s changed that. In others it appears that there is a point of diminishing returns. And while the overstaffed PR office is an occasional management mistake, the opposite is more typical.

ORGANIZATION

A communications program needs to be put together in such a way that it is responsive to corporate goals and mission. The function can be organized and most clearly understood in what might be called the building-block method (see Figure 2–4), that is, by component. For example, a large oil company such as Shell organizes all communications activities together with the exception of stockholder and investor relations. On the other hand, Allis Chalmers puts everything together under a staff executive and vice president. Interlake, Inc., combines marketing and external relations in the same office

- *Public Relations*—generally handles primary contacts with news media and major business publications. It also can provide publications development and management of major events. Speechwriting for top corporate officials often is based in this office.
- *Product Publicity*—sometimes found in the marketing department, coordinates and manages the publicity relating to new or existing products.
- *Customer Relations*—deals with the activities relating to customers/consumers. It includes various activities from hot-lines to letter answering to product recalls and also can be attached to marketing.
- *Employee Relations*—includes communications relating to various constituencies within the firm. Employees can be divided by function (production, sales, etc.) or treated as a generic group.
- *Community Relations*—pertains to corporate relations in each community where a facility is maintained. It covers the gamut from sponsorship of charitable activities to helping the community get by after a plant closing.
- *Financial/Investor Relations*—the part of the communications program dealing with analysts, major stockholders, small investors, and financial press. It sometimes is located in the office of the comptroller or finance vice president.
- *Public Affairs*—a generic term referring to relations with external constituencies of the firm. It includes issues management, governmental relations at various levels, and foreign intelligence acquisition.

FIGURE 2-4   Building Blocks of Corporate Communications

under a vice president, while Whirlpool Corporation organizes to coordinate consumer and public affairs tightly. Other examples abound that show split staffs reporting to different offices.

There are two basic approaches to organizing the corporate communications function. One example, shown in Figure 2–5, depicts a highly decentralized organizational structure in which the various communications activities report to staff or line. In a second example, Figure 2–6 shows a totally central-

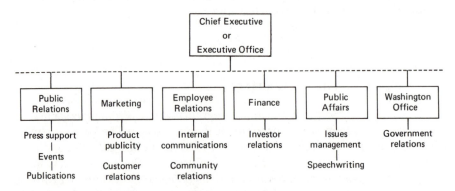

FIGURE 2-5   Decentralized PR Organization Chart

NOTE: This decentralized corporate communications office emphasizes maximum involvement in the communications function by the chief executive or the executive committee.

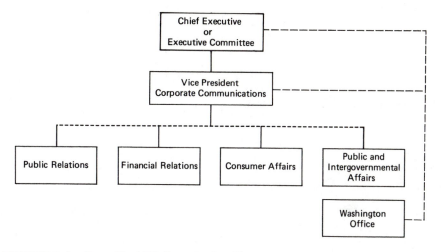

FIGURE 2-6   Centralized PR Organization Chart

NOTE: This centralized corporate communications office emphasizes maximum control of the subelements and minimal direct involvement by the chief executive or executive committee in program management. Notice dual reporting function of Washington office.

ized approach. This structure acknowledges that communications is a full-time management function and centralizes responsibility in one place. The downside is that now there is a new layer or filter to the process. Modifications of this second approach may provide a better solution. For example, investor relations no longer report to the VP for finance, nor does customer relations report to the VP for marketing.

FINANCING CORPORATE COMMUNICATIONS

Financial controls for corporate communications are often directly related to their location in the firm. In one model communications services are provided to all units and charged to corporate overhead. In a second model there is a charge back to each profit center, sometimes based on a percentage of sales produced by the unit. In a third situation each profit center assumes charge of its own communications activities, as at GE (see Figure 2-7). While this plan solves the problem of costing out communications, it works to reduce overall corporate communications effectiveness and can create duplication of effort and lack of coordination. For example, one division of a company was about to settle with a union on a 5 percent salary increase just as the corporate communications department, with its separate staff, sent out a press release announcing high profits. The final settlement was double the original.[11]

In a fourth model each profit center is charged back either the out-of-pocket costs for each project or the actual cost, which includes salaries and overhead. This arrangement creates a situation where the profit center might

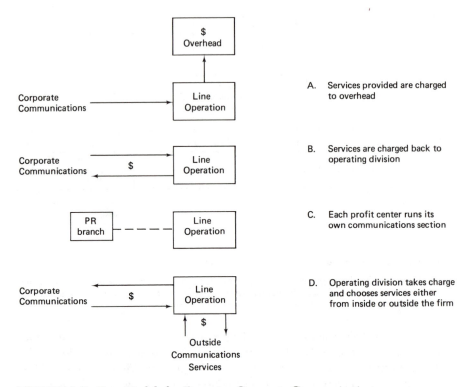

FIGURE 2-7   Four Models for Financing Corporate Communications

argue successfully that it should be able to use an outside firm. In terms of certain kinds of product and consumer PR activities, that is an arguable point. For the bulk of *corporate* assignments involving overall corporate image, however, location and control must be centralized at corporate headquarters.

Though moves to office automation are changing this, costs associated with running an in-house communications function are mainly *salaries* and *overhead*. Capital expenses are minimal. One of the major distinctions between advertising/marketing and communications is costs. Most communications activities use "free" channels of dissemination—magazine stories, radio-TV reports, newspaper coverage—as opposed to bought space. This generally is a plus in terms of cost but a minus when it comes to evaluating impact.

Traditionally PR activities were run out of the corporate administrative budget. When the PR chief needed some money for a project, he or she received clearance from the administrative officer or the chief executive and worked without a budget and with fairly loose fiscal controls.

Today the most common system is to determine hourly cost of the operation and bill out services to divisions.[12] Overhead is usually figured at twice the total cost of salaries and is normally determined by adding the costs of the manager and secretarial help. While figures are all variable, depending on employee efficiency, a common final figure is $50 per hour plus expenses. It might be noted that most outside PR counsel bill at three times the hourly rate they pay employees, plus expenses.

Competent PR professionals will be able to estimate billable hours and expenses in advance of a project with a reasonable amount of accuracy. Submission of daily time sheets, which log fractions of an hour worked on specific activities, will help track costs. This method further serves in employee evaluation. A good plan, especially for a large project, will also be organized on a modified time-line chart. It should be understood that there are certain communications functions that are difficult to track, especially the fire-fighting kinds of PR often demanded in a pinch.

PERSONNEL
QUALIFICATIONS

The backgrounds of persons in the corporate communications department are quite varied. Traditionally PR jobs went to journalists who wanted to come in from the cold: tired of long hours and poor pay and the newspaper life. Over time and through the efforts of the Public Relations Society of America, accreditation in PR has been established, and professionals trained in their field are certified with the initials APR (Accredited Public Relations). As corporate communications has become more important, top jobs have gone to specialists in other fields, such as law, finance, and marketing. The majority of corporate communications directors, however, still come from PR and journalism backgrounds.

A factor in the background of many communications professionals is the amount of time they have been with a company. Some companies, for example, promote only from within for upper-level communications jobs.

One function that *absolutely* requires professional background is media or press relations. No matter what kind of business the firm is engaged in, the person who occupies that position should be one with experience in the news media. It is well worth the extra money to find such an individual, someone who can relate well to the news media. Even the highest paid, sharpest professionals in the communications business can stumble with the media, so it is important that the top press relations person be able to deal with *both* top management and the media. An individual can be trained to relate to management but can't be trained to relate to the media. Lawyers or MBAs are not qualified for this job unless they have solid press credentials. An ex-reporter can instinctively understand where reporters are "coming from," what they want, how fast they need it, and even how the company may appear in the story.

But an ex-news reporter creates potential problems: he or she will always be considered an outsider in the company because of background and affinity. On the other hand, there are former news people who have forgotten what the news business is about and have become too "corporate." This can cause a problem.

Communications managers should understand that the press has direct access to the chief executive in many firms and can create an organizational problem for the communications director who has an employee that reports over his or her head. The smart communications manager stays on top of press relations, *always*.

EVALUATING RESULTS

The greatest weakness in corporate communications is in the evaluation of impact. One is reminded of the story of John Wanamaker, the great Philadelphia merchandiser, who said he was sure that he was wasting half of his advertising dollars, but he couldn't figure out which half.

Traditionally PR or communications success has been measured by number of inches of space in publications or reports or how many free minutes of air time were received. A look through the recent annual survey of PR campaigns that have won the Public Relations Society of America's Silver Anvil Award reinforces the fact that these methods are still the standard. The results of one campaign, picked at random from the winners, were listed as follows:

- More than 4,000 entries (to a contest that was highly promoted), with every state entered
- A two-minute news feature on ABC-TV network's weekend report
- A five-minute news feature on NBC's New York outlet
- More than 8,000 column inches of print space
- UPI, AP, New York Times Syndicate, 'Family Week,' and 'Grit,' coverage of contest results

The purpose of this $75,000 campaign was to put together a program to breathe life into an annual national contest that seemed to be dying off. The objectives of the campaign—to attract national media attention and to make the contest fair and important for entrants—were modest and achievable. If one purpose, as stated in this campaign, was "to attract maximum media attention," that's a pretty vague term and can be easily adjusted for various kinds of results. This example is typical of the current state of measurement and evaluation.

One of the people attempting to develop more serious PR measurement techniques is Dr. Lloyd Kirban of Burson-Marsteller, New York. He says that with communications budgets reaching six and seven figures, managers are becoming more concerned with results than with creativity or quality of the materials produced. "The question they want answered is not what kind of material is being produced but rather what result it is having." Kirban feels that the entire profession of PR is slowly moving toward "effectiveness measurement" but that the day when measurement techniques are in routine use is still some time off. "At Burson-Marsteller we have measured enough programs that we are close to the point where we can begin to match programs to results," he adds.

The standard system of evaluation measures the distribution system or channels with numbers that show only potential audience impressions, not any data on how many people are being reached or the quality of the message that is reaching them. The question remaining is, What impact is the message having and on whom? Kirban feels the day of judgment is close at hand especially in the product-publicity area of consumer goods, where communications techniques are being used to supplement marketing and advertising. Optimally, marketing, advertising, and PR practitioners would like to be able to measure changes in behavior as they relate to sales, productivity, and higher price/earnings ratios.

The real need, says Kirban, is to begin measuring communication variance—that is, the specific impact a message has on people. Does it increase awareness, or does it go beyond and increase knowledge, or does it go even further and increase attitudes or achieve a level of interest? Further still, does it provoke action? Awareness, the lowest order of impact, is the easiest to measure, he says. But one has to be careful not just to set a goal of "increasing awareness," he stresses. Rather the goal should be to measure awareness vis-à-vis a standard based on historical comparison. For example, did we do better or worse than we did in the past regarding awareness? At some point, Kirban feels, there will be a need to tie dollar expenditures to an expected increase in awareness levels.

Other possible approaches to evaluation call for establishment of goals based on observation. A neutral target audience is selected, and the evaluator attempts during the campaign to measure at various milestones how much the group is learning and in what direction they are leaning. Research methodology here calls for taking readings before and often during a campaign, especially if it is long, as other external events take place that might affect the outcome.

Kirban observes that more and more frequently communications activities are involved with marketing and advertising. *Test markets* with and without communications techniques will be tried, especially when at some point large sums of money may be invested in a new product rollout. Managers will want to use the test-market approach to determine how much bang they can get for their dollar with communications techniques. Costs for evaluation, says Kirban, usually come out at about 10 percent, at most, of a campaign. In small campaigns evaluation expenses might not be cost effective, he notes.[13]

Some communications/PR practitioners do not subscribe to the importance of evaluative techniques in measuring communications effectiveness. Among that group is Donald Stroetzel, manager of communications programs for Mobil Oil Corporation, a company that spends in excess of $20 million annually on corporate communications.

Stroetzel says Mobil's strength is that it is out in the "marketplace of ideas" every day—with ad-vertorials, as the company calls them, running on the opinion editorial pages of the *New York Times* and other major dailies on a weekly basis; a column, "Observations," which runs regularly in Sunday supplements; and hard-hitting full-page counterattacks when it feels the press has unfairly attacked it with bad press coverage. While the company has conducted readership surveys of "Observations," Stroetzel says, "I'm suspicious of statistical evaluation." He says that communications professionals at Mobil trust their "instincts." "Our efforts have shown a change in the op-ed policy in the *Times*," he maintains, though he admits "we can't prove it."[14] A side effect of the campaigning, says Stroetzel, is that about 10 percent of the company's new stockholders brought shares on account of this advertising. "I trust my gut reaction more than anything else," he adds.

Northwestern University marketing professor Philip Kotler, who suggests there are many similarities between marketing and communications, believes that common behavioral measures such as focus groups, concept tests, and copy and media tests can be used to evaluate communications programs.

While pressures continue to increase for better evaluation of internal communications programs such as product support, there remains significant interest in the Mobil Oil position that external communications activities are difficult to measure and that a manager goes on gut feeling. The 1976 Conference Board survey found that while many firms hold communications activities accountable to established and formalized objectives, there is less emphasis on quantitative evaluation. Most managers look for improvement in such broad areas as "improved business credibility" or "a positive corporate image." The *impressions* or *feelings* that a chief executive has about the impact of a communications program seem to account for much of the internal evaluation. Said one executive, "I have eyes and ears. I see and listen."[15] Employees, customers, friends, family, the board of directors—all contribute to this evaluation. The problem, obviously, is that such evaluation is extremely subjective and easily inaccurate.

A more accurate method of evaluating communications efforts, particularly those that are externally oriented, is through opinion surveys of the targeted publics. Some companies do polling on their own, but more often outside firms are hired to measure such things as customer satisfaction, changes in attitudes of investors, employee perceptions of management, and overall corporate credibility.

Evaluation of public-affairs activities—grassroots campaigns, lobbying, and other activities designed to influence legislation—also is difficult, though many managers find that evaluating "level of effort" rather than actual success of the project is equitable. Some managers evaluate the number of complaints coming in or the creativity and innovation of the communications effort. Others do no evaluation at all, since they consider PR/communications activities a cost of doing business.

Nevertheless, in the long term corporate communications activities will have to move more toward quantifiable objectives that can be more precisely monitored and evaluated. It is unlikely and undesirable to believe that communication with people and organizations can ever be fully quantified as to impacts, but corporate communications activities must become more than black magic.

SUMMARY

1. Competency in communications principles and practice is becoming requisite for managers.

2. Managerial concerns in communications relate to overall philosophy, policy, strategy, and management considerations.

3. No communications program is going anywhere without support from the boss.

4. Communications functions can be in many different locations in the firm: marketing, finance, personnel, and so on.

5. The press relations person must be a former journalist.

6. Very little quantitative evaluation is conducted on corporate communications programs.

NOTES

1. James L. Horton, "Strategic Communications and the Future of the Corporation," paper delivered at the World Futures Society Conference on Communication and the Future, Washington, D.C., July 1982.

2. The Conference Board, "Managerial Competence: The Public Affairs Aspects," 1981, report #805, p. 4.

3. Ibid., p. 7.

4. The Conference Board, "Managing Corporate External Relations: Changing Perspectives and Responses," 1976, report #679, p. 49.

5. Ibid.

6. *BusinessWeek*, "The Corporate Image, PR to the Rescue," January 22, 1979, p. 47.

7. The Conference Board, report #679, p. 11.

8. H. W. Close, "Public Relations as a Management Function," *Public Relations Journal*, March 1980, pp. 19–20.

9. B. G. Yovovich, "Skills Needed, Status Growing", *Advertising Age*, January 5, 1981, p. S1.

10. Adapted from Lloyd M. Newman, "Essential Preliminaries to Public Relations Actions," in "Tips and Tactics," April 4, 1977, a supplement to *PR reporter*.

11. Bruce Pennington, "How Public Relations Fits into the Puzzle," *Public Relations Journal*, March 1980, pp. 19–20.

12. Jack Tucker, "Budgeting and Cost Control, Are You a Businessman or a Riverboat Gambler?" *Public Relations Journal*, March 1981, pp. 14–17.

13. Telephone interview with Dr. Lloyd Kirban, July 24, 1981.

14. Donald S. Stroetzel, remarks to Chicago chapter of the Public Relations Society of America, February 27, 1981.

15. The Conference Board, report #679, pp. 64–69.

Internal Communications

3

Making internal communications work is a major corporate challenge for the 1980s. In Chapter 1 we stressed the importance of creating a corporate vision. In Chapter 2, we looked at the reasons for a communications function in the organization and discussed some basic management issues. In this chapter, we look at the communications activities of the firm that are tied directly to its economic mission, including: press relations, product publicity, speech writing, employee communications, consumer/customer relations, and publications. One very obvious omission from this list is financial communications which is covered in detail in Chapter 7.

PRESS RELATIONS

Press relations simply means dealing with the media. It was the original reason for having someone in the firm to handle communications activities. In the early days of PR, it was called publicity and press agentry. The purpose of the publicist was to get favorable stories into the media on events, such as the arrival of the circus. The Hollywood film studios and the big stars of today still rely extensively on publicists and press agents to hype their activities in the news media. Judging by the coverage on radio and TV, this technique has always been very effective. To turn around John D. Rockefeller's negative image as a "robber baron" years ago, a publicist suggested the aging entrepreneur pass out dimes to kids to show generosity.

George Westinghouse is thought to be the first chief executive to have hired PR people when he brought in two men to promote use of alternating current instead of direct current. The father of modern PR, Edward Bernays, saw PR as three functions: informing people, persuading them, and improving relationships among them.

Reporters in the working press have dubbed PR people over the years with two uncomplimentary nicknames—*flacks* and *shills*. The term flack comes from "flack jacket," an item of military and police clothing designed to ward off shrapnel or bullets in a battle. The "flack" takes the heat from the press that is directed at the company. Traditionally a shill was the person who hyped up the price at an auction. A corporate shill is someone who hypes up the company's image to the media. Reporters who left journalism for PR were said to have sold out—gone to work for the "enemy" at higher pay. While some of this sentiment seems to have died out in recent years, there is still a low-key animosity many reporters feel toward PR people. On the other hand, a credible PR or communications professional can easily overcome this negativism by being responsive to media needs.

How does a public relations person operate? Some managers think that all such a person does is take reporters to lunch and buy them drinks. Others believe the press person's job is to shield management, and they become upset when asked to talk to a reporter. Another perception is that the press relations staff is busy putting out releases all day long. In the well-run office, all and none of this is true.

Good press relations people perform two main tasks: They *sell* stories, and they keep management honest. Good press relations people do not go around simply issuing press releases. They work from a strategic plan and zero in on obtaining a certain type of coverage in a certain type of media. It took the press relations people at Continental Illinois Bank two years to get a prominent story in the *New York Times* "Business Day" section, but another story followed quickly in the *Wall Street Journal.* Such stories bolster image, impact stock price and bring in customers. (This new visibility became a liability for them when they were burned in the Penn Square Bank collapse.)

The press person is the spokesperson for management but also the gate-keeper who tries to bring manager and media together and attempts to smooth out the natural antagonisms in the interests of both the firm and the press. It is not an easy job. The reactive role of the press relations person—answering calls from the media and representing the firm—is extremely important. How that transaction is handled can reveal everything about a company's communication policy.

MARKETING AND
PRODUCT SUPPORT

Product publicity is a major staple of corporate communications activities. It is an effort to obtain unpaid media coverage of a firm's goods or services to enhance credibility and sales.

More often than not it is used to back up marketing efforts and defray marketing costs. There are many possible relationships between marketing and PR. According to Professor Kotler, the two functions can be granted separate but equal status, or they can have overlapping responsibilities, or one function can have dominance over the other, or they can even be considered as the same thing.[1]

A small manufacturing company might be strong on marketing, but weak on PR activities, while a hospital or university would normally have strong PR and weak marketing. Professor Kotler emphasizes that marketing exists to sense, serve, and satisfy customer needs, while PR exists to produce goodwill in the company's various publics so that these publics do not interfere in the organization's drive to satisfy its customers. Marketing stresses selling to customers. PR serves the corporation in the social marketplace. One might not completely agree but the distinction is worth noting.

Kotler sees three major differences between marketing and PR:

PUBLIC RELATIONS	MARKETING
1. Communications	Communications + needs assessment + product development + pricing + distribution
2. Influence attitudes	Elicit specific behaviors
3. No involvement with corporate goals	Defines mission customers service

SOURCE: Adapted from unpublished materials supplied by Dr. Philip Kotler, Northwestern University.

The rising cost of advertising in the 1970s forced many companies to consider using other channels for product introductions. "As advertising costs have gone up, more companies have turned to PR techniques in order to broaden the reach of their marketing programs," says Morris Rotman of the Chicago office of Ruder, Finn and Rotman, a PR firm.[2] Another marketing executive observes that PR agencies are getting involved earlier on in the "conceptual positioning of products, even to the extent of submitting names for new products."[3]

Product-support activities provided through publicity efforts pose a control problem. Editors have the final say as to what is run. Therefore great care has to be taken in designing a communications component to a marketing effort. Some techniques include news releases, features or human-interest stories, photos, packaged interviews or film clips for radio and TV, talk show participation, and staged media events.

The Heublein Company, attempting to sustain its strong market share for Harvey's Bristol Cream Sherry in New York City's black community, organized a major fashion show in tribute to unrecognized black fashion designers. The event was designed as a fall fashion event rather than a testimonial because Heublein felt it would command more space in coverage. The black-tie affair drew more than one thousand black community leaders, buyers, and members of the press. Significant media coverage resulted nationally, including pickup by syndicated news services, major national papers, and the black press. A one-minute TV clip was reported shown 208 times on 56 stations with an estimated audience of 10 million. Radio interviews distributed nationally were heard by nearly 3 million people, and a five-minute TV film feature reportedly was seen by 24 million viewers over 78 stations.

Total cost to Heublein for the entire program was $150,000. Because of the success of the show, it became a popular annual event.[4]

Much of the success of the project was attributed to high-level media fashion critics who selected the garments, and influentials in the black community who helped organize the event. Proceeds went to charity. Extensive coverage, especially by black media, and identification of the Heublein participation strengthened the market position of the product, according to the company.

When the Entenmann baking company was looking for a way to introduce itself into a new market—St. Louis—its PR firm came up with the idea of having the company bake a replica of a giant paddlewheel boat, the *Admiral*. The real *Admiral* was in the news at the time because local residents were attempting to save it from the scrap heap. The Entenmann cake was sold at one dollar a slice, and proceeds were used to help the fund-raising effort to save the boat. The baking company contributed an additional $4,000, and publicity surrounding the cake reportedly helped galvanize public support for the city to buy the boat. Both the unveiling of the cake and the fund-raising effort attracted significant media coverage.[5]

Publicity can be tied to events, as in the above two examples, but it can also be conducted under the auspices of "public service" in support of marketing efforts. (The "Come to Shell for the Answer" campaign is an example.) Johnson's Wax, which manufactures *Raid*, found that attitude was one of the biggest problems it faced among potential users of that product. Many people were ashamed to admit they had cockroaches because they felt roaches were associated only with unsanitary conditions and filth. To overcome this problem, a campaign was designed to address the pest problem. Public-service announcements were developed and distributed through the National Homeowners Association for radio and TV use. Also, a 250-pound actor dressed as a humanoid-cockroach for a publicity road show. Additionally, the company developed pamphlets, brochures, and consumer education materials for distribution.

Communications experts agree that publicity brings credibility to a product that cannot be bought with any amount of paid advertising. Says one senior ad agency executive: "The beauty of product publicity is that you get an editor to endorse a story and that greatly enhances believability." Observed the communicator who worked on the Johnson campaign, "When a magazine or newspaper runs an article on how to get rid of your bugs and attributes it to *Raid*, it's almost like them saying 'go out and buy Raid.' You can't beat that kind of endorsement."[6]

The rollout of "diet Coke" in 1982 was totally PR—a glitzy show at Radio City Music Hall.

An excellent example of public relations in product rollout occurred in February of 1982 when Kodak showed the world its new disc photo system. One major challenge that faced the company was keeping the product secret until the announcement. Kodak felt it had to do this without alienating media or analysts. Kodak also wanted a rollout that would be especially impressive to give the camera a good start. A strategic communications plan was put together that had a number of major objectives:

1. to show consumers that the new products were affordable, attractive, easy to use, and took good pictures.
2. to convince dealers and photofinishers that this would be a good volume builder for them.
3. to assure business and financial communities that Kodak had a state-of-the-art product that would do well in the marketplace.
4. to demonstrate to technical and scientific types that this was an advancement in photography.
5. to get employees excited about the product, while protecting security.
6. to improve Kodak's attractiveness to the investment community.
7. to build the company's image in communities where its plants were located.

In its efforts to maintain secrecy, Kodak deflected inquiries with comments to the press such as "We have made no such announcement" or "We have read those reports with great interest."

The press kit weighed three and one-half pounds, contained seventeen different stories and twenty-five photographs, plus a disc camera. The actual announcement on February 3, 1982, began with a worldwide release at 8 A.M. EST and was followed immediately with an appearance on the TV show "Good Morning America." A couple of hours later a full blown news conference was held in New York and seven other major cities. Later in the day the entire presentation was repeated for 230 financial analysts and portfolio managers. That evening a dinner was held for about sixty institutions that hold about a quarter of the company's stock. Each of the company's forty international offices were asked to send in their own PR plans for the disc announcement. For consumers, Kodak put together special film clips and radio tapes and arranged appearances on daytime talk shows in key cities, generated articles through camera columnists, and set up interviews with business magazines. There was a total of seventeen presentations in the first three days following the announcement. For employees, Kodak set up special displays in employee areas, blanketed employee publications with information, sent out a management letter, presented an audio-visual program to employee groups, and gave out stick-on lapel patches. For its communities, Kodak put on presentations for the local service clubs and other organizations. Also it announced a record increase in employment in 1981 attributable to the camera.

Kodak PR professionals involved claimed the announcement of the disc system was nearly perfect and that the coordinated "one voice" approach worked extremely well. It would be interesting to try and compare what comparable advertising would have cost. And that would not have generated credibility in any where near the magnitude that good PR did.[7]

SPEECH WRITING

In the past it was not unusual for the person who did press relations work to serve as speech writer as well. In today's corporate setting, it is becoming more common for speech writing to be a separate responsibility.

Executive speeches range from significant, thought-provoking, policy-setting, and newsworthy to hackneyed, cliché-filled Babbittry. (In the recent past I have listened to addresses by chairmen and chief executives of some of the top U.S. corporations. In each case the remarks could have been prepared by a food blender rather than a speech writer!) It is hard to understand why the chief executive of a major U.S. corporation will take the time to fly halfway across the continent to deliver a speech that is an insult to the rank he holds. The fault, to be sure, is not that of the speech writer, who has been told to put together the usual diatribe against big government stifling free enterprise. More likely the problem is that the company does not have a clearly articulated sense of its goals and mission as they relate to society.

A speech writer, like a press relations person, needs to have a special knack for putting ideas into a context that creatively sets forth the company's viewpoint. At the same time, the chief executive should be adaptable to the speech writer's style. This approach is indeed unorthodox and a reversal of traditional thinking, but a really savvy chief executive knows whether or not his or her speaking style needs help and will work with the speech writer, as politicians do, to develop a "voice" that effectively melds message and delivery.

Speeches by top managers should be considered opportunities to articulate policy, make news about products or processes, and even gaze into the future. A veteran speech writer, Nariman N. Karanjia, suggests that following the general wisdom of sticking to familiar topics should be avoided.[8] Rather, together the speech writer and the chief executive should consider topics of immediate interest to the general public. The perfect mix is to find topics that have general interest and also relate to concepts the firm needs to address.

A good speech writer will make suggestions based on current ideas and trends. One method of attracting attention is to do a speech that runs *against* the tide of what others are saying or arguing.

An effective approach is for the chief executive and speech writer to sit down together and prepare a press release rather than an outline of the talk to force themselves to concentrate on content and impact. Such a technique also gives the chief executive a chance to see in what direction the speech is going.

One final bit of advice Karanjia gives is to work hardest on the first four minutes of the speech. Those few minutes will deliver the first, and lasting, impression of the chief executive *and* his remarks.

Speeches are not the bread and butter of management, but their impact on the perception of the public, the financial community, the government and other publics of concern to the firm can have long-term consequences in the cumulative impression of credibility and viability that people ascribe to the firm.

EMPLOYEE RELATIONS

A 1982 study of employees by the International Association of Business Communicators showed that while about 50 percent described their company's communications program as candid and accurate, more than one-third called them poor. Nearly half said management did not act on their ideas. Face-to-face discussions with an immediate supervisor, small groups, or top execs ranked as the top three preferred sources of information. The office grapevine ranked fifteenth as a preferred source. But it was the second major source for news. The survey covered 32,000 employees in twenty-six domestic and Canadian firms.

Employees said they wanted information about future plans, productivity improvements, personnel policies, advancement opportunities, and what impact external events have on their jobs. Workers said they were least interested in human interest stories and news about other employees, long the fodder of many corporate communications programs. Finding out what employees think about their company and their jobs, how they are treated by their supervisors, and the like is becoming a higher priority as companies attempt to deal with a new generation of workers who are smarter, more interested in solving problems, and less interested in finding a single niche in the corporate pyramid. In addition, companies faced with a need to improve worker productivity, effectiveness, and profits are realizing that their workforce can make or break the company at the bottom line.

One analytical tool being used more and more these days is the communications audit (or employee opinion survey, as it is sometimes called), which aids a company in looking at its policies and programs regarding communications. A good audit looks at both formal and informal communications channels, upward and downward flow of information in the organization, and employee preferences for information dissemination. Audits model how the communication process works in the organization, based on stated goals, resources committed, programs in place, and perceptions of employees. Techniques used can include opinion sampling, focus groups, management climate assessment, and content evaluation of published materials.

Audits are especially useful tools when companies are in the process of reorganizing, after a merger or acquisition, during periods of labor unrest, or when there is simply a need perceived. Communications audits are not just limited to the internal communications of a firm. They can be externally focused as well, with attempts to determine perceptions of the organization by various constituencies.

THE NEED FOR BETTER MANAGEMENT

Managers are finding they have not only a radically changing economic environment to deal with, but also a new generation of workers who want to work with their heads, as well as their hands; are better educated, more sophisticated; are media-smart; and want to know what their company is doing and how they contribute.

The Japanese have clearly brought home to Americans the lesson that worker involvement leads to better productivity. Improved communications is a major component in increasing worker productivity. Today's problems, according to Daniel Quinn Mills of the Harvard Business School, can be attributed to too much downward communications, too much talking and not enough listening by management, unclear and often irrelevant messages, and lack of credibility and honesty.

Some ideas for turning this around include:

1. Increasing management/employee contact and communications.
2. Making supervisors/managers accountable for relaying information.
3. Developing channels that get information to supervisors and managers quickly.
4. Telling employees how their unit is doing, vis-à-vis the company as a whole.
5. Expanding upwards communications: Listen more, talk less.

One very underutilized employee communications device is the motivational campaign. This technique gives employees an opportunity to buy into the change process in an organization. Most campaigns are designed to achieve results in a short period of time (a few weeks to a few months). Some campaigns go on for years—such as safety on the job—but they must be updated regularly. Goodyear came up with a "paper dragons" campaign to try and reduce computerized reports that were totaling up to 2.5 million pages annually. Holiday Inn, Inc., got employees to cut back on long-distance phone use with a campaign featuring "Sherlock Phones and Dr. Watsline."

Productivity, energy conservation, morale, even corporate survival—there are many elements that motivate a company to embark upon a program to communicate with employees more effectively. For example:

•An Anaconda safety program resulted in a 50 percent drop in medical-treatment cases and major reductions in both the incidence and severity of accidents.[9]

•An energy-saving program at Allied Chemical resulted in a $45 million drop in energy costs for the firm.[10]

•A publicized agreement between Indianapolis builders and unions reduced construction costs and use of out-of-town contractors.[11]

Examples of how much could be saved or is lost because employee relations are ignored are harder to come up with.

According to Cliff McGoon, director of communications for the International Association of Business Communicators, surveys among chief executives of 50 major corporations have found that more than 80 percent believe a communications program can have a positive effect on labor relations, productivity, quality control, safety, and absenteeism.[12]

In recent years, employee relations has matured from the stereotypical newsletter filled with birth announcements, gold watch presentations, and bowling scores. Today's employees are media sensitive and sophisticated about issues like inflation, business, and economics. "If they see a story on television about fraud or corruption [in their company], they look to the newspapers or magazines to deny that information," says one corporate communications director. "We call it the outside-in theory," she adds. "If you tell employees something, they'll look to the outside media to confirm it, or vice-versa."[13] One company, attacked in the local media for its marketing practices in the community, had a morale problem. The communications department, through its in-house television service, put on top executives who rebutted the attack. People want to say, "I still work for a good company."

Companies are starting to build their in-house communications systems to match the speed of external systems. In-house television "news" shows presented weekly in five- to fifteen-minute formats are becoming more common. Rather than produce one magazine for all audiences, companies now produce up to a half dozen different publications, destined for various employee groups, mirroring the "narrowcasting" of commercial magazines in the external environment. One goes to the sales force, another to office staff, still another is destined for retirees.

Employees, it has been said, used to be the last to know about what was going on in the company. As information becomes more of the "currency" of our society, inside information may soon become a union contract demand. The naming of the president of the United Auto Workers to the board of Chrysler, for example, may have been a step in that direction. A five-year study by two professors at Kansas State University has shown that employee perceptions of top management can affect their work and attitudes more than any other factor. The study, by Ronald Goodman and Richard Ruch, emphasizes that the chief executive "must be willing to face up to the powerful role top management has to play in internal communications and become more directly involved."[14]

A study conducted by AT&T showed that employees expect top management to:

- Tell them ahead of time about changes that will affect their jobs
- Care about how employees really feel about their work
- Seriously consider employee suggestions
- Delegate authority to supervisors
- Be committed to customer service
- Be socially responsible
- Possess the ability to solve problems
- Provide new products or services[15]

Through use of new technology, television, for example, the chief executive can communicate more directly with employees. An organization that uses TV finds that it strengthens other communications activities and makes them more effective. (See Figure 3–1.)

Communications consultant David Brush believes that in-house TV "allows

FIGURE 3-1   Allstate Employees View TV

NOTE: Allstate Insurance Company is among hundreds of U.S. firms now communicating regularly with employees via in-house television shows produced by their communications staff.

SOURCE: Courtesy Allstate Insurance Co.

executives to see themselves as others see them, and often the result is more relaxed and self-assured personal styles."[16] Brush argues, however, that any organization that wants to get into video should first do an analysis of its internal communications needs.

Such an analysis looks at formal and informal communications systems, defines and profiles various audiences and locations, and looks at message flow and content. What comes out of such an analysis are recommendations on what subjects should be covered, media systems to be used, feedback needs, and costs. Brush recommends a combination of internal management and outside consultant to do the work.

COMMUNICATIONS AND PROFITS

Is there a link between communications and profits? The answer is yes. Good communications improve employee productivity, organizational effectiveness, and, ultimately, profits.

The Weyerhaeuser Company has studied the impact of communications on its profitability and has found, for example, that its most profitable plants have the most open and effective communications programs. Concludes a 1982 company report on the subject: "Research and experience show that employees are most highly motivated and make their greatest contribution to the business when there is full and open communications at work. The evidence also shows that where there is an adequate flow of information and ideas among employees, productivity is enhanced while confusion, duplication, and unproductive conflict are minimized. Further, because improving communication requires no capital, the productivity gains that result become total profit."

In its study, Weyerhaeuser came up with a number of recommendations which can apply to almost any type of organization that wants to improve communications:

1. BUILD A POSITIVE COMMUNICATIONS CLIMATE. The assumption here is that: (a) each employee in the unit is a member of the same team, with the right to hear and be heard on things that affect the group, (b) talking about issues and problems is more helpful than not talking about them, and (c) an information void in areas of employee interest will be filled quickly with misinformation.

Said one plant manager, "We have found that employees are very interested in plant detail, not only how it works, but how it's doing. They want to see comparative information on a day-to-day basis . . . this kind of detail . . . makes people interested in their jobs rather than just putting in time."

Weyerhaeuser's report concludes that the key is upward communications channels—hotlines, crew meetings, suggestion systems, attitude surveys, and so on. This is consistent with the company's feelings that workers in the 1980s want more control over their jobs and, when they have it, they are more productive.

Supervisors at some mills have gotten rid of their perqs—white hats, reserved parking, separate offices, and so on. They want to be accessible. At one plant there are regular plant communications meetings where rotating representatives from each work group sit down with the assistant mill manager and other management representatives on a weekly basis for an exchange of information, ideas, and feelings about the operation. With certain exceptions, such as personnel matters, anything can be discussed: profit and loss statements, sales statistics, production plans, cost items, feedback, supervisory practices, and so on. Minutes from each meeting along with management responses are circulated throughout the mill.

2. DEFINE MANAGEMENT RESPONSIBILITIES.   Managers at Weyerhaeuser work to accomplish three things:

a. to provide clear communication of what must be accomplished and what is expected of employees. (If customers are having a problem with a plant product, everyone who can impact improvement is involved.)
b. to provide feedback on how employees meet management's expectations, and timely, candid responses to employee questions and concerns; some experts suggest that feedback must be: *specific, given as soon as possible, reserved for key payoff areas, and provide employees with information they can use to improve performance.*
c. to provide information to do the job: As Weyerhaeuser designs the corporation "to move decision-making to lower levels and to expand the scope of supervisory responsibilities, we need to bear in mind that the information needs of people at all levels are increasing," the report notes. The rule of thumb is "Who else needs to know about this?"

3. SUPPORT SUPERVISORS.   Some subjects that supervisors told Weyerhaeuser management they would like to be informed about include:

a. short-term operating objectives and production plans
b. actual or anticipated changes in plant policies, procedures, or products
c. long-term plans for the operation
d. how business is doing
e. how other shifts are doing
f. success of the product at end sale

One manager in the Weyerhaeuser study discovered that because his supervisors had never had a clear explanation of the work agreement, all answers to employee questions about the union contract had to come from the shop steward. He remedied this by bringing in labor attorneys for both union and management so everyone had a clear understanding.

4. COMMUNICATE WITH WORK GROUPS.   The report concluded that "one trademark of the leading units visited . . . was frequent and regular opportunities for face-to-face communications between people in work groups whose functions are related . . . often these meetings require as little as fifteen–twenty minutes." One plant reportedly reduced its costs by more than a million dollars annually through better communications between two departments. If a meet-

ing is clearly focused, the report concluded, it can be a money and time saver, not a waster.

Each plant has at least a low budget newsletter on 8-1/2 x 11 inch paper. An employee communications committee with representatives from each department helps the "editor" put it out. Members of the communications committee wear "press" stickers on their hard hats and other employees feed them information. Typical stories include: changes in plant procedures, new hires, safety reports, production figures, "well dones," capital project progress, business outlook, and employee questions/management answers.

New employee orientation is both general and specific. It's the best time to communicate, says one official, and "It's the only time we have his undivided attention." The general orientation includes a film about the company and what it does, a presentation on company-employee relationships (pay practices, benefits, expectations), the relationship of the company to the community, and an overview of the region that the employee is working in.

The specific orientation covers plant management, organization and philosophy, unit processes and procedures, introduction to supervisors and co-workers, explanation of the union contract, communication channels, and specifics of the job and why it exists. The whole thrust of the presentation is from the employee's perspective.

SOURCE: The Weyerhaeuser Company, "Communicating for Productivity," May 1982.

Thousands of companies are now doing in-house video programming on a regular basis. Costs on equipment continue to drop, and the same equipment can be used for in-house training programs and orientation.

At Ohio Bell a system called RSVP has used monthly video programs as a method of involving employees in discussions and feedback exercises regarding company issues. Written material is integrated into the system, and at group meetings tapes are viewed and discussed. The tapes contain news clips, executive forums, treatment of single issues, and feedback from previous sessions. Employee response has been favorable by a six-to-one margin.[17]

Internal communications programs do not have to rely on video programming and complex interactive processes to be effective. Simple programs focusing employee attention to corporate policies on subjects such as pollution prevention, safety, or energy conservation can be quite effective and are easy to implement.

In an industry where a good safety record can be worth hundreds of thousands of dollars in reduced insurance premiums, the Kenny Construction Company of Wheeling, Illinois, has successfully used giveaway premiums and educational films to build safety awareness among construction workers. According to manager Philip Kenny, increasingly complex technology, manpower turnovers, and more intricate building projects have added urgency to the need for greater worker awareness regarding safety. The company undertook the production of the first comprehensive film on heavy-construction safety and integrated it with a program that provides increasingly more valuable premiums to teams for safe work days. All employees must see the film before starting work.

The 3M Company in the mid-seventies initiated an in-house program called "Pollution Prevention Pays," which has encouraged suggestions for improving manufacturing processes that reduce pollution through process changes. Technical specialists are given company recognition, advancement, and rewards for ideas. Savings to the company have been in the tens of millions of dollars.

Managers concerned about "Theory Z" and the Japanese ability to motivate working forces would do well to commit more time and resources to enhancing employee-communications programs.

COMMUNITY RELATIONS

There are two faces to community relations. One is the good-neighbor model, the traditional program of open houses, special events like anniversaries, and United Fund drives. The other side is the deadly serious one involving plant closings, opposition to expansion, environmental problems, social activism, or physical calamity.

The standard approach to community relations is the good-neighbor model: Business brings prosperity and jobs to the community; it helps in civic and charitable activities; it pays taxes to support schools and government services; it sponsors baseball and bowling leagues.

In the past there was often a tinge of paternalism to this approach, but at least on the surface the relationship was one of give and take. The city provided fire and police protection, water, sewers, roads, and utilities. The company provided jobs and economic progress.

Recent events have altered this relationship. With communications speed increasing, local problems instantly become national concerns—whether the issue is pollution, community disaster, race, or jobs. For example, minutes after two suspended walkways, filled with dancers and onlookers collapsed at a new Kansas City hotel in July of 1981, news of the horror was being reported throughout the country. What used to affect residents of only one community now becomes part of the national awareness almost immediately. When the bell tolls, all hear and are affected.

In the sixties and seventies, people began agitating for higher minority employment, clean air and water, more breaks for the consumer, higher taxes from industry. Tranquil cities and towns were thrown into turmoil by "outside agitators" from community-action groups. In Rochester, N.Y., for example, the Alinsky Industrial Areas Foundation moved in at the request of local groups to organize workers seeking increased opportunities at Eastman Kodak. Citizen groups in cities across America began to campaign for a stop to company pollution. Changing economic conditions brought an increase in plant closings in the Frost Belt as companies relocated.

Though there are many traditional community relations activities of a positive nature that still dominate, company involvement in community relations today is a more serious and difficult activity. The function of community relations is moving away from being purely a communications issue and is beginning to involve line managers and senior executives. For example, following the 1973 recession, Bethlehem Steel thought it might have to invoke major layoffs in some of its eastern communities. Even though that did not happen at the time, the company embarked on a major program to deal with such an eventuality. Some major pieces of that plan included:

- A detailed community profile on public and private economic characteristics of the community, as well as social and political traits
- Creation of a not-for-profit economic-development corporation with other businesses and cities to attract new ventures and lessen community tax-based dependence on Bethlehem
- Strengthening of corporate contributions and other social investment programs[18]

When the crunch finally came in 1979, the three affected cities were in a better position to handle the closedown and transition. (Unfortunately, Bethlehem's closedown of its Lackawanna, N.Y., plant two days before Christmas 1982 showed that the company had forgotten its own good example.) That is in stark contrast to the 1977 closedown in Ohio of Youngstown Sheet and Tube by the Lykes conglomerate, where there was little advance planning and five thousand workers were suddenly out of a job at the Campbell works.

Public-private partnerships have had significant impact in urban revitalization in many cities. Detroit, Boston, Kansas City, Philadelphia, Baltimore, Oakland, and Cincinnati are some of the cities that have seen center core areas reborn when business has gotten involved *economically* in community relations. In Baltimore business leaders organized the twenty-four member Committee for Downtown. Later the Greater Baltimore Committee was formed by seventy-five corporate chief executives. The group got involved in planning, studies, and needs identification. The successful Charles Center project and the Inner Harbor revitalization are among the more notable results of that effort.[19] According to Walter Hamilton of the Conference Board, retailers, local utilities, and banks often become the core for leadership because they have such a permanent stake in the city.

Part of the communication manager's function is to help identify new bumps in the community's economic and social fabric and bring them to management's attention. The manager should expect this type of monitoring from the communications staff and should regularly review community relations activities and plans. The extent of a firm's participation in a community is a management prerogative, but the wise company stores its goodwill in a community for a rainy day.

CUSTOMER AND CONSUMER
RELATIONS

Some managers consider consumer issues an external function and customer relations an internal communications function. They see consumer issues and consumerism as a specific interest-group problem which must be addressed as a generic business problem that can affect the firm. That is reasonable, but the distinction is quite arbitrary, and in this book, customer and consumer relations are treated as a single topic.

No one has to tell a business manager that unhappy customers are a warning that must be heeded. Yet many companies willing to spend millions on marketing to entice people to buy devote minimal time and effort to after-sales satisfaction. Large retail chains, for example, often devise devilish red-tape procedures to discourage customers from returning goods.

As one consumer writer has observed, ". . . companies love customers but hate consumers. Customers buy; consumers complain."[20] The low esteem in which American business was held during the seventies was attributable in some measure to a perception by customers that they were victims of the *caveat emptor* mentality. According to one report, between 1972 and 1977 there were 450 product recalls in the U.S. by the Consumer Product Safety Commission alone—about two per week.[21] Consumerism has been defined simply as "buyer's rights" and has resulted from a breakdown in the buyer-seller relationship when goods don't measure up to the marketing/advertising claims.

While attempts to establish a federal consumer agency have failed consistently in Congress, and executive-branch interest has waned considerably, there is a substantial amount of legislation protecting the consumer already on the books at both the state and federal levels. Laws governing consumer credit, auto insurance, flammable fabrics, cigarette labeling and advertising, packaging and labeling of consumer goods, and protection of children against hazards are just some examples.

A customer/consumer relations program can be run reactively or proactively. The optimum approach is proactive because it anticipates problems, thereby giving the firm time needed to develop solutions. Even when caught off guard, a company that is monitoring consumer issues and customer complaints on a regular basis is familiar with the channels that have to be addressed promptly—government, consumer groups, legislative members, and trade. Some have argued that in the controversies surrounding the Firestone "500" radial tire and the Ford Pinto gas tank cases, for example, early corporate attention to consumer complaints might have resulted in faster and more responsive action by the firms involved and would have saved those firms from the major PR disasters that followed.

Press reports in 1981 that auto companies were planning to stop announcing safety recalls and deal with them only by letter aroused a storm of protest and a backdown. Greater attention to public-opinion polls and continued consumer sensitivity in this area would have prevented the unwise announcement.[22]

For example, Allstate Insurance Company, concerned about increasing repair bills associated with fender-bender accidents, in the 1970s directed consumer-oriented campaigns for stronger bumpers and later for better passive restraints. The company was widely praised for its consumer-oriented approach, which also made good business sense.

General Foods Corporation for many years has solicited customer opinion and has responded through its staff on a personal basis to the more than one hundred thousand letters it receives yearly. The firm also has run half-day educational conferences and plant tours for community leaders.

One of the strongest consumer programs, and one aimed at *forestalling* complaints, is the Whirlpool Company's. Consumers can use its "cool line" to call the Benton Harbor headquarters free for information on appliances or service. Additionally the company itself makes good on its own warranties and does not depend on local distributors. The warranties are written in easy-to-read language. The company also provides help that lets consumers handle some of the easier problems that arise. Added to all this is an internal education program that stresses the importance of customer satisfaction. Customer satisfaction is also emphasized in national advertising. This program has been going on since the late 1960s.[23]

In establishing a corporate consumer affairs program, one expert recommends that three basic resources be used:

1. *The companys' customers.* A proactive program is used. It goes beyond answering letters or dealing with problems as they arise. The program analyzes information and feeds it to management, which incorporates it into decisions on design, manufacturing, marketing, and other questions that will be responsive to the problems raised.
2. *The public at large.* Public-opinion polls, consumer research, and surveys will provide information on consumer desires and preferences that, while generic, can often be worked into a company program. An example is the Shell Answer Books, which provide consumer information and product promotion at the same time.
3. *Consumer leaders.* Research indicates that consumer leaders are usually savvy about customer attitudes in the marketplace, even more so that senior managers. Smart business people at least listen to what is being said by these advocates.[24]

The discovery by Allstate Insurance officials in the late seventies that the company had interests in common with a citizen group which had charged it with redlining—the group wanted Allstate to increase business but to adapt its policies to the efforts of the group to prevent urban deterioration—emphasized that consumers are not necessarily antibusiness, that they do want good products at reasonable costs, and they don't begrudge companies profit on a good product. People still want value for their money, and even in these days of deregulation, government will remain a last resort for satisfaction, when the marketplace won't deliver.

RECALLS AND
ANNOUNCEMENTS

One of the more unhappy situations firms face is product recalls. In some instances the communications procedures associated with recalls are specified by government order. In other instances there are options available. For a voluntary recall of electric percolators, the Corning Corporation decided on a program in which the objectives included focusing national attention on the defect in a certain run of products, emphasis on the voluntary nature of the recall, attempts to persuade customers to replace defective items, and backup communications to maintain consumer and dealer confidence. In addition, evaluation techniques were built in to determine whether more communication would be necessary.

A multimedia announcement was made, designed to hit weekend papers and broadcast outlets. (The weekend is a slack news period when coverage is likely to be greater.) Live and taped interviews were provided. Major wire services and networks responded. Stories were also delivered to twelve hundred newspapers, to consumer writers, and to trade publications. Ready-to-use ad mats were sent to suburban dailies and weeklies, slide/scripts were sent to three hundred TV stations, and tapes were sent to radio stations. In addition, Corning sent letters to "Action-Line" editors asking them to give out information on the recall. While awareness concerning the percolator defect was considered substantial, according to an evaluation that was conducted after the campaign, only 10 percent of the percolators were ever returned. Major expense incurred for the effort was $1 million for in-store displays that would have been required whether or not communications activities were conducted.[25]

An excellent example of anticipating problems was the customer relations program of the New York Telephone Company that successfully got people in the large metropolitan area to switch over to the prefix "1" for long distance calls. The use of the prefix allowed the phone company to free up additional new prefixes for growth. Originally three-quarters of a million dollars had been budgeted for a saturation advertising campaign, but a communications-planning group decided to rely solely on PR techniques to deliver the message.

The project, called "One Plus," was announced formally in September 1980 at a press conference which received good coverage. Additionally a number of promotional items were given away to boost the effort. Appearances were arranged on twenty radio and TV talk shows, and when the cutover began in late November the story again was hyped. An insert sticker was placed in each bill, and account executives from the company visited the four hundred largest business customers in the city and passed out one hundred thousand promotional items. Hotels, hospitals, and one thousand switchboard attendants were contacted. The success of the program was measured by the fact that when the switchover came, two-thirds of the customers on the first business day did the right thing. The rate was even higher in midtown Manhattan. There was no foul-up of the system, no complaints to management, no adverse media criticism.

Customer/consumer relations should be an important part of a communications program, and managers would do well to develop systems not only to monitor complaints and trends but also to develop marketing-research techniques to crosscheck and anticipate problems.

PUBLICATIONS

Generally there are three types of corporate publications— those for internal distribution, those supporting business activities of the firm, and those aimed at external publics. Publications can be one-time documents, periodicals, annual reports, or occasional papers regarding issues facing the company.

Managers should be concerned about two aspects of publications. One relates to providing a consistent "look" for corporate material. A second relates to clearance procedures and content. Corporate identity and design are considered very valuable and important to "image." Not long ago NBC reportedly paid more than one million dollars for a new corporate symbol and design package carrying that symbol through all visual materials. Publications should reflect a consistent design as do packaging design strategies. (See Figure 3–2.)

Concerning clearance and content, a corporate communications office should have sufficient working knowledge of the firm's policies and procedures so that it enjoys management confidence and does not have to clear everything that goes out of the office. Some managers have a knack for dabbling not only with content, which is their prerogative, but also with style, an area that is not. Just as it is important to hire specialists for media relations, it is also important to use professional writers and editors and to give them creative latitude. Additionally, the writer/editor should be required to know and understand the important aspects of corporate policy, be technically accurate in his or her work, and be aware of the legal implications of the project being written about, if any.

Company publications, as part of the internal communications process, tend to reinforce other media used to communicate with employees. A sense of *community* and *credibility* should be striven for, and emphasis should be directed toward achieving the goals of the organization and the satisfaction needs of the employees. Internal communications should deal with issues facing not only the firm but society in general, including subjects that were traditionally taboo—automation, labor legislation, racial integration, price and wage inflation as they affect the firm's employees.

The better of the new publications *involve* employees through feedback mechanisms and responses to suggestions for improvements in the management process. Says one PR counselor, "The heightened shift towards more participatory management, which necessitates a greater emphasis on dialogue between

FIGURE 3-2 Good Corporate Design Can Have Strong Impact Not Only on Products, But Also on Company's Image, and Even on Stock Price
Sᴏᴜʀᴄᴇ: Courtesy Richardson-Smith Inc., Worthington, OH.

senior managers and employees down the line, [will continue], and therefore [there will be] more attention to internal communications."[26]

Companies have learned that issues are more important than bowling scores in communicating with its employees and are using these publications more effectively. Some companies are also segmenting publications to employees and other constituencies, with separate publications going to the office force, management, sales force, retirees, customers, and even shareholders. Also, publications should not be relied on too much. Many communicators feel people today are not "readers" but "viewers."

SUMMARY
1. Marketing and public relations can overlap but are usually separate

2. Product publicity is an effective means for adding credibility to marketing.

3. Employees are media sensitive and need to be kept informed on a continuous basis on company issues.

4. Consumer programs can help improve products.

NOTES

1. See Philip Kotler, *Marketing for Nonprofit Organizations* (Englewood Cliffs, N. J.: Prentice-Hall, 1982), p. 382.

2. B. G. Yovovich, "Skills Needed, Status Growing," *Advertising Age*, January 5, 1981, p. S4.

3. Ibid.

4. "Harvey's Bristol Cream Tribute to Black Designers" in *1981 Silver Anvil Winners* (New York: Public Relations Society of America, 1982), p. 15.

5. Theodore J. Gage, "PR Ripens Role in Marketing," *Advertising Age*, January 5, 1981, pp. S10–11.

6. Ibid.

7. See "Tight Focusing by Kodak," *Public Relations Journal*, November 1982, p. 16.

8. Nariman N. Karanjia, "The Nitty-Gritty of Speechwriting," *Public Relations Journal*, May 1980, pp. 17–19.

9. "Anaconda Co. with Hal Gardiner & Associates," in *1980 Silver Anvil Winners* (New York: Public Relations Society of America, 1981), p. 57.

10. Allen H. Center and Frank E. Walsh, *Public Relations Practices: Case Studies* (Englewood Cliffs, N. J.: Prentice-Hall, 1981), p. 22.

11. Ibid., p. 35.

12. Yovovich, "Skills Needed," p. S5.

13. Interview with Nan Kilkearry, Allstate Insurance, Chicago, March 20, 1981.

14. Ronald Goodman and Richard R. Ruch, "The Image Of the CEO," *Public Relations Journal*, February 1981, pp. 14–19.

15. Ibid.

16. David Brush, "Internal Communications and The New Technology," *Public Relations Journal*, February, 1981, p. 11.

17. Lee Coyle, "RSVP: The Ohio Bell Approach," *Public Relations Journal*, February 1981, pp. 24–26.

18. Walter Hamilton, remarks before a conference on "Corporate Strategy and Community Well-Being," Northwestern University, May 8, 1980.

19. Ibid.

20. Camille Haney, "Business and Consumerism: Emerging Patterns of Partnership," *Columbia Journal of World Business*, winter 1978, p. 81.

21. Roland W. Warner, "Guidelines for Product Recall," *Public Relations Journal*, July 1977, p. 11.

22. Robert L. Simison, "Detroit Runs Risk of Reviving Industry Critics," *Wall Street Journal*, August 25, 1981, p. 28.

23. See Richard A. Aszling, "Consumer Relations," in Philip Lesley, *Public Relations Handbook*, ed. (Englewood Cliffs, N. J.: Prentice-Hall, 1978), pp. 198–208.

24. Haney, "Business and Consumerism."

25. Lesley, *Public Relations Handbook*, p. 141.

26. Robert J. Wood, president of Carl Byoir & Associates, quoted in *Advertising Age*, January 5, 1981, p. S4.

External Communications Management

4

A NEW SET OF RULES

Understanding how corporate communications relates to the economic mission of the firm especially, in a society that is moving toward greater electronic interconnection is certainly an important management consideration.

But the most dramatic changes in corporate communications in the past decade and a half have been those that relate to the *noneconomic environment*: government, interest groups, the mass media. As with economically oriented communications, the approach is to target information and messages to relevant constituencies.

Because of changing public expectations, which have positioned business as a major contributor to improving society, American business has found itself more accountable. So strong have public expectations become that business suffered a drain on its economic resources in the seventies in attempting to meet new expectations imposed by society, in such areas as environmental improvement.

Business leaders were caught short. It took a while to learn that the rules of the game had changed: that it was essential to be in the marketplace of ideas, arguing the case, rather than blindly reacting to increased regulation.

Companies in many sectors of the business community found that the times required their involvement in public-affairs activities. Public-interest groups, congressmen, regulatory agencies, and others began going after business on pollution, worker safety, consumer, and minority-rights issues. The damage to business credibility, not to mention policies, was substantial. Led by highly visible advocates like Ralph Nader, annual meetings suddenly became acrimonious; lawsuits became numerous; and regulation became onerous.

Corporate chieftains found themselves defending the firm from a bewildering barrage and at the same time were unable to tell where the next assault was coming from. Having thrown millions of dollars into pollution controls to remove 90 percent of wastes, some firms all of a sudden were told they had to remove 95 percent, which might double the cost.

The old solution to such problems had been to go to powerful, friendly congressmen who traditionally had protected business interests. But Congress itself had undergone substantial changes during this period: committee systems were reformed, diffusing power dramatically. Companies learned that they had to put together large coalitions of members of Congress who now were more loyal to their districts and the interests of their constituencies than to party leaders. A new emphasis on developing grassroots support for an issue emerged as the imperative. At the same time reform of campaign laws made it easier to influence congressional races through political action committees (PACs). The 1980 election was the first time that business put such committees together in any way that had significant impact.

ENVIRONMENTAL
SCANNING AND
ISSUES MANAGEMENT

To cope with a new environment, new tools had to be created. Tools were needed to help give a firm both advance warning on societal developments that could affect it and a logical process for dealing with these developments in the public arena. Thus was born the *issues-management process*. The term was coined by public relations consultant W. Howard Chase as a process of *identification, analysis, strategy option, action program, and evaluation of results.*[1]

The real credit for development of issues management belongs to the special-interest groups of the seventies, who showed how to succeed by appealing to narrow interests, constituencies, the media, and government agencies and mount campaigns to achieve goals. Environmental groups were especially good at identifying issues, developing coalitions, gaining coverage and support in the press, and achieving congressional action in a well-coordinated and successful manner. Legislation on drinking water, hazardous wastes, toxic substances, and water-pollution control steamrollered through Congress, backed by these groups, labor organizations, and others who had effectively mobilized grassroots support and public opinion.

The issues-management process is based on the premise that opinion precedes legislation, that trying to influence opinion early can be very important to controlling an issue, that such efforts should create credibility with employees and the public, and that, when appropriate, alternatives can be put forward that will be considered in the public interest and not self-serving. Included in this definition is a sequence in which a problem arises; it is identified and given a label; there is then a hardening process in which it becomes clearly fixed; solutions are developed and presented; the solutions often recommend legisla-

Step One: *THE PROBLEM*	There is a general public *feeling* of dissatisfaction, a sense of frustration, and recognition that a problem exists, but there is yet no name for it.
Step Two: *THE LABEL*	A group, usually an interest group, grabs the issue and labels it, e.g., "redlining," "productivity," "occupational health."
Step Three: *CRYSTALLIZATION*	Attitudes begin to form, the media becomes involved, the reason for the problem becomes apparent.
Step Four: *ANSWERS AND SOLUTIONS*	As the issue is pushed by the interest groups and fanned by the media, all kinds of solutions begin to emerge. A business organization must be involved no later than this stage.
Step Five: *LEGISLATION*	Reacting to public outcry, political leadership begins to introduce legislation and hold hearings. The bandwagon is rolling. The company can only try to affect the course of events at this stage; it is not in control. Legislators become the brokers of the issue, bending in directions that reflect their constituencies and pressures.
Step Six: *IMPLEMENTING*	Judicial review and regulation results in implementation of the solutions and interpretations of the legislation. Court action is possible here.
Step Seven: *NEW PROBLEMS*	Previously nonexistent or unnoticed problems arise after the cycle is completed, and start the cycle again in a new context. Overregulation and reindustrialization are examples where the issue becomes turned around.

FIGURE 4-1   Seven Steps in the Development of a Public Issue

NOTE: This illustration is based on descriptions by Howard Chase; Yankelovich, Skelly & White; Lloyd Newman of Manning, Selvage & Lee; and others.

tion; there is an implementation phase; and finally, a new cycle begins (see Figures 4-1 and 4-2).

Issues have been organized into three general categories:

1. *Current Issues.* These are issues already being considered or acted on by government bodies. Bottle bills pending in various state legislatures are an example. At this stage companies can only *react* to an issue, though sometimes changes in public and legislative perception of such issues can be éffected either by companies or by external events in the society.

2. *Emerging Issues.* These issues will probably be acted upon in the near future but have not yet been formulated or "hardened." This is an evolutionary stage and a good point in which to influence policy. Emerging issues have also been divided into three subcategories:

THE ISSUE LIFE CYCLE

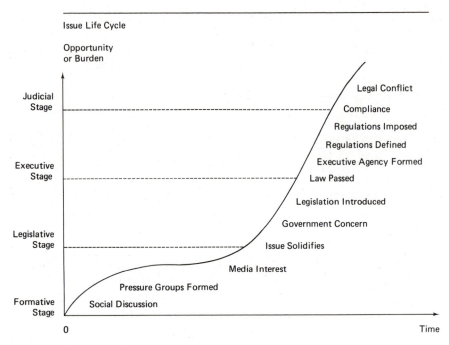

FIGURE 4-2   Continental Bank's Issue Graph

SOURCE: Adapted from "Management Insight," a publication of Continental Illinois National Bank.

a. *Operational.* Dealing with regulatory issues such as product labeling, pollution, and safety

b. *Corporate.* Involving issues such as plant-closing legislation, corporate disclosure, takeover laws, minimum wage

c. *Societal.* Broad issues such as inflation, national health care, and defense

3. *Societal Issues.* Changes involving human attitudes and behavior fall into this category, and these issues are difficult to deal with. They include demographic changes in family size, household formation patterns, reproductive rates, values, and lifestyle preferences.[2]

The general public usually does not initiate issues. Their greatest strengths are passive—passive acceptance, as in pollution controls, or passive rejection, as with Prohibition or seat belts.

Pressure groups are the initiators and activators in issue formation. A small group can be as effective as a large group, depending on its ability to form coalitions, interest the media in its cause, and get support from political bodies. The role of the media is not to create issues but rather to spotlight them—building them up or letting them die, depending on editors' perceptions as to general public interest or sympathy. Many experts recommend close monitoring of the media to determine whether involvement in an issue is warranted.

Distinctions need to be made between fad issues and issues with real public appeal.

Often a triad is formed among a governmental agency, interest groups, and media in which the agency actually encourages the interest group to get involved because it may strengthen the agency's hand. The press, always looking for a good battle, becomes interested as charges are traded. Politicians, who thrive on good press coverage, raise the volume level.

The elected official, however, will usually be smart enough to see which way the wind is blowing before making a commitment. Considerations will include the extent to which the legislator's constituency or committee is involved, the amount of pressure brought to bear by either the interest group or an opposing group, and the legislator's ability to trade support on the issue with colleagues.

The *impact* of an issue is a consideration as well. Some issues affect large segments of the public—equal rights, inflation, health care. Other issues, such as housing and unemployment, are more abstract to many people. Still other issues are quite narrow in their effect—minority rights, reindustrialization and worker safety, for example. These issues need strong leadership to move forward. Finally, there are technical issues, such as export policy and multinational taxation, which are remote for most people.[3]

INSTALLING AN ISSUES-MANAGEMENT SYSTEM

An obvious first step in putting together an issues-management system in an organization is to find out what is already being done. Is the strategic-planning unit already doing environmental scanning? Is the legal staff doing monitoring? How about the Washington office? R&D? What is going on in marketing research? Is anybody pulling it all together?

Some external issues can have an impact on production methods and costs, personnel policy, wage and benefit decisions, and finance, to name a few areas. Some executives *think* they know and understand the important issues facing their organization, but they may have what is known as the home-office perspective—the world begins and ends here in Washington, New York, fill in the blank. A field perspective, an international perspective, and a home-office perspective are all needed in monitoring issues.

Methods for identifying issues are similar to those used in technological forecasting:

1. *Intuitive forecasting.* Expert opinion, Delphi studies, or structured polling
2. *Trend extrapolation.* Plotting change
3. *Normative forecasting.* Looking at established goals and outlining efforts to achieve them
4. *Monitoring events.* Environmental scanning

5. *Cross-impact analysis.* Studying the interaction of issues with each other and with other events

6. *Scenario building and modeling.* Exploring implications of alternative actions and events.[4]

The most widely used method involves scanning of published material and public-opinion sampling. Communications departments in some corporations regularly monitor upwards of a hundred or more periodicals. Scanning also includes watching what is going on in Washington—through the company's outpost there or through a trade association—and monitoring through any of the hundreds of specialized newsletters that seek to point out trends. (One rather expensive newsletter, the *Trend Report*, monitors newspapers in key U.S. cities in California, Washington, Connecticut, Florida, and elsewhere, where trends, according to the report, generally begin.)

Environmental scanning is the "legwork," the data or intelligence gathering that underlies an issue's management or strategic planning operation. Do companies do "environmental scanning" on a continuous basis? A study by Professor Charles Stubbart of the Rochester Institute of Technology indicates that most do not. Reasons for this include continuing changes in top management, decentralization in the organization of the company, low budgets, problems in defining the precise environment, inability to handle technology forecasting, narrowly defined businesses, fire fighting surprise issues that come up, and finally, competition from the many external reports, forecasts, and other information services available to the companies. For these reasons, Professor Stubbart concludes that most scanning programs don't work. ". . . effective environmental scanning depends on the judgments and interpretations of general managers familiar with those environments," he says. "This task cannot be easily abdicated to technical specialists at corporate headquarters."[5]

Once issues are identified, they need to be classified and categorized. Robert Moore of the Conference Board has suggested a list of questions that can help this process:

- To what extent is the emerging issue due to internal as opposed to external factors?
- From a detached, analytical viewpoint, what is the content of the issue? Its inherent characteristics?
- It is a *current* issue or an *emerging* issue?
- What degree of impact is it likely to have on the company? Is it going to be a public-policy issue or a strategic issue, one affecting financial well-being?
- Will the issue affect the entire world or just a few corporations within an industry?[6]

According to Lloyd Newman of Manning, Selvage & Lee, evaluation of an issue calls for a decision on what the "worst case" impact on the company might be. It might be thought of as a present-value question: How much is preventing damage five years from now worth to the company today? This evaluation should be based on an assessment of potential impact on strategic areas: product lines, technologies, and geographic markets and the relative profit contributions of each.

The next step in the process is *planning what the company's position will be.* Factors to consider here include the *speed* at which the issue appears to be growing and potential *future impact* on the firm. In the next phase the company decides on a specific series of *actions* to take at various stages as the issue emerges. This planning should include top managers, operating managers, and the corporate public-affairs department or external communications staff involved in carrying out communications activities. Involvement at the highest corporate level is needed here, since it is part of overall corporate strategy.

In *implementing the program,* task forces move to execute the agreed-on activity. This activity can run anywhere from publishing advocacy ads to lobbying a committee of the state legislature to meeting with adversary groups. The last step, *program monitoring,* involves measuring the effectiveness of the actions undertaken. It consists simply of assessing whether the activities undertaken were accomplished.

The real focus of this process is not on *tactics* but rather on corporate decisions as to *whether* the company needs to get involved, *where* the battle will be fought, and *when* it will be fought. As Lloyd Newman observes, "Effective issues management also can prevent an issue from arising at all, or [can succeed in] redirecting its course. Most advocates of the issues-management process stress the importance of developing a system that heads off trouble."

In refining its system of issues management, a firm needs to work toward a monitoring process that can prevent surprise. The secret is in identifying "weak signals" in the environment. Three examples of strategic issues that were preceded by weak signals are the 1973 Arab oil embargo, the fall of the Shah of Iran, and the move by American consumers to smaller cars.

In putting together an issues-management system an effective "transfer mechanism" should be found to get the right information to the right people. A "user/issue matrix" that identifies which issues are important to whom at each level and function within the organization can be used for this purpose.[7]

HOW A FEW COMPANIES
MANAGE ISSUES

At Sperry Rand the decision to get into issues management came about when the company recognized that special-interest groups were having a major impact on legislation affecting industry. The purpose, according to the corporate and governmental relations VP, is "to be aware of issues and resulting proposed legislation which would in some way restrict or destroy the prerogatives of business unnecessarily—but beyond that, to establish credibility as a source of accurate information and viable alternatives."[8] Issues at Sperry are identified by managers from various disciplines sitting in "business councils," annual management communications conferences involving forty to fifty executives, and international meetings. At the division level comments and assignment of priorities are made. The list is reduced and sent on to top management, where a final review is conducted and dissemination backdown begun. Sperry also uses seventy of its managers at company locations throughout the U.S. as "congressional action managers" (CAMs) and regularly feeds them legislative-issue books, position papers, and "actiongrams" and asks them to make contact with congressmen and congresswomen on specific issues. The CAMs also meet with state legislators to provide input on local issues. Through internal communications Sperry employees are briefed on issues of concern and the firm's point of view.

Kenneth F. Thompson, group executive vice president, told *Industry Week:* "A couple of years ago everyone I talked to said, if you are going to put money in the Mideast, back Iran because it is the most solid and least likely to have a revolution. But because we were aware of the warning signals, through the international part of our issues identification, we were able to act accordingly."[9]

At Upjohn in Kalamazoo, Michigan, a corporate public-affairs committee meets at least once a month to review progress on all public-issue programs. The vice chairman of the board heads the committee. He is also chairman of the company's executive committee. Vice-presidential-level members of the public-affairs committee include operating heads of the company's three principal businesses, the corporate treasurer, the general counsel, the director of pharmaceutical research, and the director of public relations. The Washington public-affairs representative also sits on the committee, and the manager of public-policy planning, who works for the PR VP, acts as committee secretary.

Data collection and action plans are managed by the public relations unit. Reports from two major polling services are used. Tracking of issues and monitoring of publications is a full-time job for the manager of public-policy planning. Since it is an international company, Upjohn monitors activities of the United Nations, the Office of Economic and Community Development, and the Common Market. It also uses a number of commercial reporting services and funds some individual research projects on economic and legal issues. These efforts are coordinated with major trade associations.

Four times a year the PR unit prepares reports on each of the issues before the public-affairs committee. The reports cover current status of issues, impact, company position, action to be taken and the position and actions of trade associations involved. The reports, which are then made available on a confidential basis to corporate officers, deal with as many as sixty to seventy issues, even though many are only in developmental stages. About a dozen are active.[10]

In dealing with an issue, companies often use a multipronged approach involving many constituencies. For example, Standard Oil of Indiana, faced with pressures concerning the issue of divestiture in 1976, developed a strategy aimed at three major constituencies: decision makers, influentials, and communicators. Under each major heading, program elements were established with targets. Responsibility was assigned and a schedule determined.

Decision makers were identified as special persons/groups in seven states with uncommitted or unfriendly senators as well as the media and voters in those states; friendly senators and representatives and their staffs; and subcommittee members and congressional aides in Washington. *Influentials* were defined as trade associations; dealers; jobbers; *contiguous* groups such as unions, suppliers, investors, academics; and employees. *Communicators* were identified as newspaper editorial boards in cities with a strong company presence, friendly writers, and small-to-medium-size local papers of grassroots importance.[11]

GOVERNMENTAL
RELATIONS

As the above example shows, an issues-management action plan often includes lobbying, dealing with regulatory agencies, and meeting with congressional committee aides (who frequently have great influence on legislation) or administration appointees.

In the past many companies dealt with the federal government only through their local congressional representatives or trade associations. In recent years, however, firms have increased their presence in Washington. By 1979 more than five hundred major corporations had set up offices there to handle governmental relations. Also, seventeen hundred trade associations were based there, and PR firms blossomed. A veteran observer has noted, "It's no longer a matter of having an old retainer padding around the halls in the Capitol picking up press releases."[12]

The effectiveness of the Ralph Nader organizations, the environmentalists, consumerists, labor, and other interest groups in the early 1970s taught business the importance of being visible in Washington. In the late 1970s, owing to the efforts of such groups as the Business Roundtable, an influential group of top-level corporate officials who had decided to get involved in public issues, business leaders began lobbying Congress against bills concerning such issues as a consumer-protection agency, labor picketing, minimum wages, and full-employment. Access to members of Congress through lobbyists, large campaign contributions, and home-district people was augmented by the packaging of credible information that the congressional representatives could use to argue the issues. Said one successful lobbyist and door opener: "It is vital to be able to translate all that stuff into the language of the politician—into jobs, payrolls, and economic growth in a particular member's district. Then the member will listen to your case."[13]

The election of Ronald Reagan reduced these activities, since regulatory machinery was now being trimmed and the Senate had a Republican majority. Some firms reduced the size of their Washington programs but most continued to maintain a presence. A Washington office usually handles five main jobs: (1) collection of intelligence, (2) lobbying, (3) issues management, (4) business services, and (5) support to visiting "firemen," such as the chief executive.[14]

In addition to collecting information on potential activities that may affect the corporate mission both at the governmental and international levels, the Washington office also feeds back data to many of these same sources, reflecting the company's position and reasons for its support of various bills, rules, or policies. For some companies the Washington office serves the business side by handling arrangements for selling goods or services to the government, keeping track of government requirements for new products through publications such as the *Commerce Business Daily*, responding to government proposals, and sometimes working directly with engineering, legal, and production departments of the company. The Washington office also handles the red tape and government "boiler plate" often required for contracts.

The lobbying function is one of the most important that the Washington office performs. While the term *lobbying* has certain legal connotations, it is a loose word that can apply to anything from writing a letter to providing information to a congressional staffer to testifying before a congressional subcommittee. In his book *Business, Government, and the Public*, former Presidential adviser Murray Weidenbaum divides lobbying with Congress into "offensive" and "defensive." The offensive posture is used to make sure the company's views on pending bills of special interest to the company is known to senators, representatives, aides, and staffers. In the recent past such efforts have been aimed at abolishing or at least amending the flood of federal regulatory legislation. The defensive function is geared toward stemming investigations or attacks on the company by providing immediate information to Congressional allies that attempts to refute any charges.

Because of the high-level activities that the Washington office engages in and also because of its need to deal with company managers at many levels, the director of the Washington office these days is often given the rank of senior vice president. This also recognizes the need of the Washington chief to speak authoritatively on the company's behalf and to respond quickly.

While a Washington office can't be a complete substitute for the chief executive and can't handle many of the technical details involved in government operations, it can provide the connection point, the door opening, the necessary access.

NURTURING THE GRASSROOTS

The new realities of congressional lobbying go beyond the task of providing information. They also require that one attempt to influence a member of the House through his or her district—in other words, from both ends. Some companies use their own resources to orchestrate grassroots support; others use trade associations or PR firms. Most now use political action committees. During the debates in the late 1970s over energy and tax packages, for example, the National Federation of Independent Businesses used a complex system of letter alerts, Mailgrams, and telephone calls to exhort its 545,000 local members to deluge Congress with probusiness positions.

The U.S. Chamber of Commerce now has six regional offices and fifty staff members to support its issues through 1,500 local congressional action commit-tees. In addition, the Chamber began operating a nationwide satellite TV lobby for business, BizNet (see Figure 4-3), with state-of-the-art studios in Washington, D.C., during the 1982 election campaign.

Use of PR counsel for grassroots campaigns can be quite successful, as well. Hill and Knowlton in 1979 was retained by the American leather industry to wage a battle on two fronts—to help stem the export of cattle hides to foreign processers and to get the American government to negotiate with South Ameri-can countries to do more exporting of their hides. The strategy developed came to be known as the Hide Action Program.[15] It created a national grassroots campaign to "raise the issue to national prominence in order to get congressional or White House intervention." The congressional strategy was to generate enough support to get legislation imposing export controls on cattle hides, to protect the domestic industry. (Only oil and cobalt were embargoed by the government at the time.) The White House strategy was to get the executive branch to negotiate with Argentina, Uruguay, and Brazil to sell a percentage of their hides on the world market. The U.S. was the only country with a free-trade position on cattle hides.

In anticipation of the Senate vote on an embargo, two grassroots-workers rallies were held, letter-writing campaigns were initiated, pressure was exerted by local and state officials, and direct lobbying was begun by industry officials.

FIGURE 4-3 News anchors Meryl Comer and Carl Grant on the set of "BizNet News TODAY," one of numerous programs sent via satellite to members and cable systems from the U.S. Chamber of Commerce studios in Washington, D.C.

Source: Courtesy of BizNet, The American Business Network, Chamber of Commerce of the United States of America.

While the Senate vote was a negative 46–38, against the embargo, it was bipartisan, and the number in favor forced action in the House, which had been considered doubtful from the start. Direct communications were initiated with each House member. Newsletters and notes from industry executives were sent every few days to members of Congress. A "march on Washington" of workers and managers was orchestrated, and visits were paid to representatives. One hundred and fifty thousand letters poured in.

As the situation began to improve in Congress, new pressures were put on the White House. According to Hill and Knowlton, a "New Hampshire strategy" was pursued to get to the Carter White House politically. The industry used the threat of anti-administration advertising and grassroots rallies in that key presidential-primary state to prod the White House into negotiations. It worked. Argentina, for the first time in seven years, opened up to the world market with $12 million in hides, relieving pressures on the American supply. Cost for the program was $165,000, including advertising.

Such successes have meant a boom for the Washington PR business. The success of these firms has encouraged wide-scale buy outs of PR firms by major advertising agencies, who see profitability in the coming years and better access to business leadership through these agencies.

The Washington PR firms, working for corporations, have put together many campaigns similar to the Hide Action program in such areas as food and drugs, proposed bans on television advertising for children, and landing rights for the Concorde. Many firms work for foreign clients as well as domestic ones, representing companies or governments before Congress and the executive branch. PR firms also involve themselves in training clients for appearances before congressional committees and reporters.

While the thrust of this chapter has been directed at the federal level, interaction with state and sometimes local units of government requires giving thought to location of public-affairs offices and staffs. State legislation affecting taxes, health, safety, and the environment often requires governmental relations activities at the state capital. Industries such as insurance, banking, and utilities are significantly affected by the power of the state and they perceive that the power of the state is growing as Washington cuts back.

PACs

If environmentalists and consumerists have taught business how to fight back and deal with the public issues process, surely labor unions have taught business how to get candidates elected through the use of political action committees (PACs). Originally, PACs were "educational" organizations set up by unions to funnel money to candidates. In the wake of Watergate, Congress amended the federal election laws to limit the role of wealthy contributors and end secretive payoffs by corporations and unions by institutionalizing the PAC process. But instead of solving the problem, PACs *became* the problem. In 1982 there were 3,371 PACs, up from 2,551 in 1980. A PAC can give

$5,000 to both a candidate's primary and general election campaign, whereas an individual can give only $1,000. During the 1982 campaign, PACs gave a total of $183 million with $80 million to House and Senate races. Congressman Thomas Downey of New York told *Time* magazine, "You can't buy a Congressman for $5,000, but you can buy his vote. It's done on a regular basis." A study by the *New York Times* showed that one-fourth of the House of Representatives raised more than half of their 1982 campaign money from PACs.[16]

There are also "idealogical" PACs that run campaigns on issues, such as environment, women's rights, balanced budgets, and so on. The most notorious is the National Conservative Political Action Committee (NCPAC), which has run numerous negative campaigns against liberal candidates. Such PACs can spend unlimited amounts of money on their own advocacy campaigns as long as their activity is not authorized by any candidate's official organization, giving them a license for mischief during a campaign.

In addition PACs have raised the cost of campaigning. A campaign for the U.S. House of Representatives has gone from $50,000 to almost $500,000 in the 1982 election. Most PAC money goes to incumbents, not challengers. Bills to limit PACs have not fared well in Congress, though more and more people are recognizing that PACs are close to "legal bribery".

The 1982 campaign saw more state initiatives to alter business practices than ever before. Issues brought before voters included nuclear waste disposal, handgun registration, bottle deposits, and shutting down a nuclear power plant. Initiatives were conceived as a way to take issues directly before voters in order to sidestep heavily financed business and special interest lobbying groups in state legislatures. In the fall 1982 election business spent $25 million to influence voters regarding initiatives. State laws to limit corporate spending on initiatives have been voided by the Supreme Court and there is no limit on ballot-issue campaign spending.[17]

TRADE ASSOCIATIONS

Trade associations can be a very useful adjunct to the government relations activities of the firm. Associations look out for members' interests by keeping them informed on government actions affecting the industry. Associations develop positions on regulations and laws and represent their constituents with position papers and testimony before legislative, regulatory, and advisory bodies.

Trade groups also sponsor conferences and seminars to help members cope with laws and policies once they are in place. Sometimes trade groups will go to court to fight for their members. Also, such groups undertake studies of the potential effect of laws and regulations and use that information for lobbying. The effect of returnable-bottles legislation on jobs, the impact of imported steel on American firms, the cost to utilities of complying with sulfur oxide regulations are typical examples.

In complex areas, such as occupational health and safety or pollution control, trade associations can provide important advice and guidance to members who might have trouble wading through the Federal Register. Voluntary codes put together by trade groups can often have a blunting effect on proposed government rules, as in motion picture ratings or chain saw kickback standards. Beyond trade associations, there are large umbrella groups like the U.S. Chamber of Commerce and the National Association of Manufacturers, which represent broad-scale business issues. Business policy research is accomplished by think tanks like the Conference Board and the American Enterprise Institute.

The currency of trade associations, as with governmental relations offices in Washington, is *information*. Associations provide Congress with detailed analyses of proposed legislation unavailable elsewhere. This information often encompasses consequences of the legislation in home districts of members of Congress.

ADVOCACY ADVERTISING

Question: What do the following headlines all have in common?

- "Why does every emerging nation want its own steel industry?"
- "American consumers know a good product when they see it"
- "Trial by television"
- "We get more radiation in our livingrooms than from nuclear power plants"

The answer: Each represents an attempt by a company to deal with a public issue through a full-page newspaper ad. The term given to such efforts is *advocacy advertising*. (See Figures 4-4a through 4-4d.)

The first headline above was one of a series of ads run by Bethlehem Steel over the years on various themes—environmental controls, foreign trade, productivity, and inflation. The second ad, a defense against a *Consumer Reports* critique of kerosene heaters by the CEO of Kero-Sun, Inc., the market leader, emphasizes health and safety aspects of the product.

The third headline, "Trial by Television," was a response by Kaiser Aluminum to an attack on its aluminum wiring as unsafe. The ad called coverage of the issue by ABC News a kangaroo court. According to Kaiser, at least one thousand responses were received, with 96 percent in favor of the company's position. The fourth headline, regarding radiation, was published by a utility-contractor group called America's Electric Energy Companies and ran in January 1980, ten months after the accident at Three Mile Island.

All four headlines and the ads that accompanied them dealt with issues of importance to the companies involved, some more directly than others. In the case of the steel ads the campaign was part of a continuing company commit-

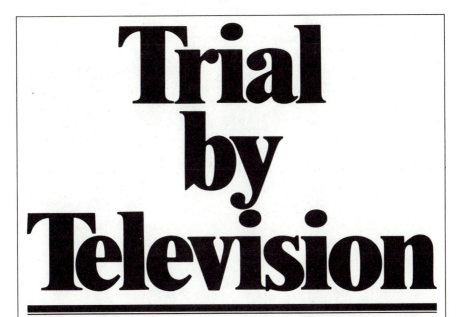

Trial by Television

The American system of justice is founded on a simple principle: The accused has the right to be fairly heard in his own defense, and to confront and cross examine his accuser.

This principle, more than any other, defines the difference between freedom and tyranny.

Yet today, here in America, charges are aired before tens of millions of people without fair opportunity for the accused to respond.

They call it "investigative" television journalism. We call it "Trial by Television."

Much of investigative television journalism is solid and responsible reporting—but much is not. Many producers of "news magazine" programs too frequently select story segments with their minds already made up about the points they want to make. Then they proceed to select the facts and quotes which support their case. "Interview" opportunities are sometimes provided the "accused." But the edited "interview" format puts the producer (i.e. the accuser) in full control of deciding what portions, and how much of, the accused's defense the public will be allowed to see.

Rarely does this result in balanced and objective coverage.

The television production team becomes the accuser, judge, and jury. With no real recourse for the accused to get a fair hearing in the court of public opinion. Yet the viewing public is led to believe that the coverage is balanced and objective. This is a deceptive and very dangerous practice.

"Trial by Television," like the kangaroo courts and star chambers of old,

needs to be examined. If we decide, as a society, that we are going to try issues, individuals, and institutions on television, then some way must be found to introduce fairness and balance.

Here's what we're doing about it.

Recently, Kaiser Aluminum was the victim of grossly misleading and inaccurate statements on a segment of ABC's "20/20" program. On its "20/20" segment of Thursday, April 3, the announcer accused aluminum house wiring of being unsafe, and Kaiser Aluminum of intentionally marketing an unsafe product. These accusations are blatantly wrong.

Although we were offered an opportunity to be "interviewed," "20/20" reserved the privilege of editing any part of our statement. Any defense we might have made would be subject to their sophisticated editing techniques, and to their commentary. Since it was evident to us that the producers had already formed their opinions, we declined their offer. How can a defense be fair if it is subject to censorship by the accuser?

We have been advised by many to ignore the "20/20" attack on the basis that you can't fight the network, and to prevent further harassment. We will not allow ourselves to be maligned or misrepresented by any group—even television.

Here is what we are doing:
1. We have demanded a satisfactory retraction from ABC-TV.
2. We are asking the Federal Communications Commission, under their "Personal Attack" doctrine, to order ABC-TV to provide us with time and

facilities to present our side of the story to the same size audience in a prime time segment.
3. We have asked Congressman Lionel Van Deerlin (D-California), Chairman of the House Sub-Committee on Communications to consider Congressional hearings to examine the implications of this increasingly insidious and dangerous practice.

Here's what you can do about it.

Unfortunately, not all victims of "Trial by Television" have the resources to defend themselves, as we are trying to do. Their only defense is you.

If you believe the rights of the accused to fairly defend themselves are more important than sensational attempts to increase TV ratings; if you believe the right of the public to get balanced and objective information on issues of importance is as important as it has ever been, please speak out and let your elected representatives know.

America was conceived to prevent tyranny by providing checks on the power of any institution. Today, a new power is dispensing its own brand of justice—television. There's only one check against it. You.

If you are upset by the unfairness of "Trial by Television," write your elected representatives, or us at Kaiser Aluminum, Room 1137KB, Lakeside Drive, Oakland, CA 94643.

One person can make a difference

KAISER ALUMINUM & CHEMICAL CORPORATION

FIGURE 4-4 Four Advocacy Ads Covering Government Regulation, Nuclear Safety, Press Coverage, and Product Safety

SOURCE: Courtesy Kaiser Aluminum.

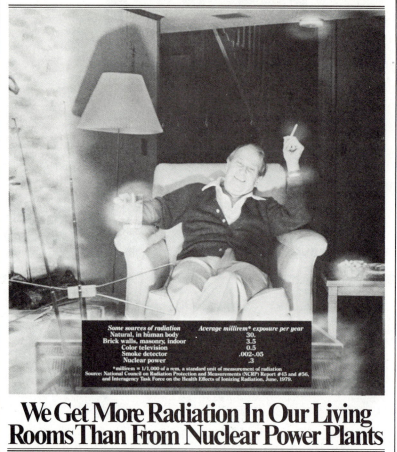

Some sources of radiation	Average millirem* exposure per year
Natural, in human body	30.
Brick walls, masonry, indoor	3.5
Color television	0.5
Smoke detector	.002–.05
Nuclear power	.3

*millirem = 1/1,000 of a rem, a standard unit of measurement of radiation
Source: National Council on Radiation Protection and Measurements (NCRP) Report #45 and #56, and Interagency Task Force on the Health Effects of Ionizing Radiation, June, 1979.

We Get More Radiation In Our Living Rooms Than From Nuclear Power Plants

Radiation is a subject of deep concern to many Americans. Because of the potentially harmful effects from prolonged exposure to *all* types of radiation, this concern is understandable, particularly since we all receive constant exposure to some radiation from sources ranging from the sun to household appliances.

Yet because most of us do not understand radiation, this concern is often turned into unjustified fear. For example, some people say that nuclear power plants should be banned because they release radiation into the environment.

Without a full understanding of radiation, some of us might tend to agree with that premise. But that kind of thinking ignores some very basic *facts* of life—facts which we should all understand before jeopardizing our nation's energy future.

Radiation: A Fact Of Life

Scientists and medical experts have been studying radiation for eighty years. We know more about radiation and its effects than we do about most harmful substances in the earth's atmosphere.

We know, for example, that radiation is a *natural* part of the world in which we live. It comes from the sun. It has always been a part of the earth. We even have radiation in our bones.

In addition, man has invented many devices to improve our lives—items which also release radiation. X-rays have been of enormous medical benefit to mankind. . . yet they also release radiation. Jet travel is another example. A person receives twice as much radiation during one round-trip flight from New York to San Francisco than if he lived next door to a nuclear power plant for one year!

Yet you don't hear anyone suggest we should ban x-rays or air travel. The offsetting benefits to society are simply too great.

Many other sources—some found in our own living rooms—contain levels of radiation much higher than those found near nuclear power plants. (See inset).

Nuclear Radiation: Risks And Benefits

By comparison, nuclear power plants release very little radiation. Even during the accident at Three Mile Island—which nuclear opponents have called the worst nuclear "disaster" in history—the average person living within a fifty-mile radius of the plant was exposed to only 1.5 units of radiation. That's even less radiation than a person receives from living for one year in a house made of brick.

Yet what about a serious accident at a nuclear power plant? First, a nuclear plant *cannot* explode like a bomb—it is physically impossible. Second, every nuclear power plant is designed with a series of redundant safety systems so that even if one system fails, there are others to prevent any harm to the public or the environment. The ultimate safety system is a concrete structure several feet thick—strong enough to withstand major earthquakes or even the crash of a commercial aircraft. So when malfunctions occur, the containment structure prevents the release of any harmful amount of radiation into the atmosphere—which is exactly what it did at Three Mile Island.

When considering the *facts* of radiation—and the radiation risks of nuclear power, we must also remember the *benefits* derived from those limited risks. Nuclear power is already supplying 13% of America's electricity needs. We need all the energy we can get. Radiation is a natural part of our lives and should not be used as an excuse to deprive Americans of one of our most valuable energy resources.

Nuclear Power. Because America Needs Energy.

SOURCE: Ad created by Smith & Haroff, Inc., on behalf of the U.S. Committee for Energy Awareness.

The 1970s model won't meet America's needs for the '80s

The Clean Air Act is up for reauthorization this year. As a nation, we must decide whether the legislative solutions tailored to the needs of the '60s and '70s are the correct solutions for the '80s. Clean air, of course, remains a key national priority. But today's environmental and economic conditions have changed. The law should adapt to reflect these new needs and realities.

To help update the Clean Air Act, the National Commission on Air Quality was asked to submit recommendations. The commission endeavored to reconcile a host of conflicting interests. But we believe it overlooked certain key facts and gave insufficient weight to America's pressing energy requirements and the current state of our economy.

The report does admit that the act "can affect energy development in certain areas." It acknowledges that newcomers—presumably energy developers as well—"will sometimes have difficulty" establishing major facilities. It concedes the act "could affect the number, size, and location of oil shale facilities" in the West and may be blocking the recovery of heavy oil in California. It admits that coal conversion in the Northeast "could be limited by the air quality standards." But then, having said all that, it concludes that "energy...expansion can proceed largely as planned" under current law.

Frankly, we fail to see how such a conclusion can be justified. The original Clean Air Act was formulated at a time when air quality was rapidly deteriorating in key areas of the nation. Energy was cheap and plentiful, and the economy was thriving. It made good sense then to channel more of the country's wealth into alleviating America's environmental problems. But three major events have since taken place:

1. The country has made enormous strides in improving air quality. Between 1973 and 1978, average annual concentrations of sulfur dioxide decreased 20 percent and carbon monoxide by close to a third. Moreover, today's new-model cars produce over 75 percent less emissions than 1967 models.

2. The oil embargo of 1973-74 and the curtailment in supplies caused by the situation in Iran have brought home the need to reduce U.S. dependence on foreign oil.

3. The U.S. economy has fallen off—so much so that the electorate has clearly demanded a new emphasis on making the country more productive again.

Instead of trying to modify the ground rules so as to allow greater U.S. development of conventional fuels, the commission sticks with the same panaceas that fell short, even in the '70s, of meeting America's energy needs: namely, conservation and the development of renewable energy sources. But this falls far short of what's needed. With the bill for foreign oil nearing $100 billion a year, inflation in excess of 10 percent, and some major industries in deep trouble, the nation can no longer afford the sky-high price of single-minded environmental zeal—especially since the benefits from incremental improvements in air quality have become progressively smaller relative to the cost. U.S. energy development can be encouraged, not discouraged as it has been. This can be consistent with air standards which protect public health.

Despite the sharp climb in OPEC oil prices and improvements in industry's ability to burn coal cleanly, the Clean Air Act has inhibited switchovers from oil to coal. In 1980, coal accounted for about the same share of U.S. energy use as it did in 1968. In New York, Consolidated Edison has been trying for the past eight years to convert three oil-fired plants to coal, the fuel they were originally designed to burn. Although the utility has finally obtained a key air quality permit, at least 26 more potential regulatory roadblocks still loom.

And the current Clean Air Act is complex, often redundant: A proposed energy facility may have to run the gauntlet of dozens of potential roadblocks and delays, for up to 17 different pollutants. Vice President Bush, who heads the President's regulatory-relief task force, is developing proposals to relieve some of these problems. But other, more serious problems can only be fixed by Congress.

The Clean Air Act has made a valuable contribution to America's environmental health. But we think that, in its present form, it does and will continue to impede development of America's energy resources. Congress should adapt the act to the '80s so it will not only protect health but also allow the nation to meet its economic goals and social priorities. And both require adequate energy.

Mobil

SOURCE: Courtesy of Mobil Oil Corporation.

SOURCE: Courtesy of Kero-Sun, Inc., Kent, CT.

ment to speak out on public issues. The third ad was a direct response from the company to an attack by the media and was initiated in self-defense. The final ad, taken by a trade association on behalf of its membership, addressed the psychological fears the public has regarding nuclear power.

The change in political administrations in the U.S. in November 1980 cut down dramatically on the anti-government rhetoric in advocacy advertising. A report by the Association of National Advertisers released on October 6, 1981, while noting that 1981 corporate advertising expenditures might top $1 billion for the first time, said that the use of advocacy advertising had reached a plateau. The major thrust now appears redirected toward corporate identification.

Nevertheless most any day of the week there is some kind of advocacy advertising carried in the major daily newspapers in the U.S.—especially the *New York Times* and the *Wall Street Journal*, each of which has a national audience. The idea is not new. The Warner & Swasey Company of Cleveland began running ads that talked about economics and the importance of free enterprise as far back as the 1940s. Playtex Company sponsored ads signed by its president, A.M. Spanel, in major newspapers for many years. Those ads addressed personal views on domestic and foreign affairs.

Advocacy ads are distinguished from *institutional* ads. The latter attempt to strengthen the corporate image to shareholders, analysts, customers, or the general public. (See Chapter 7.) Examples of institutional ads are: "We're in business today . . . and we'll be here tomorrow" or "We're providing energy for tomorrow" or "Expanding today . . . to serve you tomorrow."

University of Texas at Dallas professor S. Prakash Sethi has defined advocacy advertising as concern with the "propagation of ideas and the elucidation of controversial issues of public importance in a manner that supports the position and interests of the sponsor, while expressly downgrading . . . opponents and the accuracy of their facts." He says an advocacy ad has three components: identification of sponsor interest; intensity of advocacy; and specificity in identifying the adversary: big government, activists, foreign competition, etc."[18]

The acknowledged big spender in this form of communication has been Mobil Oil. As noted earlier, Mobil is one of the giants in corporate communications, with an annual PR budget in excess of $20 million. Two-thirds of that money goes for sponsorship of arts programming on public and commercial television and the purchase of space in print media ($5 million) for its advocacy program. This large amount of money became available when the company decided during the 1973 oil crisis to stop its consumer advertising. Mobil, like other oil companies, had traditionally been a low-visibility company, though it had started running ads on the opinion-editorial (op-ed) page of the *New York Times* as early as 1971. With the energy crisis and a new management commitment to getting out front and speaking in the industry's defense, the op-ed advertising was expanded to other newspapers in major cities and the *Wall Street Journal*. The ads, which now run weekly, occupy about one-eighth of a page and cover many subjects. The company believes the ads have had a subtle influence over time on the editorial slant of the *New York Times*.

Mobil openly acknowledges that its op-ed pieces are directed specifically at opinion leaders in the U.S.

A 1978 study of editors and reporters by Opinion Research Corporation ranked Mobil fifth of all U.S. companies for "most effective image with the press corps." Mobil's soft-sell advocacy program, a weekly Sunday supplement column called "Observations," is regularly evaluated and comes out with high readership percentages. "Observations," written in short paragraphs and featuring clever woodcuts, costs about $3 million annually.

Mobil's strategy has been to position itself as the policy leader for the oil industry. Since it attempts to appear *different* from other oil companies, the company believes, it has a better chance to get its case across to critics. But an evaluation by *Fortune* magazine concluded, "When it gets down to fundamentals, however, Mobil has no message substantially different from that of the rest of the oil industry or indeed from that of large corporate enterprise in general."[19]

Though Mobil's communications chief, former labor lawyer Herbert Schmertz, has made many efforts over the past few years to expand the company's advocacy efforts to commercial television, he has not met with much success.[20] In addition to its awareness that commercial television reaches so many people directly and effectively, Mobil's concern over what it has perceived as unfair news coverage by the networks has been the driving force behind efforts to get its noncommercial messages on the tube. Schmertz began his campaign on this issue with a request to run a rather mild ad on offshore drilling. Only NBC agreed to run it. CBS argued against accepting such advertising by claiming that "those with the most money would get to talk the loudest."[21] Schmertz countered that Mobil would even pay the cost for critics to rebut the ad.

The Mobil conflict with the networks over advocacy ads was part of a long-standing feud between corporations and television over news coverage and fairness. (See Chapter 5.) Among Mobil's more famous run-ins was its rebuttal to a five-part miniseries about the oil industry, which aired on the NBC station in New York City, and a rebuttal to a CBS News report on oil industry profits, filmed in front of a Mobil gas station. Both rebuttals were published in the *New York Times*, the *Wall Street Journal*, and other major newspapers. The headline used to take on the miniseries was titled simply "Hatchet Job" and used little hatchets for paragraph indentations. The response to CBS was titled "How CBS on October 24, 1979 Prefabricated the News." These kinds of counterattacks, Schmertz feels, gain respect from people both inside and outside the media. "People know that if they take a swipe at us, we'll fight back," says Schmertz's boss, Chief Executive Rawleigh Warner, Jr.

Schmertz has noted candidly that Mobil really doesn't feel it has moved public opinion concerning specific issues. The downside risk of such ambitious visibility is that when problems arise as they have for Mobil over the years, the press comes on with a vengeance, and credibility suffers.

Mobil's two-fisted approach is worth a book in itself. The approach is born of management's feeling that being unconventional is an important ingredient to being successful. The company has gone to such lengths as taking ad space to go after a satirical piece by Russell Baker in the *New York Times*. Such an approach, flippant at times, however, sends mixed signals to the public and may bring out the urge among regulators, journalists, and others to "even things up" with the town bully.

PREACHING TO THE CHOIR

Most PR professionals feel that advocacy advertising is merely preaching to the choir, that the ads are seen by the chief executive's peers and not by those who should be reading them. Commenting on Mobil's approach, Charles Knapp, chief executive of Financial Corporation of America, noted: "They shouldn't be spending a lot of money on ads in the *Wall Street Journal* to justify what they do. People who read the *Journal* don't need that. The companies like Mobil have to appeal to the guy who's buying three gallons of gas for his '57 Chevy."[22] A quantitative evaluation of advocacy advertising, normally aimed at "influentials" or "opinion makers" has yet to be undertaken.

Professor Sethi observes that the choice of media for advocacy ads—major dailies and national papers—indicates that the intended audience is better informed than most but that most ads deliver superficial messages that preclude their effectiveness. "Too often," says Sethi, "advocacy advertising is confined to what the corporation wants the world to hear rather than what the world wants the corporation to address."[23] His solution is for outsiders to evaluate and approve the ads. Others argue that a focus group approach would be more practical. The real answer, though, to whether advocacy works is found in the reservoir of credibility that the firm achieves over time.

Writing in the *Harvard Business Review*, Vassar College Professor David Kelley argues that business uses issues ads in strictly a defensive way that does not challenge the assumptions of those attacking it. "We should not assume that business can adapt to any environment just by being nimble and pragmatic [via external relations] . . . if the public demands are accepted as right against the corporation, then workers and consumers will not hesitate to enlist the aid of government in securing them," he asserts, in urging that business be proactive in defending its rights and not accepting anti-business ideology.[24]

The potential for advocacy advertising is dynamic. With the new telecommunications media opening scores of broadcasting and receiving options for home and office, advocacy certainly will find new options for delivery.

The real issue for the future is equal access for opposing views. Deregulation will not solve that question for broadcasting. The established news organizations argue that they provide this equal access because they are objective. The push by business for access to advocacy is based upon a perception of unequal news coverage.

Nuclear power advocates, such as The Committee on Energy Awareness, and its foes, such as the Safe Energy Communications Council, have squared off in many of the major U.S. markets, running paid TV commercials supporting their position. In some areas where pro-nuke advocates have bought time, anti-nuke groups sometimes have sought free response time via the Fairness Doctrine. This may portend the nature of future issue skirmishes on commercial TV. The networks remain on the sidelines, afraid of having to give out free time.

INTERNATIONAL
INTELLIGENCE

Many large international corporations routinely gather intelligence on political situations in foreign countries where they operate. Sources of information include personnel on the scene, governmental relations offices in Washington, and staff assigned to information gathering at the home office.

It can be argued that political intelligence should be part of strategic planning instead of corporate communications. But it also can be argued that political intelligence is a part of the issues-management process. A decision on placement should be based on how the firm is organized for gathering and processing information from outside sources.

The structure of this function varies, but it can fall under the communications heading and fits well with issues-management and public-affairs responsibilities. The incumbent in such a position should be a specialist in such areas as foreign affairs or intelligence collection. Gulf Oil Company, for example, has a four-person international studies unit, which is completely separated from the rest of the company in order to insure objectivity.[25] That unit was responsible for giving the company early warning concerning the downfall of the Shah of Iran, allowing the company to make adjustments, since Iran at the time was providing 10 percent of the company's oil supplies.

That same group at Gulf, working on its own, decided to recommend going into Marxist-run Angola. This action was recommended despite U.S. government analyses that the country would be merely a Russian satellite. The arrangement has reportedly proved satisfactory. Another company, Xerox, relies heavily on local managers abroad although it does use outside experts. American Can uses a computerized matrix system to measure risk investment.

The Conference Board has been working on ways to improve political analysis for countries. An initial survey of 193 companies doing substantial business abroad found that half did not use any formal means of assessing the political and social situations in the countries they do business in. This can mean not only trouble for a company attempting to locate or maintain a plant but also missed opportunities for business that could be uncovered with good analysis.

Various approaches have been developed for monitoring risk. E. T. Hanner, who has developed a business-environment risk index, evaluates ten variables for three periods: the present, five years out, and ten years out. A second step involves giving additional points to factors that might have special impact. A rating panel of country-specific experts is used to make the assessment.[26]

Another system uses experts whose estimates are based on "precursive conditions" for adverse actions in each country.[27] Probabilities are established and a cross-impact analysis is conducted.

SUMMARY 1. The most dramatic changes in corporate communications in the past decade are related to increased involvement in public issues.

2. An issues-management program can help a firm monitor and identify issues in which it may need to become involved.

3. A firm must consider a number of audiences when attempting to communicate on public issues, and it should target its involvement to only those that are relevant.

4. Advocacy advertising is of marginal benefit in corporate communications.

5. The gathering of foreign intelligence can help a firm in its international activities.

NOTES

1. Raymond P. Ewing, "Issues, Issues," *Public Relations Journal*, June 1980, p. 14.

2. Lloyd N. Newman, "Issue Management," in *Public Affairs Manual*, National Association of Manufacturers, September 1980 pp. 2–3.

3. Robert H. Moore, "Scanning the Horizon for Emerging Issues," remarks to the CNA Life Reinsurance Conference, Chicago, September 1978.

4. James R. Bright, *A Brief Introduction to Technology Forecasting*, (Austin, Texas: Permaquid Press, 1972), pp. ix–x.

5. Charles Stubbart, "Are Environmental Scanning Units Effective?" *Long Range Planning*, June 1982, pp. 139–45.

6. Moore, "Scanning the Horizon."

7. John Hargreaves, "Issue Management: Its Rationale and Discipline," *IPRA Review*, 1978, pp. 13–15.

8. Donald B. Thompson, "Issue Management: New Key to Corporate Survival," *Industry Week*, February 23, 1981, p. 79.

9. Ibid.

10. Ibid.

11. Interview with Joseph Hammond, VP Public and Government Affairs Department, Standard Oil Company, conducted by John Hatcher for unpublished paper, August 1981.

12. See "The Corporate Image, PR to the Rescue," *BusinessWeek*, January 22, 1979, p. 54.

13. Walter Guzzardi, "How to Win in Washington," *Fortune*, March 27, 1978, p. 55.

14. Murray Weidenbaum, *Business, Government, and the Public* (Englewood Cliffs, N.J.: Prentice-Hall, 1981) pp. 290–95.

15. "Hide Action Program with Hill and Knowlton, Inc.," in *1980 Silver Anvil Winners* (New York: Public Relations Society of America, 1981), p. 39.

16. "Running With the PACs," *Time*, October 25, 1982, pp. 20–26.

17. Steven D. Lydenberg and Alice Tepper Marlin, "Business and Votes," *The New York Times*, October 27, 1982, p. 25.

18. S. Prakash Sethi, "Advocacy Advertising and the Multinational Corporation," *Columbia Journal of World Business*, fall 1977, pp. 32–46.

19. Irwin Ross, "Public Relations Isn't Kid-Glove Stuff at Mobil," *Fortune*, September 1976, pp. 106–11.

20. ABC television in July 1981 announced it would accept advocacy advertising for late-night viewing only. There had been no takers through early January 1983. Most television stations, according to one study, will accept issue advertising in some circumstances. The FCC on September 16, 1981, announced it would seek congressional approval to eliminate the Fairness Doctrine, which would remove the requirement of equal coverage for both sides of an issue and open the way for advocacy advertising, at least in theory. See "The Fairness Doctrine a Subject at Seminar," *New York Times*, September 16, 1981.

21. Mobil's Style Strikes Some Bosses as Arrogant, Others as Admirable," *Wall Street Journal*, July 28, 1981.

22. Ibid.

23. Sethi, "Advocacy Advertising."

24. David Kelley, "Critical Issues for Issues Ads," *Harvard Business Review*, July-August 1982, pp. 880–87.

25. Louis Kraar, "The Multinationals Get Smarter About Political Risks," *Fortune*, March 24, 1980, p. 87.

26. F. T. Hanner, "Rating Investment Risks Abroad," *Businesss Horizons*, April 1979, pp. 17–23.

27. D. W. Bunn and M. M. Mustafaoglu, "Forecasting Political Risk," *Management Science*, November 1979, pp. 1157–67.

Meeting the Press

5

You're writing a book on media for managers? ... All businessmen need to know are three little words: tell the truth.

—Frederick Klein
Wall Street Journal

BUSINESS ENCOUNTERS MEDIA

How does a firm communicate its credibility and argue its case on public issues? The primary communications channel, the main broker for society's attitudes towards business, is the news media (referring primarily to television and newspapers).[1]

The media are channels for disseminating information, but at the same time they are independent businesses and, collectively, a major institution: the fourth branch of government, as they have often been described. And while the media are a channel of information, they also process and filter information, so that what is fed into the channel does not always come out the same way. This is not to say that one cannot communicate effectively through the media; it does mean that one must understand how to do it.

In Chapter 1 we established ground rules for successful communications: The organization must be both legitimate *and* credible. A company can be legitimate by finding a role in the economic and social well-being of the nation or world. It can be credible by stating its case positively and in the public interest. It is truly credible only as long as it continues to tell the truth. If a company proceeds to base its communications program on these two principles, it should be successful in dealing with the media. Eventually. This does not happen overnight. And further, it must be remembered that over time there has been a lot of bad blood between the media and business that must be taken into account.

The cat-and-mouse antagonism between the media and business is legendary—remember Irving Shapiro's rule (see Chapter 1) that to get ahead in business one shouldn't talk to reporters. Summing up the business/media conflict, Howard Simons and Joseph Califano write: "To the businessman, too often the antagonism boils down to this—business builds up; the media tears down. To the media, too often the antagonism boils down to this—business always hides its wrongdoing; only the media penetrates this stone wall."[2]

The antagonism grew louder during the seventies as the media, reflecting changing public opinion, began treating business more and more like a public institution instead of a private one. People began realizing that business decisions had tremendous impact on their health and well-being, the quality of their lives, what their kids watched on TV, and on the health of children yet unborn.

As the media grew more demanding, business leaders were unprepared to discuss their decision making or its impact on the media or the public. The media, used to the give-and-take of dealing with government and politicians, found business people defensive, antagonistic, and hidden behind their corporate doors. Business people, on the other hand found out the media were very powerful, that they sometimes got things wrong, and that controversy sells newspapers.

From the perspective of the news media, business people were unprepared for increased public interest and additional scrutiny by the press. They didn't know how to talk to reporters, they didn't understand television, they weren't able to communicate their position on issues without using jargon and they didn't like explaining themselves or their actions to the outside world. Mostly, however, business people did not understand that the public no longer regarded business as a "private" sector but rather as a sector that had a great effect on their lives.

Business also discovered that all institutions are not equal: that while the news media are businesses as well, they have special protection under the Constitution. Business unhappiness with what it perceived as unequal status with the media was summed up by a businessman at a conference on media and business:

> . . . what . . . disturbs me the most, is the double standard between the press and business on matters of responsibility. I was, frankly, surprised to hear a television executive say that he wouldn't wait a day or two to go to press, or go on the air, with a story about an [CIA] agent, even though it might cost him his life, for fear of competition. Whereas I don't think the press would stand for it if a drug company rushed its product out quickly for fear of competition.
>
> I heard it said that the press will protect confidentiality at almost all cost, whereas if a business tries to, it will be considered a cover-up.
>
> I heard it said that the press will one way or another buy information, while business will be castigated for questionable or sensitive payments.
>
> And finally, I heard . . . that the press reserves its right to observe the orders of the courts, even when none of us would tolerate the fact that the

president of the United States raised that reservation. No businessman could say, "I will reserve the right to observe an order of the court."

I think, in looking at business, perhaps the press could look at it from its own perspective of its engaging in competitive practices and perhaps the coverage might be a little more balanced."[3]

The rising importance of economic issues in the late seventies and the realization that "big government" had been unable either to solve social problems or curb inflation, began to raise public expectations for business performance. The public, faced with increasing economic pressures and disenchanted with government, allowed business an expanded role in solving the major pressing societal problem. Responding to this change in public attitudes, the media began to strengthen coverage of business issues.

"A decade ago," notes Seymour Topping, managing editor of the *New York Times*, "the business/financial editor of [the paper] seldom ventured into the daily news meetings of the executive editor or the managing editor. Today, no front-page conference convenes without the . . . [business] editor."[4]

JOURNALISM CHANGES
SHAPE

In 1964 when the U.S. Supreme Court ruled in the the *New York Times* v. *Sullivan* that virtually anybody in the news was a public figure and would have to prove malicious intent to win a libel case, the media hailed the decision as a major step forward in protecting freedom of the press. In the years since then, that protection granted the media by the High Court has become, as Judge Irving B. Kaufman has said, "a stunning if well-intentioned failure." A study by the Libel Defense Resource Center found that out of a sample of fifty-four defamation and invasion-of-privacy cases brought against the media since 1978, the defendants were ordered to pay damages in forty-seven cases. Thirty of the awards totaled more than $100,000, twelve exceeded $259,000, and nine went beyond a million dollars. This clearly shows that the protection of the Sullivan case no longer applies, concludes Judge Kaufman, and "the spector of virtually unlimited damage awards in defamation suits obviously has a substantial chilling effect on the media's performance of its vital role."[5] Front page cases such as the Carol Burnett victory over the *National Enquirer*, the major win by the CEO of Mobil over a *Washington Post* story, and suits by Vietnam military notables like General William C. Westmoreland and Colonel Anthony Herbert against CBS show that the litigation is not letting up.

As times change, so often do the fortunes of institutions. And while business was on the defensive throughout the seventies, reaching a low point in the public-opinion polls following Watergate, the ITT affair in Chile, overseas bribe scandals, and concern over environment and consumer issues, the tables appeared to have turned in the early eighties. A poll conducted after the *Washington Post* conceded that one of its reporters had concocted a Pulitzer-Prize-winning story about an eight-year-old drug addict, showed that 61 percent of those responding said they believed "little" or "only some" of the news. One-third said they thought most reports were valid and only 5 percent said they believed all news reports. In a Gallup Poll taken for *Newsweek* magazine, one-third of those who had heard about the *Post* incident said reporters "often make things up."[6]

An attack by a Chicago television station on ABC's "20/20" news magazine for its investigation into arson-for-profit focused attention on the fuzzy area between news coverage and entertainment on news magazine shows.

In the wake of such incidents, *Harper's* then editor-in-chief Lewis Lapham wrote that "the lines between fiction and fact have become increasingly difficult to distinguish." Lapham said he felt that the public expects a certain level of theater from public events and that journalists are under pressure to deliver not only facts but drama as well. Lapham contended that "the previously distinct genres of journalism, literature, and theater have gradually fused into something known as 'the media.'"[7]

But the dilemma is that the public expects this "drama" to be credible. These strong pressures for creative writing and juicy investigative stories in recent years have produced high ratings and readership and a rash of "information" shows on television as well as problems of credibility. This problem of "drama" has been especially pronounced in the field of "soft news"—that is, feature journalism—as opposed to "hard news"—the day-to-day reporting of events.

Meanwhile, coverage of business dealings has moved closer to center stage. Seymour Topping says the *Times* has found that readers of the business pages have "pervasive" interests because many of them are "reader-investors" who have to decide among many options. To respond to an audience perceived to be "desperately" looking for more guidance, the *Times*, like many other U.S. papers, began expanding its business coverage in the late seventies. A section called "Business Day" was inaugurated and now is published seven days a week by a staff of seventy, including thirty-six reporters plus help from national and overseas bureaus. "All our new reporters have advanced degrees in fields like energy, technology, accounting and business," says "Business Day" editor John Lee.

Complaints from business people about news coverage have become less frequent, according to Lee. "The complaint is mostly with TV news," he says, noting he rarely receives complaints regarding fairness of coverage. Lee thinks that business is generally "paranoid about the press" and for good reason: "They have had single or multiple experiences that are unfavorable. . . . They want the press to be a 'house organ.'" Lee says the *Times* is trying to emphasize achievement and technical change in its coverage now and not routine developments, which he characterizes as "background noise": earnings, new products, promotions, mergers. Lee also believes that business people like to read about the problems of others.[8]

THE TURNING POINT

The acrimony between the media and the business community came into full flower during the Arab oil embargo of 1973, and it was out of this crisis that the American business community began to learn the rules of the new marketplace. The public, doing a slow burn in long lines at the gas station pumps, was furious. The politicians had to pin the blame on someone other than themselves, and the oil companies were totally unprepared for problems either at home or with their Arab partners. Few reporters or editors knew anything about energy matters, and coverage was often uninformed, or it merely repeated charges. The oil companies, who traditionally had been tight-lipped, were under siege by the media and politicians.

Topping recalls January 1974, when a group of senior oil executives were summoned to Washington and berated by Senator Henry Jackson and his colleagues. Looking for an industry spokesman on the following day to lay out the industry's case, all Topping could find was one executive who had given a local news conference in Houston. That oilman found himself on the front page of the *Times*. Later that year, and in subsequent years, the oil industry went through trauma as it reported earnings. The public was shocked at record high profits, and the press interpreted them as confirmation that the companies were in league with OPEC in price fixing.[9]

The upshot of the embargo was a fast education for corporate communicators in the oil business. Shell started a television school for managers to help them overcome their fear of meeting the press. Mobil began spending its heavy advocacy advertising. Gulf started protesting bad coverage and sent a "truth squad" around to visit editors and editorial writers. Anthony Hatch of Arco observed, "Oil companies did not know how to communicate when the embargo hit, and they still have trouble. The oil companies have low credibility. Justifiably. And it's questionable if they're ever going to catch up."[10] One new strategy Arco pursued was to begin producing its own TV news features.

At the same time, other industries that had traditionally been tightlipped— grain shippers, steel manufacturers, drug companies and banks, to name a few—began developing new media strategies to communicate their points of view as charges concerning such issues as profits, pollution, redlining, and unsafe drugs began appearing frequently in print.

BUSINESS, MEDIA, AND THE PUBLIC

The public is concerned about business honesty but also about press fairness. According to pollster Daniel Yankelovich, Americans retain "bedrock support for many freedom-of-expression values." Yankelovich says the public rejects government censorship of the media and vigorously supports the rights of groups whom they detest—like Nazis and Communists— to freely express their views. Yankelovich says the public views the media's obligation as a fair, balanced presentation of all points of view. But he goes on to say that people feel "media autonomy"—total freedom to publish—is *secondary* to the goal of "fairness"—presenting all sides of an issue. This contrasts with the views of media leaders, who feel that the press's right to autonomy is paramount. Yankelovich feels there is a tendency for communications professionals to misinterpret public calls for fairness as potentially intrusive. "This misconception has caused some leaders to discount public criticism of the media and to cast the public as outsiders with no legitimate stake in freedom of expression issues."[11]

If the public wants the media to be *fair*, it wants business to be *honest*. Public-opinion sampling in the early eighties indicates people are showing more and more support for free enterprise. But they are still strongly anti-institutional. They feel that truth and openness are the cure to rules and regulation and that disclosure is a key concept in keeping business honest. The idea is that if institutions have to tell everything, then nobody will get away with anything. The emphasis in the seventies was to "clean up your act." In the eighties it is to "do the right thing."[12]

Business leaders are sensing these changes in public opinion, and they realize that the clock cannot be turned back. Further attempts to weaken environmental laws have also been met with negative public reaction. This lends credence to public concerns that business "do the right thing." And while business people generally sense a shift in public support toward them, they realize that such support can do a quick turnaround.

A study by the *Wall Street Journal* and the Gallup organization released in August 1980 showed that business people still believed the public had a low regard for their institution. The study reported that only 13 percent of those interviewed thought the public's image was favorable to business. Two-thirds of the executives polled in thirteen hundred large and medium-sized companies held a negative view.[13]

Solutions suggested by respondents in that survey were that business should take the lead in educating and communicating better with the public. This seems to reflect a perception that the source of low esteem is ignorance. Suggestions offered by the executives for improving the image included:

1. Education about profits
2. More corporate involvement in community affairs
3. More teaching about free enterprise in high school and college
4. Establishment of a better working relationship with the press
5. Use of good PR and advertising to project the truth about a firm

One interesting result of the survey was that owners of small firms did *not* share the perceptions of executives of medium-sized and big businesses. According to the study, more than half the small-business owners believed that the public's opinion of business was favorable. Their suggestions for improving image included improving product quality and maintaining ethical standards.

"We must be more militant in policing business," said one retailer. Business leaders must "act with integrity" said another. Only 10 percent of large corporation heads mentioned ethical standards, and even fewer talked about quality.

In the last decade, executives of many of the Fortune 500 firms have opened their companies' doors to the new world. This has been especially true with firms that have become involved in major issues and need public support: AT&T, U.S. Steel, the oil companies, to name a few.

Attempting to strike a balance between the interests of business and media, Arthur Sulzberger, the publisher of the *New York Times*, said, "I would never suggest that good news is no news, but I would suggest that bad news is often big news." Sulzberger said it was not the function of the press to play up the good news. "Our job is to give the reader accurate information he can use about what is important and what interests him. This is also an important goal of business." From his perspective, Sulzberger said, America's business is no longer business. "We've gone beyond that." And, he added:

> For the journalist that means the freedom to get to the root of truth, the freedom to criticize, the freedom to goad and stimulate every institution in our society, including our own.
> For the businessman that means the freedom to compete fairly on the basis of value and service. And it means the freedom to defend themselves against unfair charges by pressure groups, to assert the principle of the profit motive, and to fight off excessive or stultifying government regulation.[14]

WHY THERE IS CONFLICT

There are many theories about the reasons so much traditional, almost organic, hostility exists between business and the media. A few of those theories are listed below.

THEORY	DESCRIPTION
"I'm boss"	Business people, especially senior managers, are used to having their way. "Just run it the way I sent it in, Sonny."
Reporters as labor	Reporters view business people as labor views management, since most reporters are salaried employees of a large news organization.
The business of business	Management feels its primary responsibility is to shareholders and not to the public, à la Milton Friedman.
Too many bottom lines	Businesses report profits in confusing ways. Reporters don't understand nuances and report figures simplistically.
You're hiding something	The business bureaucracy and its reluctance to divulge information makes reporters suspicious that someone is trying to hide something.
Two different worlds	Reporters need immediate access to high-level officials for comments on issues. Corporate officials aren't used to such demands.

Medium distortion	The media, especially television, are apt to try and show things visually—especially confrontation. Reasoned arguments are not often interesting. TV reporting is not a clear channel of communication, but by its very nature distorts, according to Marshall McLuhan. Newspaper reporters tend to distort by arranging facts and processing information according to the inverted pyramid system.
Priorities	Business people judge stories by their effects—good or bad—on business and assume that if the story is harmful to their business, the reporter must have intended to do damage. But reporters and editors judge a story on whether it is interesting and significant, not by its effect on business.

Standing alone none of these theories wholly explains the problem. Together they offer some insight that helps to explain the conflict. These theories might be better understood when seen in the context of such day-to-day problems as *access, reporting of profits*, and *PR tricks*.

ACCESS TO BUSINESS NEWS

In the public sector there is a tradition of disclosure of information, based on the theory that since the public pays the bills it is entitled to know what the government is up to. In the case of the federal government, a powerful law, the Freedom of Information Act, governs release of information and stipulates a bias toward full disclosure. No such tradition or law applies to American business. Release of business information is governed by the Securities and Exchange Commission and the various stock exchanges and requires disclosure only of information that materially affects the firm's well-being or profitability. The goal is to insure that everyone in the marketplace has equal access to information (see Chapter 7).

The tradition is that the private sector is *private*. Maximum disclosure, it is argued, would hurt competition. Reporters, usually trained in public-sector reporting—from police beats and the courts, to city, county, and state government—are used to operating in an environment where release of information is either routine or regularly demanded.

When assigned to the business beat, these reporters find that the rules are not the same and that many company officials don't even talk with reporters, let alone release any but required information. Coca-Cola Company, for example, rarely dealt even with stock analysts until just the past few years. Procter and Gamble, continually involved in hush-hush marketing research for its consumer-goods business, is famous for being tightlipped, as is Sears. Until just the last decade, corporate officials did not perceive a constituency base outside the firm's stockholders. As firms have come under greater government regulation and public scrutiny they have found that such a low profile can hurt their public image, turn public opinion against their products, deflate stock prices and do other economic mischief. Firestone in the late seventies got into a big fight with the government over the safety of its "500" radial tire and disclosure of information relating to that issue.[15] Press and congressional interest promptly accelerated, sales and credibility were hurt, and the company eventually had to deal not only with a recall problem but also with a problem of rebuilding its image as a tire maker. While Firestone felt it was legitimately defending its interests, the public perception was that the company was stonewalling by refusing to turn certain data over to the government.

There are legitimate business concerns regarding proprietary information. Neither the public nor the press always understands this. However, a policy to disclose only what's required by law can play havoc when the company becomes involved in a public issue. Some businesses affect public health, safety, and welfare more than others and have a greater obligation to be up front in the release of data.

Business often looks to government to protect its interests. Recent business concerns have centered on information disclosure required by the Freedom of Information Act. Many business groups have sought to weaken the Act because they feel it does not adequately protect proprietary information that has been submitted to the government under regulatory laws. The Justice Department's antitrust division estimates that more than half of its Freedom of Information Act requests are from actual or potential litigants in private antitrust suits. And the FDA reports that 85 percent of the thirty-three thousand requests it received in 1980 were from companies that are regulated. Businesses are concerned with industrial espionage.

Public-interest groups fear the government is withholding data that relates to public health or safety. For example, the Nuclear Regulatory Commission released to the Union of Concerned Scientists, a public-interest group, documents that indicated that a former NRC chairman was aware of serious safety problems at some nuclear plants during the 1970s but downgraded the problems to expedite licensing.[16]

Disclosure for a firm is a two-edged sword: If it does release information, that information could affect proprietary matters, but the information also could be of such a nature as to imply management misfeasance or, in some cases, malfeasance. This could put the company into a bind with the concept of "materiality"—disclosure of information that affects the health or profitability of the firm.

Attempts to stonewall an issue that is perceived as affecting the public automatically spurs efforts by the press to "get something" on the company and arouses public suspicions. It's like Br'er Rabbit playing with the tar baby—the more you try to avoid the problem, the deeper you get into it. Furthermore, the firm runs the risk that the press will go to other, less credible, sources and start running hearsay and circumstantial information filled with innuendo. In these kinds of situations, the press positions itself as guardian of the public interest, and the firm finds itself on the wrong side of the issue.

The advice you get from corporate communications people on handling such problems usually will emphasize disclosure. If there is a problem, get the information out and get it out quickly.

REPORTING PROFITABILITY

Business people often get angry at the media for the way they report profit. Mobil Oil once felt compelled to take out a two-page ad in the *New York Times* to rebut a CBS Evening News report by Ray Brady on oil company profits. Brady feels the term *profit* is not as good as the term *revenue*. "People don't turn off when they hear that word [revenue]," he says. A. Kent MacDougall, a *Los Angeles Times* correspondent, in a series of articles on business and the media said, "A close look at profit-reporting practices indicates that the news media's most serious shortcoming is not that it reports profits unsympathetically but that it does so simplistically."[17]

Corporations tend to report high net-income figures to the public and stockholders through straight-line depreciation accounting. But they report lower numbers to the IRS through the use of accelerated-depreciation schedules. Another trick has been to use different inventory accounting measures (FIFO over LIFO) to show higher profits through lower cost of goods sold.

This financial-accounting gamesmanship seldom fools Wall Street, but it does confuse reporters trying to accurately summarize a company's financial posture and outlook. MacDougall admits that it is easier to generalize about bookkeeping manipulation than to prove it. Some observers suggest that business concentrate on other reporting methods, such as return on capital or return on stockholders' equity. One solution is to report profit margin—net income as a percentage of sales and other revenues. But many believe the most reliable indicator is *return on total capital*—annual net income as a percentage of stockholders' equity plus borrowed funds.

PR GAMES

Some business managers remain convinced they can control media coverage and access, and they do it with impunity. This is the "run-it-like-I-sent-it-in-Sonny" attitude of company chieftans not ready to accept the fact that some salaried employee of a news organization can really do harm to a high-ranking chief executive. In some corporations the chain of command is so long that a reporter on a tight deadline might as well forget any serious effort to get the company side of the story. Ray Brady describes a typical instance when a story comes out of Washington at 10 A.M: "The consumer group has a statement ready at 9 A.M. The corporate guy is called at 10:30, but he never gets any statement back until sometime in the afternoon. Then he complains about lopsided coverage."[18] This may be intentional on the company's part, or maybe it is ignorance.

Some try to manipulate the timing of their story. To bury a story, it is sometimes released on a Friday afternoon, when the media are generally swamped. To play it up, it should be released on a Monday morning or even a Sunday, when there is a really big news hole to fill.

Another way some companies handle the press is simply to refuse to comment on a story. Mobil often does this because it feels coverage, especially TV coverage, is stacked against it. Some companies refuse even to admit a story exists, as the Disney organization did when a group of top animators quit en masse.

HANDLING THE PRESS

A look at some of the most often quoted, highly visible people on the public stage reveals that by "being cooperative, quotable and confident, a clever public figure can often get the media to make him look good," as *Newsweek* put it. *Cooperativeness* is a key factor. In many instances this means being there, being available to answer calls from the media, not hiding behind the PR person. Some companies like AT&T have a policy to try and make top people available for all reasonable interview requests. And it's not just answering calls, but returning them, too, being sensitive to a reporter's particular deadline. Also, it's a matter of knowing how to handle yourself and what to say in an interview with a newspaper reporter versus an interview before a TV camera.

The second key element is to be *quotable*, to use colorful language that is succinct and is easily understandable. Some personalities are so good at this you can just ask them one question and they'll take it from there, giving a reporter all they want, and on the speaker's terms. Reporters, like everybody else, enjoy being entertained, and a good speaker will "put on a performance" for the press.

Thirdly, a person who is *confident* in what he does and in what he knows will come across that way with the media. "The press has an animal instinct that smells fear," says former Democratic Party chief Robert Strauss, who is well known for slick press relations.[19]

Also, CEOs might get along better with the press if they understood that newspaper people like to gather around power, that they like the intimacy of contact with people at the highest levels. (There is an old saw about reporters that they are "overprivileged and underpaid.") A reporter's perq is a certain "privilege" to mingle with the famous, the wealthy and the powerful. Making reporters part of their world, giving them the intimacy of access and knowledge is an excellent way to get great press coverage. (But remember to tell the truth.)

Another game is to bury the key information in a news release. MacDougall relates how one deficit-beset computer company led a news release with the good news that it had received "waivers of certain financial covenants from its banks and institutional lenders" and buried the bad news that its losses would be substantially greater than earlier forecast.[20]

A very demoralizing game is for managers, especially top managers, to blame corporate communicators for bad press coverage. Gulf & Western has had a revolving door of PR chiefs in recent years because senior management has expected them to make a silk purse out of a sow's ear in the media with a firm that has had its share of problems with both Wall Street and federal regulators. Blaming the communicators is especially prevalant in companies where there is either "backwater" understanding of communications issues or a domineering entrepreneur in charge. Even more dangerous is a situation where senior management presumes it can control media coverage. When things go wrong, the blame is quickly pinned on someone who really may be only a PR technician.

TELEVISION—A SPECIAL PROBLEM

When the Roper Organization asked two thousand adults what medium they relied upon most "for information about business," TV newscasts were their top source (60 percent) followed by newspapers (44 percent) and radio (31 percent) with business publications only 16 percent.[21] Yet television news is an awful environment for serious coverage of business news. MIT Professor Edwin Diamond terms today's newscasts "disco news," with young-looking people, high noise levels, flashing lights, the "Eyewitness" brand of information/entertainment. Industry professionals sometimes call this approach "Newszak," a term for an essentially entertainment program presented in a news format. The first generation of TV news journalists—the Cronkites, Chancellors, Severeids—were newspaper and wire service trained. Today's generation of TV news journalists have only a television background. They tend to follow the "story" model of journalism—telling a story that people enjoy or relate to their own lives—as opposed to the "information" model that sticks to the facts. The "story" model, says Diamond, emphasizes style over substance. The stereotype that "disco" journalism caters to—short attention spans, low political interest, unsophistication—is slowly being replaced, however, with a much more sophisticated audience that cable TV, with its emphasis on diversity, appeals to, such as the Cable News Network.[22]

If there is a real battleground between the media and business, it is television. On the one hand there are the entertainment shows, which on the whole portray business negatively. (See Chapter 1.) Then there are the news shows, which have paid scant attention to business news, providing at best little more than headline information. Also there are the "feature journalism" shows like "60 Minutes" and "20/20," which have shown a fondness for tripping corporate people and berating them with prosecutorial interviews.

Also it has often been noted that information dissemination on television is subject to serious distortion. A corporate official who stutters or nods his head while being asked damning questions may be truthful, fair, and honest, but he *looks* as if he's guilty or agrees with the charges. Because of the time constraints on stories (rarely more than two and a half minutes) set by the networks, a complicated issue is reduced to its most simplistic elements.

The tight time constraints on television plus the visual nature of the medium—the need to show pictures—make business coverage difficult. The anchor on a network evening newscast is rarely on the air for more than six minutes in a thirty-minute newscast. It is not unusual for an interviewee to spend a full eight-hour day with a news crew and then have only 30 seconds of the interview used on the evening newscast.

One oil company official, Charles Kittrell of Phillips Petroleum, looks at the situation realistically, "We have to recognize that there's a difference in what you can accomplish with different media," he says. "We feel intimidated when we have to summarize for TV. But we're going to have to learn how to summarize. Unless we can help TV get our message across, we're going to leave the field open to the competition.[23]

Selective editing with an eye toward visuals poses another problem. In 1979, when there were new gas lines following the fall of the Shah of Iran, an oil company president spent several hours explaining his company's position on price controls and a proposed windfall-profit tax. All of a sudden, a New Jersey congressman held up a poster demanding "No Decontrol" for the benefit of the ABC news cameras that had arrived late, declaring that he had received thousands of such messages from unhappy voters in his district. He then attacked the oil companies. The chief executive tried to defend his company but decided he'd had enough and walked off. Guess what appeared on television that night? Not the hours of patient testimony.[24]

Michael Arlen in his book *The Camera Age* attempts to draw a distinction between the evening newscasts, or "hard-news" programs, and "soft-news" shows such as "60 Minutes," "20/20," and "NBC Magazine." Arlen contends that soft news, or "feature journalism," is the most difficult for business to deal with. The soft-news shows, says Arlen, place emphasis on "portraiture, anecdote, and intimacy." When television news departments were made up of former wire-service and newspaper reporters, this approach was resisted. But TV news and especially shows like "60 Minutes" have today become victims of their success in the ratings.[25]

Arlen says these new shows have made a transition from the world view, that official acts make the world turn, to a new view that people account for everything. Because of its ability to create intimacy, TV overuses interviews, profiles, anecdotes, exposés. Is this news or entertainment? Don Hewitt, executive producer of "60 Minutes," responds: "Our purpose is to make information more palatable and to make reality more competitive with make-believe. We're not interested in heavy Environmental Protection Agency stuff. I'm not in the business of broader social awareness. I'm in the business of covering news. I'm interested in finding a small town that has to comply with EPA rules and what happens there. I want to deal with stories about people grappling with issues."[26]

This feature journalism is a style in which the reporter concentrates on one aspect or instance of a major problem rather than on the problem as a whole. One of TV's problems is not being disposed to putting a particular issue into a wider context.

60 MINUTES VS.
ILLINOIS POWER

Few clashes between the television news media and business are more instructive than the one that occurred following the November 25, 1979, telecast of "60 Minutes" on CBS. In that broadcast there was a sixteen-minute piece on the skyrocketing cost of building nuclear power plants. The story, titled, "Who Pays? You Do!" zeroed in on an Illinois Power plant going up in Clinton, Illinois.[27]

The company's public affairs manager later described the aftermath of the broadcast to *Industry Week*: "The show was simply devastating to us. . . . We began getting hate telephone calls minutes after the broadcast. The next day, Monday, more than three times as many shares of our stock were traded in a single day than ever before, and the stock price dropped by more than one dollar. And our employee morale hit rock bottom. We knew we had to do something, and fast."[28]

Illinois Power had some misgivings when it let CBS on its property to do the story in the first place. Just to cover itself, the utility stipulated that it would make its own videotapes of all interviews with executives.

"We wanted a record," said company PR chief Harold Deacons. "It became obvious they were after overruns, which our executive vice president, Bill Gerstner, admitted, were considerable. But [Harry] Reasoner—he was a helluva guy, good listener—told me before he left it was amazing how different the facts were from what you heard, after you went to the scene and talked to people. 'I hope you'll feel you were treated fairly by us,' he said. Then, we were bombed."[29]

After seeing the broadcast, Illinois Power felt it had been had, with gross distortions of fact, a sensationalized approach, use of disgruntled employees—in other words, a hatchet job.

Realizing that statements to newspapers were hardly going to change anybody's opinion, the company, following the "60 Minutes" format, replete with stopwatch, put together a rebuttal. It used the videotapes it had made while "60 Minutes" was on hand, plus testimony, exhibits, and other material from rate cases before the Illinois Commerce Commission. And of course it used the sixteen-minute broadcast tape as well. Titled "60 Minutes/Our Reply," the forty-two-minute rebuttal initially was produced for use with employees and community groups. Since then it has been seen by groups nationwide, including business school classes and business organizations—among them "60 Minutes" sponsors. More than two thousand requests for copies have been received. (See Figure 5–1.)

FIGURE 5-1   Opening Frame of Illinois Power Company's Rebuttal to "60 Minutes"
Source: Courtesy of Illinois Power Company.

Harry Reasoner later gave some grudging respect to "Our Reply," calling it a "planned, smart, preemptive-strike sort of thing. . . . Obviously you make people mad in this business. They were prepared before we got there."

Among Illinois Power's complaints in "Our Reply" was that less than two and a half minutes of a one-and-a-half-hour interview was shown on its side of the story. Another was CBS's statement that the utility was seeking a 14 percent rate hike to cover a jump in construction costs for its planned power plant, which had risen from $430 million to $1.4 billion. Not so, said IP. Only a fourth of the rate hike was going to the new plant, and that was going for interest payments, not construction.

Other factual errors were noted by IP, but the company really bristled at the critics of the project who were interviewed by CBS. "Two of these men were fired for cause, and the third resigned because he was not satisfied with a 7 percent pay increase. All were associated with the Clinton project for short times only," said Wendell J. Kelley, chairman and president, in a letter to stockholders following the broadcast. One of those fired went to work for a local antinuclear group. One of the three interviewed by CBS was identified only as "Mr. X," who told CBS he feared retribution if his identity became known. He was filmed in shadows with a voice-distorting microphone. Introducing Mr. X, Reasoner said, "This man was a construction superintendent at Clinton. He has a crack reputation. Works elsewhere now. But fears retribution if his identity becomes known."

Observed the IP spokesman in "Our Reply": "There's something theatrical about this kind of lighting and voice distortion. It's as if the illusion is more compelling than the reality of what's being said." IP said it knew the man's identity anyway, but "The implication is that Illinois Power has some sort of goon squad that runs around the country to 'put heat' on former Clinton workers."

The most damaging part of the IP counterattack, as far as "60 Minutes" was concerned, dealt with the Reasoner interview with IP Executive Vice President Bill Gerstner. In the session, Gerstner trotted out numbers to back up his claim that Clinton's cost overruns are lower than those for similar facilities. In fact, he said, Clinton had the lowest overruns among seven similar projects. CBS contended in its report that Clinton's costs were "well ahead of the pack," which directly contradicted the unused portion of Gerstner's interview. "Our Reply" showed Reasoner asking the question and Gerstner giving the answer, which was never used. Finally, CBS stated that a request for a new rate hike by the utility had been opposed by anticompany forces and that the Illinois Commerce Commission staff had asked that the increase be denied. That, said the company, was the opposite of what had happened, and CBS had been informed four days before the broadcast that the staff had recommended an increase.

The "Our Reply" show did what few, if any other, industry rebuttals have ever been able to accomplish: document clearly a news editing process that fit conclusions to a premise rather than to the facts. It has damaged the credibility of feature journalism and possibly broadcast journalism in general and has made many corporate officials wary of appearing on "60 Minutes" and similar shows.

CBS newsman anchor Bill Kurtis, who while at WBBM-TV in Chicago went after ABC's "20/20" for its techniques in a piece on arson for profit in that city, observed, "What bothered us . . . was not the research . . . but efforts to bring nonvisual data to a level where it can compete with entertainment. Also there is the ethical consideration of devices such as entrapment."

ON MEETING WITH
THE MEDIA

It is no mystery why a young person with an MBA entering the profession of management is most adept at communicating in that rather structured environment where people understand a common tongue and pecking orders are firmly established. Chester Burger wrote in a well-regarded article for the *Harvard Business Review*: "A corporate president is not chosen for his outstanding ability to articulate corporate problems. He is selected by his board of directors because of his management know-how."[30]

Of course the world of the chief executive is changing, and CEOs more often are finding themselves out dealing with public issues. Managers at many firms have been run through crash training programs in recent years on how to deal with the media and other contentious groups. Companies such as Adolph Coors, Standard Oil of California and Gulf have put thousands of employees— down to the level of refinery manager and ship captains—through media training. That training, run by independent consultants, PR firms, and professors, shows managers how to stay cool and make points while under attack. Topics that managers are taught include developing credibility, interview techniques, how to anticipate questions and respond to them, and turning negative questions around.

Many training programs are developed specifically to address a company's unique characteristics. For example, handling crisis situations would be included in a session for chemical company managers. Responding to regulatory actions might be covered for a pharmaceutical company.

Learning to meet and communicate through the media is an *acquired* skill for most people. It is acquired on two levels: dealing with the media generally and dealing with the visual medium, television.

Before a firm plunges into learning how to deal with media, it ought first to make sure it has adequate tactical *policies* and *procedures* for doing so.

Should all media requests for information or interviews be funneled through the communications office? Is the organization decentralized so that calls go directly to the affected operation? How should top management be kept informed of inquiries? What publications or other media should the chief executive speak to, as opposed to a subordinate? If there is going to be a spokesperson named for the firm who will it be? With what authority will he or she speak?

The policy should answer these questions and reflect the level of public involvement necessary to maintain the firm's position in the marketplace. Further it should mesh realistically with public and press interest in the affairs of the organization.

The statement of tactical communications policy does not have to be elaborate, but it needs to be comprehensive enough to prevent problems from arising. It is up to the corporate communications staff to insure that the policy is understood, clarified, and interpreted when necessary. The needs of the media usually are quite simple: When they call they want a prompt authoritative response that directly relates to the question. If reporters wish to speak to senior management, they should be able to speak to senior management or to a spokesperson who represents the position of senior management on the issues at hand.

There should be a policy as to which officials in the firm handle which kinds of questions. General-information questions might go to the communications director; financial-information questions might be handled personally by the chief executive; consumer issues might be handled by a product-information specialist.

Within the communications policy should be a central-point mechanism that tracks information requests and responses. If the chief executive has just spent ten minutes on the phone with *Barron's*, the nature of the questions and answers should be relayed to the communications office so that what appears can be compared to what was said. If any new policy was made on the telephone, which sometimes happens, this can be duly reported to the senior staff through this central-point procedure.

Emergencies and disasters (the subject of the next chapter) should be covered by separate contingency plans, which may be quite different from regular communications policy. Employees who could be affected by emergencies or disasters should be familiar with the criteria for changing from the policy to the plan (see examples in appendix 3).

Where outside public relations counsel is to be involved on a regular basis, this decision should be included in the policy as well. If the call from *Barron's*, for instance, is related to a takeover attempt on the firm, the outside PR firm involved should be routinely notified of such a contact and the nature of the interview.

Also *a good communications policy more than anything else should reflect a positive corporate attitude regarding dealings with the media or other constituencies*. It should not be defensive or reflect an "us vs. them" attitude but should be a positive tool for representing the company externally.

Finally *a good communications policy ought to be followed*. If a bank has touted to its employees and the press that it has a positive, open communications policy and then tries to hush up the fact that a senior officer has had to quit because of a conflict-of-interest problem, then that policy loses its value and becomes basically worthless. It doesn't help corporate credibility either.

PASSIVE VS. ACTIVE STRATEGIES

The questions, often arises, When should we speak out? and Whom should we not talk to? One rule of thumb regarding the second question is that you generally ought to stay away from soft-news television programs like "60 Minutes" or some of its imitators. The evidence is fairly strong that the payoff from such encounters is not worth the hassle. But even this rule has its exceptions. For example, the Silicon Valley-based Osborne Computer Company and its outspoken president, Adam Osborne, were sought out by "60 Minutes" for a profile. Almost from the first call it was apparent that the angle was going to be "brash young entrepreneur makes good", so the company decided to go ahead with the project. A reasonable gamble.

When a company should speak out on an issue is an interesting question. As stated in Chapter 4, if the company has determined that it should get involved in an issue that can affect its interests, then it should speak out. This is especially true where there is a new issue to deal with. It should be an issue that affects the company or the industry it is in and is important to the firm. The firm ought to weigh what the downside risks are of speaking out on the issue: Will your stand on an issue be publicly credible? Will you support your words with deeds? What will happen over the long term from your involvement in the issue? And what will happen if you decide to do nothing? Finally how will it play in Peoria? That is, what will be the public reaction to your taking a stand or to taking no stand?

The kind of attitude that a firm has toward the media will often determine whether its communications strategies are active or passive. There is some feeling that because of the actions of the Reagan administration, business can get out of the political-social marketplace for a while and go back to the business of business, which could mean turning back the clock on consumer, environmental, health, and safety issues as well as on economic regulation. This scenario would dictate returning to a passive, reactive communications policy as well.

The smart firm, however, understands that administrations can change every four years. The smart firm also understands that public expectations for improved business performance and economic achievement are very high and that if those expectations are not met, the attitudes that support relaxing regulation might change as well. Also public-opinion polls continue to show that clean air and water, a safe work place, consumer protection, and other hard-earned accomplishments should be maintained, even if final achievement is somewhat delayed.

The environmental movement appeared to be sputtering out towards the end of the Carter administration, but the Reagan appointment of James Watt (as Interior Secretary) and Ann Gorsuch (as EPA administrator) jolted environmental groups back into action. The Reagan appointees, said environmental leaders, did more than anything else to resurrect the movement. For businesspeople trying to slow down clean air and water regulation through amendments to the national pollution control laws, the timing of those appointments could not have been worse. Business got caught in the crossfire, with the general feeling among moderates that business needed to communicate its proposals better in the public forum. In other words, the smart firm understands it must maintain a presence in the marketplace of public issues.

New York Times publisher Arthur Sulzberger's advice to the Economics Club of Detroit back in 1977 regarding corporate communications argues for an active strategy and remains relevant. He made four suggestions:

1. *Get out front.* Businesss leaders need to be just that—leaders. The public perceives them as "the *bland* leading the *bland.*" Sulzberger argues against the "faceless official spokesman" and for visibility of top corporate leaders, although he points out vulnerability often follows renown.

2. *Stop talking jargon.* Jargon is a problem mentioned before. But it is also a problem for the press, which needs to understand business jargon in order to report it more accurately.

3. *Go look for complaints.* He suggests that most people don't believe business claims about its products but that almost half of the people who complain to companies are satisfied with the responses they get.

4. *Do some complaining yourself.* Business as much as anyone else has a right to be heard, says Sulzberger, and it ought to take advantage of opportunities to speak out. "News is not only what happens but what people think has happened and what values they attach to what *has* or *has not* taken place." Tension between the press and government is "healthy," he contends, with business and journalism sharing certain values: Both are pro-opportunity, proconsumer, proprofit and profreedom.[31]

PREPARING FOR A MEDIA ENCOUNTER

In preparing for a media interview, one should note that there are different classes of reporters and different types of media.

At the supposed head of the journalistic pyramid are the star reporters—the Mike Wallaces, the columnists, the first-string Washington reporters for the major general-circulation papers and periodicals. This group is a mixed bag. Some of them, like Wallace, are tigers; others, including many first stringers and columnists are pussycats. Washington reporters are often part of the "system"— they are beat reporters—and they pretty much go with the press releases. Local reporters in some cities, however, are extremely aggressive. Cities like Chicago and Philadelphia are towns whose reporters are known as hard-nosed "door-kickers" with a tradition of going after a story aggressively. Ironically in Washington there may be only a handful of really tough reporters, while in some less heavily covered areas, there may be a dozen or more.

As far as importance goes, lowly wire-service reporters are among the most important, since AP and UPI wire services together serve almost every radio and TV station and newspaper in the U.S.

One consultant on TV appearances talks about the Donahue "Chorus Line," referring to the interviewing technique of talk show host Phil Donahue. The technique—"one, two three, kick"—is based on observation of Donahue's interview methods. He asks three "soft" questions, and then lowers the boom. The advice to an upcoming guest: broaden your answer on the third question to blunt the kick."[32]

Another bit of advice: if you make a blooper in an interview, it's often wise to let it lie. If you try to go after it, you end up creating a two-day story that will be more memorable.

One should be aware of what the reporter's reach will be and understand that unless that reporter is a star, it is not easy to know how tough or easy he or she going to be.

Also there are substantial differences in dealing with TV and with print. Newspapers and magazines have more space to convey complicated information and therefore will be more receptive to it—the full script for a half-hour TV newscast covers less than half a page of type in the *New York Times*. Also it will be easier talking to print reporters since it is more likely that one will be dealing with a business specialist. Consider the irony of the fact that the *Chicago Tribune* has a business news staff of nearly forty, while network newsrooms in New York have only a half dozen or so devoted exclusively to business news. Also with print media there will be less medium distortion—they don't have to show pictures and cover the story in ten lines or less of copy.

Coverage in the *New York Times* or *Wall Street Journal* will usually be more informed than in the local press. A financial relations PR specialist at one Chicago bank said: "You have to be very careful dealing with local reporters. It's a slow process; you have to walk them through it." With national press, it's much easier. Another financial PR person added: "It's a tough situation. Reporters don't know much about the company's business. They quote you out of context. They come in with a story idea, and you have no idea what they're going to write. You're sticking your neck out in trying to cooperate. The problem with dealing with the press is that it's a nonwinner. You can take the point of view that anything said about you, pro or con, is putting your name before the public and therefore is going to be good for you. On the other hand, with the expenditure of time, it's worth absolutely nothing; they're just trying to get a story. I think the attitude around here is antipress. Not that we're against the press, but there doesn't seem to be anything they can write that we're really in favor of unless it's a glowing article and very accurate and those don't come around very often."[33]

With television one almost always will be working with a general assignment reporter. That doesn't necessarily mean they won't be experienced in business-news coverage, but it is not a specialty with them. The TV camera will focus on appearances and mannerisms, not on words.

MEETING THE PRESS

There are four distinct phases in preparing for a media interview: Attitude, advance preparation, execution, and critique.[34]

ATTITUDE.   It is important to realize that in an interview, especially a TV interview, the skills of the person asking the questions are probably sharper than the subject. The interviewer doesn't know more about the topic but most likely knows more about conducting interviews. The interview subject is on the interviewer's turf, even if it's in the subject's office. Nevertheless the interviewee should be enthusiastic for the cause and believe in the company and in what it does. He or she should reflect the company's credibility.

ADVANCE PREPARATION.   It seems obvious, but not everyone realizes how important it is to prepare for an interview. If it weren't so sad, it would be funny that many new government appointees start off their careers with foot in mouth—totally unaware of the history of their agency or past policy or current staff thinking, giving interviews with no advance thought that what they say will end up being reported in the papers as policy. A skilled manager, when faced with an upcoming interview, will brainstorm with associates every possible tough question that might arise. In the 1980 presidential campaign, for example, a Michigan congressman named David Stockman made quick friends with candidate Reagan when the former was brought in to "play" John Anderson in mock debates.

The mock interview is a moment for total candor on everyone's part. One associate should ask tough questions, while another times the response if preparing for TV. Notes and documents are helpful when dealing with a print reporter, but at most, 3-by-5s, (or maybe large idiot cards) should be used—and sparingly—for TV. The mock sessions should emphasize plain English over jargon. If possible, the best way to do this mock interview for TV is *with a video-tape recorder* so that the subject and PR specialists can get a preview of how the company representative will appear.

Another technique for preparing is to write down some very negative and uncomfortable things about the firm or its policies in one column, then draft a list of favorable things in the other column and try to work out ways of "bridging" from one column to the next.

Figure 5-2 discusses many common interview traps and techniques.

FIGURE 5-2   Interview Techniques

---

1. *The "set-up"*. A long preamble precedes a question, sometimes loaded with misinformation or a "when did you stop beating your wife" question.

    EXAMPLE   "Considering the low regard that people have for the oil industry, how do you, as a major oil company chief executive, expect people to believe you're not ripping them off?"

    SOLUTION   There are two schools of thought on how to deal with this problem. One is to break in politely to challenge the premise. (By the way, don't nod your head when the question is being asked . . . it makes viewers think you agree with what's being said.) The second approach is to wait until the question is finished, then go back and knock down the preface: "Yes, it's true that some people don't think much of our business, or business in general, but in fact, our profits have been flat for the last two years. . . ." or simply: "What you've said is just not true. Let's look at the figures. . . ."

2. *"Either . . . or"*. The interviewer poses two unacceptable alternatives.

    EXAMPLE   "Either you're naive, or you're protecting someone higher up. . . ." Another example: "Now were those irresponsible statements due to ineptness or greed?" or "Are you for or against takeovers?"

    SOLUTION   One solution is to answer the question directly: "Neither. The real issue here is. . . ." and move to the points you want to make. Or you can just ignore the trap and respond the way you want to.

3. *Irrelevancy*. In this situation, you are called upon to answer a question in an area unrelated to your own. The problem is that you can end up being quoted out of context. The memorable remark of Jimmy Carter in the *Playboy* interview about lusting in his heart is a classic example of what can happen when you get into an area far afield of your own, as it were.

    EXAMPLE   "Mr. Jones, besides being marketing director of Widgets Unlimited, you're also on the Youth Commission. Do you think the drinking age should be lowered?"

    SOLUTION   You might simply remark that your youth commission believes in supporting the laws in existence, then launch into some information regarding the good works of the commission.

4. *The empty chair*. In this situation, the interviewer quotes an opponent or person with a different point of view who has criticized your view but is not present.

EXAMPLE   "Mr. Nader has said that your product is a health hazard and should be recalled immediately." or "Congressman X says your industry is notorious for price-fixing. . . ."

SOLUTION   You can respond simply "I haven't seen those remarks." or "I don't understand in what context those remarks were made." or "I can't believe the Congressman said that, but I believe the facts will show. . . ." You should make sure not to attack an opponent who is not present.

5. *The broadside*. This is the "ad hominem" argument, in which you are attacked directly.

EXAMPLE   "You're a polluter, aren't you?" (or a liar, or racist, or redliner, etc.)

SOLUTION   The best advice: deny it straight out, if it's not true; or be candid if there's some truth in it: "We previously did have a pollution problem, but in the last two years we've licked it," or "Redlining has no place in our loan operations."

6. *Let's pretend*. This technique involves the interviewer asking a hypothetical question, a "What if . . ." question.

EXAMPLE   "What if gasoline goes up to two dollars a gallon. Should the government take over the oil companies then?"

SOLUTION   Politicians are constantly asked these types of questions. The best advice is to demur and move to the point you want to make: "I think such a question is pure speculation. I think our real problem is conservation. . . ."

7. *Inconsistency*. If you or your organization has changed opinions or policies over time you might be asked about that change.

EXAMPLE   "Your firm issued a press release previously, indicating that you would not leave this community and move to Arkansas. . . ." or "You previously stated that there were absolutely no health problems with your new drug. . . ."

SOLUTION   You should clearly explain the reasons for the change, whether it was due to a change in policy or circumstances. "Our intentions have always been to maintain a plant in this community. However, the difficult economic conditions nationally and the flood of competing imports have forced us to consolidate operations. . . ." or "Our research until recently indicated that our new drug had sufficient safeguards. . . ."

8. *No comment*. "No comment" is not the same as "I don't know." "No comment" can be stated a number of ways. If you don't know, you don't know.

EXAMPLE   "Is it true your company is considering buying our local TV station?"

SOLUTION   If the answer is "No comment," it can be done smoothly: "Our firm has a history of attempting to expand into many new areas. We look at over five hundred companies a year for possible acquisition. But it's a major decision in every case and one in which there must be consensus within the company. There has been no decision at this time about buying your local TV station."

---

*See also "Learning to Shine on TV," *BusinessWeek*, January 19, 1981, pp. 114–16; and Jack Hilton and Mary Knobloch, *On Television! A Survival Guide for Media Interviews* (New York: AMACOM, 1980).

By all means, the interview subject should have a clear idea of the points he or she wants to make. Statistics, anecdotes, and examples to highlight these points should be in mind.

EXECUTION.   When talking to a reporter, the subject of off-the-record comments frequently arises. Most experts advise against *any* off-the-record remarks. Yet the system is used every day. The "capital" of off-the-record remarks is Washington, D.C., where there are even degrees of off-the-record statements:

- "Off the record"—Reporters cannot use the information given to them.
- "Background"—Reporters can use the information but can't name the source (an administration official suggested today. . . .).
- "Deep background"—Reporters can use the information but can report it on their own authority only (it appears that no missiles will be sent to . . .).

Stephen Hess in a study of Washington reporters found that roughly a third of interviews in that city are either off the record or background. This figure generally does not apply to business, though off-the-record interviews are not uncommon. There are times when it is necessary to go off the record, to clarify a point or to maintain credibility with a reporter. It is not wise to do so unless there is a trusting relationship between the subject and the reporter.

CRITIQUE.   This is the final phase of the interview process. If a record of what's been said has been made with video or audio tape (some newspaper reporters audio tape their interviews), it should be examined to see how one might have done a better job. It is a good idea to ask associates to go over their impressions as well of how the interviewee came across. Decide what should be worked on for the next interview and work on the skill. If somebody "sticks you good" during the interview or does a hatchet job in editing, complain to his or her boss, but do so in a reasoned, well-documented manner. There are organizations, such as the National News Council, that arbitrate complaints concerning bad press coverage. Then there's always the option of spending thousands of dollars on an ad to complain about the coverage. The best bet, however, is to complain to the interviewer's boss.

APPEARANCES AND MESSAGES

When dealing with television, unfortunately, appearance is sometimes as important as what is said. The camera moves in and out, catching things that go unnoticed in regular conversation. Eye contact with the interviewer and the camera, the pace of speech, voice inflection, body movement are all fair game for a camera. This author once took a new boss to a television station to offer a rebuttal to an editorial attacking his appointment. He was sincere, argued that he should be given a chance to succeed, and came across sounding like the honest person he was. However, he had never used a teleprompter before and kept moving his eyes back and forth to read from it. He came across visually looking shifty-eyed and guilty.

One should not always expect the interviewer to be "after you," especially if the appearance is on a TV talk show. Many such programs are overrun with writers trying to hype their latest books. And talk show hosts over time become indifferent. It is important that an executive in such an interview know exactly what message to deliver. Use props when necessary. The official talking about a new plant or product should have something visual to show.

One should expect to be a little nervous. It's natural. Talk shows are not a manager's area of expertise. He or she should be credible. Arrangements should be made, as at Illinois Power, to tape all interviews, if possible, for a record of what was said. Most important, responses should be condensed into twenty- or thirty-second statements. It takes practice, but it may insure that the message gets through.

The general rules for dealing with interviews:

1. Tell the truth, even if it hurts.
2. Don't beat around the bush or exaggerate.
3. If you don't know an answer, say so.

Also state the most important facts first. Don't let anybody put words in your mouth.

Preparation is the most important factor. Anticipate questions but have two or three points ready to get across, no matter what questions are asked. Come on with those points early, in the first minute or two of the interview if possible.

SUMMARY

1. There is a long tradition of business-press animosity.

2. Developing credibility over time is the best strategy in press relations.

3. In the early eighties the news media have been finding themselves more on the defensive. Part of the problem has been introduction or evolution of "soft news," which emphasizes telling interesting stories.

4. News coverage of business in the eighties has increased substantially, and competence in covering that type of news is improving among reporters.

5. There should be clear policies for managers on dealing with the media.

6. Media encounters should be prepared for, especially when dealing with the electronic media.

NOTES

1. See Louis Banks, "Taking on the Hostile Media," *Harvard Business Review*, March-April 1978, p. 125.

2. Howard Simons and Joseph A. Califano, Jr., *The Media and Business*, (New York: Vintage Books, 1979) p. ix.

3. Ibid. p. xv.

4. Seymour Topping, "The New York Times Approach," in *ASNE Bulletin*, October 1980, p. 10.

5. Irving B. Kaufman, "The Media and Juries," *The New York Times*, November 4, 1982, p. 29.

6. Associated Press wire dispatch, April 27, 1981.

7. Lewis H. Lapham, "Gilding the News," *Harper's*, July 1981, pp. 31–39.

8. Interviews with Seymour Topping and John Lee conducted on March 27, 1981.

9. Remarks by Seymour Topping at Cox School of Business, Southern Methodist University, 1975.

10. Quoted in Frank Donegan, "Networks vs. Big Oil: Why TV News Is Coming up Dry," *Panorama*, August 1980, p. 92.

11. Daniel Yankelovich, "A Public Perspective on First Amendment," *Editor & Publisher*, November 1, 1980, p. 15.

12. Florence Skelly, executive vice president, Yankelovich, Skelly & White, to Public Relations Society of America Chapter Conference, Chicago, February 27, 1981.

13. Frank Allen, "Big Companies Blame Public's Ignorance for Bad Image; Most Small Firms Don't," *Wall Street Journal*, August 21, 1980.

14. Arthur Ochs Sulzberger, "Business and the Press: Is the Press Anti-Business?" Speech to Economics Club of Detroit, March 1977.

15. Elliot Zashin, "Strategic Action in the Regulatory Environment: The Case of the Firestone '500'," *Research in Corporate Social Performance and Policy*, Vol. 4, 1982, Lee E. Preston, ed. (Greenwich, Conn.: JAI Press, Inc.), pp. 189–214.

16. Wendy Swallow, "Has the Freedom of Information Act Worked—or Has It Worked Too Well?" *National Journal*, August 15, 1981, pp. 1470–73.

17. A. Kent McDougall, "In Reporting Profits There Are Many Bottom Lines," *Los Angeles Times*, February 7, 1980.

18. Ray Brady, interview with author, March 27, 1981.

19. "How to Handle the Press," *Newsweek*, April 19, 1982, pp. 90–94.

20. A. Kent McDougall, "Firms Often Learn Hard Way It Doesn't Pay to Clam Up," *Los Angeles Times*, February 8, 1980.

21. "Survey Finds TV Favorite Business News Source," *Advertising Age*, October 25, 1982, p. 42.

22. Connie Lauerman, "Has TV's Disco News Danced Too Far From the Facts?" *The Chicago Tribune*, July 6, 1982, Sec. 3, p. 1.

23. Donegan, "Networks vs. Big Oil."

24. A. Kent McDougall, "TV Business Coverage Is Struggle Against Superficiality," *Los Angeles Times*, February 5, 1980.

25. Michael Arlen, *The Camera Age: Essays on Television* (New York: Farrar, Straus & Giroux, 1981), p. 268.

26. Paul Good, "Why You Can't Always Trust '60 Minutes' Reporting," *Panorama*, September 1980, p. 40.

27. A transcript of the Illinois Power Company production, "60 Minutes/Our Reply," is available from the company's headquarters in Decatur, Ill. On September 27, 1981, "60 Minutes" devoted its entire program to a discussion of journalistic ethics of the investigatory techniques it uses, such as ambush interviews, confrontation, dramatic techniques in story development, and establish of sting-type operations. Conspicuously absent from the program was any mention of the Illinois Power story, in which the company charged that facts were ignored to preserve a story's thesis. There was,

however, a statement in the show by Don Hewitt, the show's producer, that there must be a strong case against a target, which has been developed by research, before a story proceeds.

28. William H. Miller, "Fighting TV Hatchet Jobs," *Industry Week*, January 12, 1981. p. 62.

29. Paul Good, "Why You Can't Always Trust '60 Minutes.'"

30. Chester Burger, "How to Meet the Press," *Harvard Business Review*, July-August 1975, p. 63.

31. Sulzberger, "Business and the Press."

32. Mark Brown, "Worried Execs Get Advice on Facing Up to Television," *Chicago Sun Times*, October 13, 1982, p. 63.

33. From interviews conducted by Richard Hall and Kathy Amundsen for the author, November 1981.

34. Michael J. Connor, "Teaching Businessmen to Face the Nation Is a Growing Business," *Wall Street Journal*, March 7, 1975.

Crisis Communication

6

EMERGENCIES HAPPEN

Among the important lessons business learned in the seventies was one about the need to be prepared for emergencies. The nuclear accident at Three Mile Island is a case in point.

Any company or organization can face crisis at almost any time. An airplane can go down carrying with it the firm's top managers. A hotel fire can occur, like the one in Harrison, New York, in 1980 that ended in death for most of the senior management of Arrow Electronics Corporation. A major bank robbery or embezzlement, an oil or chemical spill that threatens life or property, natural disasters like Mount Saint Helens, a wildcat strike, civil disorder, an unexpected attack in the press, a surprise takeover bid, can all come about at the spur of the moment.

Research conducted by my students of Chicago-area firms has shown that in many instances the upgrading of the communications function in a firm has directly followed a corporate crisis or a dramatically changed environment.

After getting burned by the competition when it announced an upcoming cutback on its Cleveland runs, United Airlines became tight-lipped in the new deregulated environment—to the extent that one reporter characterized the new policy as "extreme" compared to the rest of the industry. Having averted a near takeover by Seagram, Quaker Oats significantly upgraded its financial relations programs. Bell & Howell put some PR emphasis on its educational division when it started having troubles with the government over student-loan programs. J. D. Searle, a pharmaceutical company, brought in highly respected Washington veteran Donald Rumsfeld and some PR pros to help rebuild the company's image after problems with regulatory agencies.

Two issues are involved in any crisis situation: *anticipation* and *reaction*. Monitoring the environment (covered in chapter 4) can help in anticipating some types of crises: takeover of foreign operations by a hostile regime, civil disorder, an unfriendly takeover bid.

Anticipation through crisis planning is the major subject of this chapter. And while there are limits to any attempt at trying to predict, let alone manage communications or any other problems in a future setting, there are many things that can be done in advance. The second component of crisis management is reaction, or execution of a plan. The mere existence of a crisis plan is by no means a guarantee that such a plan will be executed effectively. For example, whatever crisis planning had been done before the Three Mile Island (TMI) accident, the execution of that planning was a disaster in itself. No matter how good a job a communications manager does or how competent the manager and the staff are, one can lose control of a situation. Consider the uproar after the president of Union Oil was erroneously quoted as having said "What's a few birds" when being questioned in Congress while the Santa Barbara oil spill was going on.

Also there are human factors that can impede crisis planning in the planning and execution phases. In a planning phase, people calmly sit down and draw up chains of command, lists of responsibilities, "If this . . . then that" statements. In the heat of crisis, there is significant emotional stress, and unanticipated problems arise that can easily throw off a predetermined series of responses. Fatigue, anxiety, fear—all difficult problems to handle in themselves—compound in a crisis situation. Judgment blurs, people are tired, they don't think straight, mistakes are made. At TMI the VP of engineering, who had been thrown the ball as spokesman for the company, Metropolitan Edison, failed to tell reporters there had been a small off-site radiation release and that more could be expected. The lieutenant governor, upon learning of the radiation release, asked the VP why he hadn't told the press about it. "Because the press did not ask about it," the engineer reportedly said.[1]

CARDINAL RULES

There are a number of important rules to follow in crisis communication, but the cardinal one is, TELL IT ALL AND TELL IT FAST. Get it out quickly and all at once.

When information gets out quickly, rumors are stopped and nerves are calmed. A continuing flow of information at least indicates that, while there are problems, at least someone's getting a handle on it. The idea is that if information is getting out, somebody knows what's going on and somebody will solve the problem.

Dealing with rumors is an important aspect of crisis management. Rumors, whether they are true or false, should be answered immediately with the truth. Experts suggest that setting up hotlines or trying to track them down is a waste of time, that it's better to treat rumors head on. A "no comment" does nothing but fuel rumors. One suggestion is that companies should establish timetables for making important decisions and stick to them. "If no buyer is found for our plant by next month, we will close" would be an example of using a timetable and dealing directly with a rumor. The collapse of Braniff Airways may have been due in part to the impact of rumors about its possible grounding, which caused customers to stay away from the airline and hastened its folding.[2]

Some other major rules:[3]

- *Be sure that all sources speak from the same platform about a situation at a specific time*. It is better for one blind man to describe the elephant than six. Credibility can be easily destroyed. Too many people telling different stories at Three Mile Island provided all kinds of red flags for the press. Too many spokespeople during the Reagan assassination attempt created all kinds of confusion that resulted in a terribly botched reporting job by the media.[4] In a confrontation crisis, the problem becomes overwhelming when two sides of an issue are fighting to be *the* credible source. A labor battle or activist group confrontation are examples. When Ford Motor Company closed its Mahwah, New Jersey, plant in the spring of 1980, there was great acrimony between the company and the United Auto Workers. The UAW charged that Ford was trying to send a message to labor and the country by closing down a plant near the New York media center. The company kept tight control of communications by issuing its comments out of Detroit. It even tried to block press interviews with current and former plant managers. This created a credibility problem, even though high cost factors and the inefficiencies of the operation were well known. [5]

- *Make everything possible public*. Cover all the bases and all the important subjects, as long as security or confidentiality is not breached. This should have been done by the official at TMI who didn't give some crucial information to the press because "nobody asked about it." Reporters at TMI, when they later found out about the information, became more and more dubious about company comments.

- *Update the information regularly*. When a situation is fluid, frequent updates of information are important. In a crisis situation, overkill is better—there are few situations in which there is too much public contact. Frequent accounting builds trust and confidence. Lapses in the flow of information stimulate speculation and can increase anxiety.

- *Increasing complexity can mean more crises*. A power failure can shut a whole city down in a matter of moments. A computer breakdown can halt a major business or governmental operation. A heavy snowstorm can wreck the transportation infrastructure of an entire region.

- *The less people know about what is going on, the more they fear the possible consequences*. The national hysteria that followed the oil embargo of 1973, the hysteria that followed the swine flu episode, the craziness of the McCarthy era can all be attributed to a lack of understanding of the facts involved. Newspaper and TV reports of large oil tankers waiting off the Atlantic Coast while people couldn't get gas at the pump was an excellent example.

- *Get management involved early in the planning effort*. A common mistake is to allow the lower-level managers to handle all crisis planning. History repeatedly shows that when emergency strikes, the top person should become involved immediately and should stay that way.

Also, crises don't necessarily end quickly. The DC-10 crash in May 1979 near Chicago, in which 260 people died, and the collapse of the suspended walkways at the Hyatt House Hotel in Kansas City, Missouri, which killed more than 100 people, continue in the courts, in the public's collective memory, and in the individual lives of those involved. Television transmits visual images that are immediate in time and enduring in memory.

Also the demand of the public for information and greater media awareness of the complexity of crises has boosted disaster coverage. In Kansas City, for example, the *Kansas City Star* hired its own architects and engineers to determine the problems associated with the walkway collapse. In the old days most companies caught in a disaster tried to keep a very low profile, and they were generally successful. An airline PR man once related that, years ago, his first responsibility after a crash was to paint out the airline's name at the crash site. Av Westin, an ABC news executive, noted that if the DC-10 crash had happened a decade ago, "We would've just gone to American [Airlines] and to the FAA to cover the story, whereas, now we've been all over McDonnell-Douglas."[6] Westin feels that the media are now far more aggressive and cynical. In the wake of the DC-10 crash, the manufacturer of the plane had a major problem with lack of public confidence and prompted the grounding of the planes by the government. The crash also instigated press investigations into the plane's air worthiness. This affected the airline's ridership.

OTHER TACTICS

Some organizations have gone well beyond the cardinal rule of getting information out quickly. One example is the Department of Energy's Rocky Flats Research Center near Denver, which is managed by Rockwell International. The policy there was to tell the local media within a half hour of any mishap even hinting of danger. This policy can occasionally result in crying wolf if the mishap is too small, but that is a judgment call.

Getting it out quickly sometimes can become an offensive tactic when a company is faced with a possible crisis. For example, Chrysler Corporation some years back, when faced with information that in fifteen hours *Consumer Reports* magazine was going to attack the steering mechanism in its Omni and Horizon subcompacts, quickly made its own videotapes demonstrating correct handling of the cars and also taped interviews with company officials, who defended the autos. When the *Consumer Reports* attack came, Chrysler was ready. This approach can be escalated one more step to what is known as a preemptive strike. In this instance, the company being attacked strikes first. That was done quite effectively by the Tobacco Institute, which took the initiative in announcing (and attacking) the impending release of a new surgeon general's report on smoking and health hazards.

THREE MILE ISLAND
LESSONS

The mistakes of Met Edison at Three Mile Island bear study because the company did violate the basic rules of crisis communication management. At first the incident didn't appear to be very significant. Initial press coverage, as a matter of fact, was quite routine. The press had little inkling that anything was seriously wrong until Lieutenant Governor William Scranton held a press conference and indicated that Met Edison was putting out conflicting information. That was a "red flag" signal to reporters, who had not yet grasped the magnitude of the situation. As Professor David Rubin wrote in the aftermath of TMI: "Reporters who didn't know the primary system from the secondary system in the reactor *did* know when conflicting information was being put out, and that's all a good reporter needs to scent a story."[7]

A second mistake, Rubin notes, was inadequate logistic support for the press. Met Ed was unprepared when reporters got to the scene. There was one pay phone—no press center, no background information on the plant. Also a phone line to company headquarters, which was set up to handle all inquiries, was constantly busy. It was sixty hours into the crisis before a press center was established. Because the company did not *physically* and *administratively* centralize press operations, the hundreds of reporters who streamed into TMI were left to their own devices. They turned their attention to getting information from the NRC, outside researchers and academics, people in the community, and antinuclear groups.

Adding to the synergy of this crisis was the coincidental release of a movie, *The China Syndrome*, just weeks earlier starring antinuclear activist Jane Fonda, which drew some eerie parallels with TMI.

There was some confusion in the nuclear industry as well. The company that had designed the plant refused to talk to the media, although it could have given some helpful information. The industry lobby—the Atomic Industrial Forum—kept a low profile.[8] Finally Harold Denton, the head of the Nuclear Regulatory Commission was named by President Carter to assume the role of primary on-scene coordinator and spokesman.

Denton's first major assignment was to attempt to calm fears generated by his own agency that a hydrogen bubble inside the plant was potentially explosive. That rumor caused more than one hundred thousand persons to temporarily flee the area. Before Denton's arrival on the scene, the NRC had worked hard, according to reports, "to make sure that mainly 'reassuring' information would reach the public."[9] When the bubble story emerged, the NRC consistently tried to play it down. The more it did so, the more the press magnified the story's importance. It wasn't until the arrival of Denton, whom reporters judged as "disarmingly frank" and "can probably be believed," that the crisis began defusing. While Denton was not especially knowledgeable or good at speaking, he had the convincing and reassuring manner, which was absolutely necessary to calm the crisis.

In the wake of TMI the nuclear industry, which had been caught off guard to say the least, decided to take the offensive and try to right its tarnished image. Industry groups moved quickly to bolster governmental affairs and especially lobbying efforts in Washington, to shore up public acceptance of nuclear power through creation of a special industry committee, and to coordinate research, speakers' publications, and announcements. On the lobbying front the industry realized it needed to provide more than just lectures to Congress, as in the old days. One official said, "We have to be more sophisticated than that and supply them with accurate, credible, timely information, so that they use our data for decision making."[10] Other techniques used by the industry included an "energy truth squad" of youthful executives put together for the purpose of going around to campuses to counter antinuclear activists such as Jane Fonda. Even so, the large credibility gap had already done serious harm in Congress and on Wall Street for the nuclear industry.

Attempting to dig out from under this long-term problem would be difficult for the industry. Richard C. Hyde, a senior VP for the Hill and Knowlton public relations firm, who was involved in trying to help Met Edison at TMI, suggested four strategies:

1. Reassess the industry message in the wake of public opinion following TMI. Communications, he said, had been too simple and too confident.
2. Communicate the hard, bad facts as well as the good ones—talk about radiation in cold, hard terms.
3. Involve the public in the decision-making process—give better information to the public and let it make decisions on the future of nuclear power.
4. Prepare new ground rules for crisis management. The industry must resist the temptation to cover the flanks. It should develop good background information to help the press in emergencies and change its method of communicating: opting for candor, completeness, and an approach that recognizes that TMI has produced a new and sophisticated public.[11]

STRATEGIES FOR CRISIS PLANNING

Communications planning for crisis management is not done off in a corner somewhere. All crisis planning is based on a modification of existing routines and procedures. If a company does not have a communications program or has one that is "loose" rather than well defined, it must first develop good internal organization before attempting crisis planning.

The development of a plan to handle crisis must be done in the organization by its own staff. It should not be totally delegated to an outside firm. It cannot be done by one staff or line group in a vacuum. It *can* be facilitated by an outside consultant. When put into effect, a crisis plan suspends many of the procedures, alternates hierarchical relationships, and calls for actions that are generally outside the normal operations of the organization.

For example, on a regular basis the chief executive and the PR director might be separated by one or two levels of management. In a crisis, however, there may well be nothing separating them, and the chief executive might end up taking his cues from the PR chief. Therefore the relationship needs to be developed and worked out earlier. In some industries, like the airlines industry, crisis plans are updated as often as bimonthly to insure currency of information and coordination between actors.

Planning updates can also be a result of new developments turned up during environmental scanning (see chapter 4), as new information discloses a potential for crisis. For example, if monitoring indicates that consumer groups are beginning to go after makers of baby food, baby-food companies should be developing a contingency plan, as well as a shorter-term strategy.

Planning for crisis generally falls into two categories: *emergency* planning and *disaster* planning. The DC-10 crash and TMI were disasters—sudden catastrophies. A power outage in town, a water shortage are examples of emergencies. There needs to be planning for both types of contingencies. A brainstorm session among staffers from different departments should be conducted initially to list every possible problem that could occur. Some firms use gaming situations to assist in this process. Actual planning should be generic—applicable to all kinds of situations, with specific instructions for emergencies or disasters.

J&J SAVES TYLENOL

One of the most successful crisis management stories of recent times was Johnson & Johnson's handling of the Tylenol tragedy in the fall of 1982, after seven persons died from ingesting cyanide-laced Tylenol capsules. At the time of the deaths, Tylenol enjoyed a 37 percent market share of the pain-reliever market, and $400 million in annual sales. The product accounted for 17 percent of the company's earnings.

The company was first informed of the tragedy through the news media. With no advance warning of the incidents, J&J's first actions were to dispatch a scientist, PR person, and security agent to Chicago, where the deaths were reported, to gather information. Plants were checked to make sure the poisonings did not result from any action in the manufacturing processes. J&J moved swiftly to bring its CEO directly into the crisis as the lead. Two major decisions were made: 1) to recall 31 million bottles of Tylenol capsules, with a retail value of $100 million, and 2) to announce a reward of $100,000 for information leading to the arrest and conviction of the responsible party. While the company could have decided at that point to abandon the product, it decided to go to new tamper-resistant packaging.

A major press strategy used by the company was to deal with reporters on a one-on-one basis, rather than in a news conference situation. This strategy muted the possibility of an uncontrolled "media event" similar to the kind that plagued the Three Mile Island episode. The company also moved quickly to measure public opinion, not only to find out how the public was reacting to the crisis, but also to give J&J an idea of how to better handle what appeared to be a crisis that was going to be around for a while. J&J learned from the polling that 94 percent of the people surveyed knew Tylenol was involved in the poisonings. The good news, J&J CEO James Burke told *Fortune*, was that 87 percent realized that Tylenol was not responsible for the deaths. The bad news was that about 50 percent said they would not buy any Tylenol product in the future even though the deaths had been attributed solely to ingestion of capsules, not tablets. The early polling also indicated to the company that people who had used the product frequently in the past would be inclined to go back to using it in the future.

At company headquarters, three task forces began working on the image rescue effort. For internal morale, the PR department assembled a one-hour videotape of news reports on the tragedy and comments by company officials. The tape was shown to employees via the company's worldwide television network.

By late December 1982, Tylenol had regained 65 percent of the nationwide market share it had previously held. Even the company expressed surprise at the turnaround, since initially it had lost 87 percent of its customers for the product. What were some of the reasons for Johnson & Johnson's amazing comeback after the Tylenol tragedy? They included determination and smart marketing savvy as well as good crisis management:

CORPORATE VISION.   The company early on made a strategic decision not to let the brand die. There was no hesitation, no "should we or shouldn't we?" that dragged on. J&J's determination was born not only out of a realization by the company that the product was a major source of revenue, but also from polling that showed that the public did not blame the product for the deaths. By not hesitating, the company was able to move back into the marketplace aggressively with a new tamper-resistant package before competitors grabbed market share. The decision to go back into the marketplace also reflected the company's internal belief that its long-term commitment to health would save Tylenol, a thread of corporate pride and commitment that ran through the entire episode and created not only credibility but a *modus operandi* that melded public concern with marketing know-how.

SMART MARKETING.   Late in November, just weeks after the crisis ended, the company flooded the market with 40 million discount coupons, timed to when people would be going back to stores to get refills of competing products that had moved in following the recall. The generous $2.50 discounts brought many former users back into the fold. The company also offered retailers a 25 percent discount for ordering supplies in the same amounts as before the recall. This was accomplished with no advertising, save a few ads aimed at seeking public trust for the product.

GOOD PRESS RELATIONS.   The once nearly invisible (from the media's point of view) J&J management did a complete about face once the crisis hit, seeking out national exposure on "60 Minutes" and the "Donahue" shows, while its small PR staff handled thousands of press inquiries and a toll-free line manned by employees fielded 350,000 calls. Johnson & Johnson CEO Burke said the corporation, in the aftermath of the episode, "has been changed once and for all." "We've gotten strength from this, not weakness," he said. The long-standing company credo ("We believe our first responsibility is to the doctors, nurses and patients, to mothers and all others who use our products and services.") and the company's hard-nosed dedication to that credo had a lot to do with the way it reacted to the tragedy in the marketplace. In fact, when he was made chairman of J&J in 1976, Burke had initiated a series of "challenge meetings" for senior managers to make sure that credo became part of the corporate culture.

Burke disagreed with analysts who said the product would never recover its former market position. He predicted it might take two or three years to recover fully, but expressed confidence that "regular" customers would return to the product. The most amazing part of the entire episode was not that J&J had handled it so well, but that the public perception of the company was so strengthened by what happened.[12]

WHAT'S IN A PLAN?

Actual planning for a contingency requires committee work—involving top management, legal and technical staffs, communications personnel, and others. Committee assignments are given out, and various sections of the plan are put together piecemeal (for some examples, see Appendix 3), with a final committee review of the entire process, to insure coordination. A number of elements are common to these plans.[13]

CENTRALIZATION.   Any crisis plan must recognize the need for central control during a crisis. While many persons will be involved, and in some cases widely scattered, it is important that clear lines of responsibility be laid out and that release of information be centralized in one location. For example, following the Kansas City Hyatt Hotel bridge collapse, Hallmark, the company that owned the hotel, through a series of briefings, instructed *all* employees to be careful when speaking to reporters or others about the disaster and to speak only as individuals and not as employees or representatives of the Hallmark Company.

Contingency planning should include designation of an *operations-center director* and a *communications-center director*. The operations-center director can be the *on-scene coordinator* or the *home-office director*, depending on the situation. Responsibilities of staffers involved and whom they report to must be spelled out in detail. Communications assignments will include spokesperson, logistics, courier, typist, go-fors, and drivers. The need to maintain round-the-clock operations may require consideration of shift changes.

The main concept of centralization is *information* centralization. The organization managing the crisis must speak with one voice. But there must also be a point where information collection is centralized as well. Collection and dissemination of information is a disciplined activity requiring that only one person or one coordinated group be charged with controlling what is said.

Another aspect of centralization is the control of egress and ingress to the site of a disaster. For example, in the hours that followed the midair crash of two planes in a San Diego neighborhood in 1980 in which 144 persons lost their lives, police had to immediately seal off the area, evict reporters who were there, and establish a press information office (under a nearby shade tree) to offer continual briefings to news people. Access was controlled by providing the reporters with a bus tour of the devastated site.[14]

In delicate situations where there must be notification of next of kin, centralization prevents premature release of names. Also centralization insures that management gets information before it is released.

COMMUNICATION.   When doing crisis planning, it is important that responsibility for managing overall communications be assigned to a specific person or organization. That assignment usually goes to the communications director. It is then his or her responsibility to assign the job of spokesperson, fact gatherer, and press-center chief. Depending on the size of the firm and the size of the crisis, these jobs can be performed by one person or many persons. One of the more important considerations during communications planning for crisis is the development of dissemination plans and channels to be used.

The list of those who want to know what's going on can grow quickly, but priorities need to be established. The priority list should include: top managers, starting with the chief executive; the governor, senators, congressmen, and local political leaders such as the mayor, council people; the media; employees; families of employees; and influentials in the community.

When the Ball Company of Muncie, Indiana, had an emergency over the unavailability of canning lids during the harvest season of 1975, it identified target audiences as consumers, distributors, and stockholders as well as government officials and the news media. *Secondary* publics included employees, management, and the business community.[15] As a general rule, senior management, the media, and top government officials in the affected area should get first information during a crisis. When setting priorities with the press, at the top of the list should be the national wire services—Associated Press and United Press International, both of which have bureaus in every state capital and major city. Sometimes government agencies must be notified early on, as in the case of major spills of chemicals and other toxic substances.

All communications planning should be based on the idea of centralizing information at a press center that is equipped with such things as (1) fact sheets, (2) telephones, (3) typewriters and paper, (4) duplication facilities, (5) sufficient electrical power (20 amp service), and easy access. Walkie-talkies, which can help internal coordination when the scene is spread out, are also helpful. In the wake of TMI, the federal government moved to require contingency planning for such facilities at every nuclear site. (See Figure 6-1.)

The plan must identify persons in the organization who can serve as technical experts in various aspects of the potential crisis. The list of these names should be updated regularly. If there is a chlorine leak, which engineer or scientist can speak to its possible impact on health or safety? If a bank is held up, who can describe the security measures that the bank had taken? If the government is announcing a product recall, who can respond to the technical issues involved?

FIGURE 6-1 Kemeny Commission Recommendations on Communications in the Wake of Three Mile Island Nuclear Accident

---

G. *THE PUBLIC'S RIGHT TO INFORMATION*

1. Federal and state agencies, as well as the utility, should make adequate preparation for a systematic public information program so that in time of a radiation-related emergency they can provide timely and accurate information to the news media and the public in a form that is understandable. There should be sufficient division of briefing responsibilities as well as availability of informed sources to reduce confused and inaccurate information. The Commission therefore recommends:

   a. Since the utility must be responsible for the management of the accident, it should also be primarily responsible for providing information on the status of the plant to the news media and to the public; but the restructured NRC should also play a supporting role and be available to provide background information and technical briefings.

   b. Since the state government is responsible for decisions concerning protective actions, including evacuations, a designated state agency should be charged with issuing all information on this subject. This agency is also charged with the development of and dissemination of accurate and timely information on off-site radiation doses resulting from releases of radioactivity. This information should be derived from appropriate sources. (See recommendation F.1.) This agency should also set up the machinery to keep local officials fully informed of developments and to coordinate briefings to discuss any federal involvement in evacuation matters.

2. The provision of accurate and timely information places special responsibilities on the official sources of this information. The effort must meet the needs of the news media for information but without compromising the ability of operational personnel to manage the accident. The Commission therefore recommends that:

   a. Those who brief the news media must have direct access to informed sources of information.

   b. Technical liaison people should be designated to inform the briefers and to serve as a resource for the news media.

   c. The primary official news sources should have plans for the prompt establishment of press centers reasonably close to the site. These must be properly equipped, have appropriate visual aids and reference materials, and be staffed with individuals who are knowledgeable in dealing with the news media. These press centers must be operational promptly upon the declaration of a general emergency or its equivalent.

3. The coverage of nuclear emergencies places special responsibilities on the news media to provide accurate and timely information. The Commission therefore recommends that:

   a. All major media outlets (wire services, broadcast networks, news magazines, and metropolitan daily newspapers) hire and train specialists who have more than a passing familiarity with reactors and the language of radiation. All other news media, regardless of their size, located near nuclear power plants should attempt to acquire similar knowledge or make plans to secure it during an emergency.

   b. Reporters discipline themselves to place complex information in a context that is understandable to the public and that allows members of the public to make decisions regarding their health and safety.

   c. Reporters educate themselves to understand the pitfalls in interpreting answers to "what if" questions. Those covering an accident should have the ability to understand uncertainties expressed by sources of information and probabilities assigned to various possible dangers.

4. State emergency plans should include provision for creation of local broadcast media networks for emergencies that will supply timely and accurate information. Arrangements should be made to make available knowledgeable briefers to go on the air to clear up rumors and explain conditions at the plant. Communications between state officials, the utility, and the network should be prearranged to handle the possibility of an evacuation announcement.

5. The Commission recommends that the public in the vicinity of a nuclear power plant be routinely informed of local radiation measurements that depart appreciably from normal background radiation, whether from normal or abnormal operation of the nuclear power plant, from a radioactivity cleanup operation such as that at TMI-2, or from other sources.

Excerpted from Report of the President's Commission on the Accident at Three Mile Island, issued October 1979, Washington, D.C. (John G. Kemeny, Chairman).

Another very important element is *speed*. The plan must emphasize quick release of information and must not require four levels of management and three levels of legal staff to approve information prior to its release. Speed may be one of the most difficult problems to address when putting a plan together, especially when that plan must be coordinated with various staff and line offices in the company. But the purpose of the planning process is to work out clearance problems *in advance* so that information release is quick and comprehensive.

COOPERATION.   The third principle of crisis planning is cooperation, which means that everyone who will be involved in execution of the plan should be involved in developing it. This point relates especially to senior management, which tends to delegate its participation in this kind of planning. As a matter of fact, senior management must not only be involved in developing the plan but must *initiate* development of it and lend full support to launching the effort. This will help insure more than pro-forma participation by middle-management staff and line personnel.

One way of testing the plan and instilling cooperation can be through the use of simulation and gaming. Hill and Knowlton, a public relations firm heavily involved in crisis communications training, has developed a series of situations that are modified to conform with a company's needs and collectively titled "Incident at Riverton." Through the use of multimedia equipment, up to twenty corporate officials are involved in a scenario that can be made increasingly more difficult: an engine collides with a tank car; it ruptures and spills chemicals; fumes spread toward town; there are conflicting governmental instructions; the chemical flows into the city's sewers, and a call for evacuation is sounded. Complications include negative TV reports, eyewitness questioning of tank-car safety, accusations against the railroad by the mayor, a possible cover-up of misfeasance, exploitation by a state senator for personal political gain. A chemical company, which had no crisis plan, was able to deal quickly with a major catastrophe just weeks after having taken this kind of training, according to Hill and Knowlton officials.[16]

EXECUTION.   A first priority when the crisis occurs is getting people on the scene and making sure the system is functioning correctly from a management and communications point of view, first internally, then externally. Shock troops that go on the scene first need to be backed up very quickly both operationally and logistically. Getting information moving within the organization must be accomplished initially, with external release following as quickly thereafter as possible.

In the case where there have been deaths of key corporate personnel, financial emergencies, crime, or regulatory or legal emergencies the corporate office will usually be the command center. In civil disorders, labor union troubles, natural disasters, system malfunctions, and so on, there is usually some distance between that activity and the home office.

As the Three Mile Island incident showed, business managers often fear reporters' bias and ignorance to such an extent that they refuse or agree only reluctantly to talk with the press. When they do talk, they are so steeped in jargon and qualification that any communications gap is exacerbated. Reporters, on the other hand, when they get either conflicting or confusing information or see that a spokesperson is dancing around the issue, immediately suspect a cover-up.

"All an organization achieves by ducking questions," says a PR executive, "is to assure its point of view will not be presented or that someone else is going to present it—someone who doesn't have its best interests at heart."[17] In a crisis situation it is wise to be fair (no exclusive stories to favorites), to keep everything on the record and to be precise. TWA, for example, issues a little red book to employees, giving them guidance for airplane crashes, which advises, among other things, not to use colorful descriptives in reporting on crashes (slammed, careened, plowed into.)[18]

A crisis or emergency is, in this day of instant communication, a legitimate news event and one that often affects public health and safety. In the execution of the communications plan it is important to attempt to help the media make deadlines and to be responsive to the needs of different media. A newspaper needs facts, a TV station needs pictures, a magazine reporter needs details. In the San Diego crash, as mentioned earlier, police needs to control access to the crash site were reconciled with TV and photographer needs for pictures by a bus trip to the scene from outside the cordoned-off area.

In executing the plan, it is also important that the spokespersons neither speculate beyond the facts nor place blame. This should be worked out with legal counsel when the plan is being developed.

EVALUATION OF THE PLAN.   Soon after the crisis or emergency has passed there should be a total debriefing of all involved. Questionnaires should be used with those outside the organization who were involved—members of the media, community service agencies, officials—and also those within—top management, those involved in the operation, maybe a cross-section of employees. Questions should zero in on adequate access to information, timeliness and accuracy of the information, and suggestions for improvement. A meeting of the planning team should be held and changes made in the plan for the future. Also letters and memos of appreciation should be sent.

CONFRONTATION CRISIS

Some situations in crisis planning need special attention. One is handling defensive measures relating to a threatened corporate takeover (see Chapter 7). Another involves handling the potential impact of emerging societal issues (see Chapter 4). A third is dealing with confrontation.

The major model in confrontation was developed over a forty-year period by the famous social-rights activist, Saul Alinsky, who adapted union-organizing techniques to this effort and through his Industrial Areas Foundation placed organizers nationwide with community groups who were seeking political power for social change. The Alinsky organizations use group-dynamic skills to build citizen support and achieve local power and then to provoke power centers through confrontation techniques in order to negotiate for stated demands of the group. It is a process whereby an organized group seeks power, and thus legitimacy. Corporations that provide consumer goods or services often can be the target of groups seeking jobs, improved delivery of services, better goods, a clean environment, or improved health or safety conditions.

In one well-documented instance the Allstate Insurance Company found itself up against an Alinsky-style group, the Metropolitan Area Housing Alliance (MAHA) in Chicago in 1977.[19] The group had charged Allstate with redlining certain Chicago neighborhoods in regard to homeowners insurance, thus contributing to the deterioration of those neighborhoods.

The lesson Allstate learned in dealing with MAHA was that to be a good corporate citizen was not enough, that more is required of today's firm for survival in both business and social environments. MAHA had charged the company in a press conference with being the "worst redlining offender in the city." This charge was based on the number of homeowner-policy terminations made in a nine-month period. The problem from the corporate perspective was that there was indeed a problem in some neighborhoods: replacement costs had exceeded market value. And Allstate was in fact the biggest redlining offender—but only because it was also the largest insurer in the metropolitan area. Allstate officials were not ready when the charges were leveled, even though there had been some indications that such an attack was coming. "We did not have the products or statistics in hand [when the charges were made and] . . . by the time our response was ready [it was] . . . no longer news."

Requests for Allstate to attend community meetings and explain its policies piled up while the company refused comment pending completion of the state investigation (that investigation eventually exonerated the company). MAHA circumvented this Allstate policy by making enough noises at the Sears (parent company) annual meeting for the company chairman to commit Allstate to a community meeting. From those meetings with MAHA and with groups in fifteen other cities, Allstate came up with five basic conclusions for dealing with confrontation crises:

1. *Confrontation is a means to an end*. That is, negotiation and change. The faster one moves to discussions, the less hassle can be expected from the media. The cost of *not* meeting with a group is higher: in morale, productivity, and energy needed to keep fighting, plus damage to the firm's image. Decisions to meet or not meet should be made early.

2. *Not all groups want discussion*. Attacking groups sometimes just want a *target*. They want to posture and do not really represent a constituency. Allstate decided it would meet with any group that is broadbased and really looking for solutions. Sometimes the company has to refuse, but it still leaves the door open for the future.

3. *Management must be trained to deal with confrontation*. In the MAHA case Allstate executives faced some really angry people. The executives of the firm, used to giving orders, not listening to demands, at first got angry and defensive. But the company's communications department quickly put together some training, "meet the press" confrontation sessions that were worse than anything that could be expected on the outside. All executives involved in negotiations had to attend the two-day course. Also executives were sorted out. Some disliked and couldn't handle confrontation situations; others thrived on them.

4. *Rhetoric must be ignored*. The groups talked two different languages. MAHA said it had "won victories," Allstate said "we made some reasonable changes." The rhetoric at first angered management, until it realized that this was part of the group's organizing process more than anything else.

5. *Perceptions of the same problem differ*. Allstate maintained it could prove it did not redline. The citizen groups felt that the redlining, whether intended or not, was the result of business policies. Allstate said it saw practices that appeared to make its product less available. It learned, through this crisis, "to see through new eyes." The change in the corporation's perception was valuable, and in the end the real issue was how Allstate could better sell and how the people could better buy the product.

Allstate frankly told the citizens group that there were some things, such as valuation, that it couldn't change. The fact that it did change some things and that it agreed to a $1 million investment in urban economic development following the crisis attests to the success of MAHA. It might be anticipated that as economic dislocation continues in the U.S., especially in the Frost Belt sections of the Northeast and Midwest, other corporations will face similar crises as people attempt to preserve their communities.

SUMMARY

1. Many firms plan for crisis only after it happens.

2. The cardinal rule of crisis communication is "Tell it all, tell it quickly."

3. Senior management must be involved in crisis planning.

4. Crisis can also be defined in terms of attacks on a company's credibility or reputation.

NOTES

1. David M. Rubin, "Met Ed's Mistakes," *Wall Street Journal*, June 2, 1980.

2. "Killing Rumors Before They Kill a Company," *The New York Times*, December 19, 1982, p. 23.

3. See Kathleen Connelley, "Managing a Crisis Effectively," remarks to the Council for Advancement and Support of Education, Chicago, April 1, 1981.

4. Comment by Gary Deeb, TV and radio critic, *Chicago Sun-Times*, quoted in Connelley, "Managing a Crisis."

5. See William M. Carley, "Cosing of a Ford Plant Reflects Worry of Car Makers: Quality," *Wall Street Journal*, June 16, 1980.

6. See Thomas Petzinger, Jr., "When Disaster Comes, Public-Relations Men Won't Be Far Behind," *Wall Street Journal*, August 23, 1979.

7. Rubin, "Met Ed's Mistakes."

8. Ibid.

9. Casey Bukro, "How Accurate Was Press about Three Mile Island?" *Chicago Tribune*, March 30, 1980.

10. See William J. Lanouette, "Under Scrutiny by a Divided Government, the Nuclear Industry Tries to Unite," *National Journal*, January 12, 1980, pp. 44–48.

11. Richard C. Hyde, "Candor in Communication Vital to Keep Nuclear Option Open," *Electric Perspectives*, April 1979, Edison Electric Institute, pp. 6–9.

12. See Michael Waldholz, "Tylenol Regains Most of No. 1 Market Share, Amazing Doomsayers," *Wall Street Journal*, December 24, 1982, p. 1; Thomas Moore, "The Fight To Save Tylenol," *Fortune*, November 29, 1982, pp. 44–49; Michael Waldholz and Dennis Kneale, "Tylenol's Maker Tries to Regain Good Image in Wake of Tragedy," *Wall Street Journal*, October 8, 1982, p. 1; Michael L. Millenson, "Tylenol Regains Big Share of Market, Survey Shows," *Chicago Tribune*, December 18, 1982, Sec. 2, p. 5; and Michael Millenson, "J&J Gains Admiration, Strength," *Chicago Tribune*, November 21, 1982, sec. 5, p. 1.

13. See Seymour Smith, "How to Plan for Crisis Communication," *Public Relations Journal*, March 1979, pp. 17–18. See also Robert L. Barbour, "Guidelines for Drawing up Public Relations Emergency and Disaster Plans, parts 1 and 2, *Tips & Tactics*, a supplement to PR reporter, November 28 and December 12, 1977. See also "A Synopsis of Presentations at the Conference on Crisis Communications" sponsored by the northeast district, Public Relations Society of America, New York, September 26, 1979.

14. See Allen H. Center and Frank E. Walsh, "The Plight of the Police," *Public Relations Practices, Case Studies* (Englewood Cliffs, N.J.: Prentice-Hall, 1981), pp. 305–9.

15. Ibid., pp. 310–16.

16. Interview with Richard C. Hyde, Hill and Knowlton, by the author, September 30, 1981.

17. Michael L. Drohlich, "Manage PR Crises Through Advance Planning," *Scope*, May 1980, pp. 7–11.

18. Thomas Petzinger, Jr., "When Disaster Comes."

19. Nan M. Kilkeary and Kurt P. Stocker, "The Corporation and Confrontation," 1980, unpublished.

Financial
Relations

7

BASIC HOUSEKEEPING

There is a little gnawing question that seeems to be gnawing a little more frequently these days: What impact does good corporate communications have on a firm's economic condition? This chapter investigates how a good corporate communications program can improve a firm's financial position. In particular, a good program can keep managers out of trouble with the SEC and, most important, it can protect the firm against unfriendly takeover attempts.

Managers sometimes look at financial relations as basic housekeeping— filing annual reports, which now includes 10-k's, maintaining services to stockholders, and sending information to analysts and financial reporters, along with some handholding for the large-block holders. There are two major audiences here: the SEC and stock exchanges, which have some very specific requirements for disclosure of information, and the major "actors" in the marketplace— the buyers, sellers, and advisers.

This communications housekeeping cannot be dismissed lightly. There are enormous problems involved in readership and data presentation. The biggest question that faces companies in this area is how to present company results and trends in ways that appeal to readers. A major segment of the communications business wrestles with this particular problem on a daily basis.

Furthermore, as Jim Horton, a financial relations specialist with Robert Marsten & Associates notes, business managers and communicators are "involved in enormous arguments over what kinds of data to present."[1] It is a question of what data truly describe the company's results, according to Horton. Inflation accounting, foreign-currency translation, real world versus standard practice presentation of numbers enter into this question, among other issues. People at the Fair Accounting Standards Board and the SEC spend a lot of time working on this these things.

Beyond the need for detail and specificity is the greater need for those involved in financial/investor relations to communicate the *vision* that will show how the company plans to maintain viability in the future. For this reason, more than any other, investor relations is important. It attempts to communicate to the business world that the company has chosen a path, has set a course that will keep it buoyant.

More important than the need for detail and specificity is the greater need for communicators in financial/investor relations to help the corporation communicate its strategic vision to the marketplace—a vision that clearly communicates expectations for financial performance, a course that has been chosen, a path that has been taken that will bring long-term future growth.

Those communicated expectations should include:

1. the expected rate of growth;
2. reasons why the company thinks it is going to achieve that rate of growth: pricing and share strategies;
3. how the company expects to invest in new plant and working capital to achieve growth (i.e., in expansion, cost reduction, or replacement projects, and so on);
4. what kind of return the company expects to achieve.

Here is a hypothetical example of what a company's clearly communicated expectations might look like:

> We are in a business which at this point is in a cyclical trough. We had relatively poor performance in the last year or so—worse than expected. While many analysts may think that we may be able to achieve only modest growth because we are in a maturing industry, we believe that because we are concentrating on doing the things we do best—being a low-cost producer—and using that advantage to the fullest in maintaining market share, we are positioned for much more rapid growth than our competitors. Because of this we feel that we will be able to achieve growth in the neighborhood of ten to thirteen percent per year. In order to assure this growth, we will be investing roughly fifty percent of our internally generated cash in the future.
>
> We feel that by pursuing a very aggressive pricing strategy, we will be able to maintain market dominance. Furthermore, we feel that there are numerous expansion opportunities in this business and while we intend to invest heavily in capital which will sustain our low-cost market position, we expect to allocate considerable other capital to expansion into new product areas.

VALUATION

Investors and analysts are interested in the long-term financial outlook for a company. They are not so much interested in this year's earnings per share as they are the future potential for growth. Companies that don't clearly communicate financial expectations and good reasons for those expectations can find their stock improperly valued over time. And they can also find themselves a potential takeover target. Companies that look backward when talking about growth take a safe course, but it is safe only for the moment.

For those facing takeover attempts, however, the backward glance can be fatal. An amazing amount of good news about sunny skies tomorrow emerges when managers are looking down the barrel of a takeover. One person who has taken this problem on is Michael Seely, president of Investor Access Corporation, who put forth some important arguments on proper "valuation" at a conference on investor relations.[2]

Seely said that shareholder relations are evolving dramatically, from dealing with routine functions toward answering tough market questions, such as:

- Why is one firm's stock volatile and another's not?
- What is the company's intrinsic value and why is that price different from its market value?
- How do existing strategies affect stock price?
- What is the logical clientele for a company's stock?
- How can a company close the gap between market and intrinsic value before a raider does? And how does a company do this efficiently?

Seely emphasizes that *forecasts* on how a company is going to do count more for smart investors, and he even suggests that the corporate strategy function be merged into investor relations.

Seely's main concern is with *valuation* of the firm and improving it. He observes that hostile tender offers make sense only when the company is not correctly valued and where a premium can be paid to get the target at less than its intrinsic value, and that conventional defense seeks to sustain the inefficiency rather than remedy it. His approach, he says, would be to make greater regular use of opinion surveys to attempt to explain why comparable companies are valued differently and to measure perceptions of various policies and strategies of like companies. Such "soft" tools, plus information already available on the impact of advertising, the strengths and weaknesses of the annual report, and the benefits of listing or using registered representatives, can be evaluated and analyzed in a way that will produce a cost-efficient investor relations program. Looking to the future, Seely sees a day when investor relations managers, using computers, will be able to build models to answer questions relating to dividend policy and its impact on: stock prices, intrinsic value (adjusted for the prime rate), trigger prices for an exchange offer, and volume necessary to bring about a one-point move in shares.

Seely's suggestions are often radical: Abolish group meetings, publish annual reports that leave out profit and loss in favor of showing ranges of earnings possible using different accounting methods, and point out "how management decisions changed short-term results but enhanced long-range prospects." (The SEC, the FASB, and the American Institute of CPA's dictate much of what companies present in the P&L and the balance sheet).[3] Many experts recommend emphasizing projections for the future as a means of warding off takeovers and basing advertising on how the company is perceived on Wall Street. And while some people might suggest that to increase value a company may need to be restructured, experts suggest that no company is really undervalued because of its form. Undervaluing is a function of poor communication of expectations. Restructuring should come only after the company has communicated its expectations continually over a period of time and believes it remains substantially undervalued. This new approach to investor relations through valuation might have a positive impact on companies with a declining shareholder base, thinly traded volatile stock, inability to tap capital markets, and undervalued asset base. It is an aggressive vision of the role of investor relations but makes sense in the takeover-prone eighties.

IMAGE
AND ITS VALUE

Research released in 1980 by Bozell & Jacobs International pointed out that a good corporate advertising program run in key magazines can contribute 4 percent to the variability in a company's stock price.[4] The Bozell & Jacobs study showed that 55 percent of the variability in a company's stock price can be attributed to such financial fundamentals as earnings per share, dividends, net sales, debt equity ratios, and return on assets. Forty percent is attributable to individual investors, the "romance of the market," that is, the psychology of the total market, the specific category involved, PR activities, the kind of press a company receives, and the amount of "push" the stock is given from various institutions and brokers.[5]

Companies spend nearly a billion dollars a year on corporate or "image" advertising (see Figure 7-1) and yet many advertising and communications professionals are skeptical of its effectiveness. Critics claim that much corporate advertising is unplanned, unfocused, unproductive, sporadic, and limited. Adman David Ogilvy says that corporate advertising's failure is that most companies do not define the purpose of the advertising, nor do they measure the results of this advertising. Says Ogilvy, "I long to see a company describe itself as 'the company that makes money'." Thomas E. Garbett of Doyle, Dane, Bernbach, Inc., says that corporate ads can, under the right conditions, "not only aid stock prices but boost sales, hold employees, recruit professionals, and get people to understand . . . the company." A survey by Garbett showed that industrial companies are more likely to use corporate advertising than consumer product firms. (His research also showed that less than five percent of corporate advertising dollars are spent on attempting to sway the public through issues advertising.)[6] The newest kind of corporate advertising is called "market preparation." The AT&T ads following divestiture that appeared in early 1983 were that kind of ads. "Market preparation" advertising "prepares" the market for what the company is trying to sell and positions the organization as a resource for certain types of products. This kind of advertising can be of special help to conglomerates who need to explain who they are, especially to the investment community.

According to Terry Haller, chairman of the Financial Communications

FIGURE 7-1 Market Preparation Ad Following Diversification of the Bell Corporation

SOURCE: Courtesy of the Bell System.

Strategy Center in Wilmette, Illinois, most corporate ads are ineffective. Mr. Haller says that over 80 percent of all corporate ads fall into four predictable categories—growth (26 percent), new technology (24 percent), product line (17 percent), and connection to the energy business (14 percent). He faults ad agencies for the problem, asserting that "no corporate ad has ever been scientifically test marketed to register its impact on stock price." He adds, "it is impossible to see how they could inspire the investment community with any confidence in the client company's future, which of course, is the basis of any investment decision."

He suggests that ads have to talk about a company's particular strengths, what sets it off from competitors, and its ability "to navigate itself into the future."[7]

One company, International Telephone and Telegraph (ITT) spends about $10 million a year on image advertising. One of its main goals has been to differentiate itself from AT&T. Nearly half of the largest 800 companies use corporate advertising to sell ideas as well as products. The usual reasons for doing this are to make the company memorable, raise morale, and attract investors and consumers. Critics contend that at least half the money spent on corporate ads are wasted, that more often than not companies are talking only to themselves, staring at their belly buttons. ITT, however, tries to measure recognition of the company by the public. That research has shown that as long as the ads are run, the company maintains good visibility, but visibility drops when the advertising stops.[8]

A variation on corporate advertising is the use of CEOs as pitchmen, either for the corporation or for products. Among the most famous are Eastern Air Line's Frank Borman, Chrysler's ("If you can find a better car, buy it!") Lee Iacocca, and Schlitz' Frank Sellinger. In each case, these CEOs were asked by their agencies to be the spokesperson. "The credibility of the individual is extremely important," cautions J. Walter Thompson Advertising executive Walter O'Brien, "and people don't learn that, they're born with it." Iacocca received strong praise from the financial community for doing the ads, which were perceived as more corporate than product. Said an auto analyst with Drexel, Burnham, Lambert: "Without those ads, the company's efforts would go pretty unnoticed. The ads have been a big positive for Chrysler." The downside is that the CEO now becomes a "personality" who is a target for calls, upbraidings, and complaints from unhappy customers.[9]

FINANCIAL DISCLOSURE

While new approaches to valuation may still be some years away from general acceptance, there is a continuing need to cope with present SEC and exchange requirements for keeping the various publics informed on a company's financial position. The SEC was founded in 1934 as a response to the abuses in stock sales of the twenties and to prevent the conflicts of interest that rise when corporate officials gain financially from inside information. SEC legislation has established over time a process for registration of securities and companies and has mandated a shareholder's right to disclosure. SEC laws require that every public company publish an annual report and provide a specific statement of financial responsibility (the 10-k, which has now been folded into the annual report).

This legal activity has evolved over the years through major SEC decisions and changes into a policy called "materiality," which requires release of all information that can affect a company's profitability or financial position. Simply stated, the policy is, WHEN IN DOUBT, DISCLOSE. The major stock exchanges have published guidelines regarding disclosure, which emphasize, among other things:

- Immediate release of any information that can materially affect the price of the company's stock: death of a chief executive, merger negotiations that are complete, discovery of a new resource, imminent labor trouble, or significant share sales
- Quick movement to stop unfounded rumors that could affect a stock's price
- Backing off from exaggeration—not making premature announcements or overly optimistic predictions, especially in news releases
- Making sure everybody gets the same information

The legal precedent for these guidelines follows the U.S. Court of Appeals 1968 decision in the Texas Gulf Sulfur case, in which the court reversed a district judge's ruling and supported a SEC contention that company executives had used inside information to trade in a stock before that information had been disclosed publicly. Also involved in the case was the contents of a news release, which the SEC concluded did not tell the public that a major discovery of copper and zinc had been made.[10]

More recently the go-go Wall Street brokerage house of John Muir was forced out of the public brokerage business because of discrepancies between what their prospectus said about certain stocks and possible hyping of stock by Muir.[11]

Decisions regarding disclosure have to be made on a day-to-day basis and need the coordinated response of both legal and communications staffs. Examples of events that should be quickly reported include mergers and acquisitions, information regarding dividends, stock splits, gain or loss of a major contract, a new product or discovery, a major borrowing on the debt market, purchase or sale of a major asset, a tender offer for another company's securities, and a major change in management.

There are two sanctioned "disclosure" wires in the U.S. for material information—Dow Jones and Reuters. Dow Jones has a practice of doing periodical interviews with companies just before results of their year are made public. These "Dow Jonesers" are important for a company in getting out its view of the coming year. There are different DJ bureaus around the U.S. serving each major region, and it's important for firms to keep their regional bureau informed of what is going on.

DEALING WITH
SHAREHOLDERS

One of the reasons that we have shareholder relations and why there is a need to do a better job of communicating with shareholders is that the *efficient markets theory* doesn't always work as well as it should. That theory suggests that all players in the market have equal information available to them. While most major publicly held companies are well known and well studied, smaller firms, such as those traded over the counter, are sometimes lost in the shuffle. So, many stocks with good fundamental value end up sometimes being underpriced because so little is known about them—a compelling reason for good investor relations at the second tier, as much as fear of takeover is the compelling reason at the first tier.

A New York Stock Exchange Survey in 1981 showed that 29.8 million individuals owned stock in corporations or mutual funds in 1980, an 18.1 percent jump from five years earlier.[12] Traditionally the annual report has been the main method for communicating with stockholders. But new programs are now being devised for improving marketing programs for the small shareholder, with such enticements as dividend reinvestment plans with 5 percent discounts on shares bought with dividends; dividends with deferred tax features; toll-free lines for shareholder inquiries; and cumulative voting for directors, a practice that gives small shareholders more voting power. There was widespread belief that in the major battle for control of Conoco Oil in 1981 DuPont was successful, even though its dollar offer was the lowest, because of the total package of money, shares, and tax advantages it offered, indicating an increasing sophistication among stockholders beyond immediate cash enhancement.

This new sophistication is a problem for corporate officials. A study by Georgeson & Company showed that 44 percent of corporate officers surveyed admitted their companies have done a poor media communications job, that only 18 percent of institutional investors are well satisfied with present corporate financial communications, and that a mere 7 percent believe these communications activities have been excellent for individual investors.[13]

Yet small investors report that their major source of information is the *Wall Street Journal*, and many admit their investment decisions are based on what they read in annual reports, especially those sections dealing with the financial situation and management's appraisal. Some companies are establishing "listening" programs to keep in touch with shareholders. One company sends a welcome letter and survey to new shareholders. One uses professional researchers to survey shareholder likes and dislikes and then profiles the information and sends it to all shareholders. Another company uses separate surveys— one for stockholders, another for brokers. At another firm a questionnaire was printed on the back of dividend checks and received excellent response. Marketing research by still another firm found that a rapid increase in investors came from recommendations of brokers. It reoriented its program to that audience.

These kinds of initiatives point to a trend toward greater marketing activities of the firm's stock to all investors. In light of the great number of takeover attempts in recent years, such efforts are becoming a more important communications function. Firms are also finding that they need to spend more time analyzing proxy sheets to identify more clearly the kinds of shareholders they have and that they need to wrestle more with the problem of "street name holders" and how to identify them. PR counseling firms are getting more and more involved in this type of tracking.

ANNUAL REPORTS

James H. Dowling, president of Burson-Marsteller, said some years ago that an annual report should do one thing: "It should help investors decide whether to become or remain shareholders in the company."

He believes that clean, crisp writing in these reports is essential, writing that gets to the nub of the message, such as this excerpt from the 1976 annual report of Ogilvy & Mather, the ad agency:

> We had a whacking good year, as well we should have. Most advertising agencies did. More than 90 percent of the larger U.S. agencies had higher profits in 1976 than in 1975. However, Ogilvy & Mather's performance was especially good.[14]

A few words about annual meetings are necessary here. Some major conflicts have taken place in the recent past at annual meetings as activists with proxies and shares of stock have sought to use the annual meeting as a forum for raising social, political issues, and consumer issues. The model for this type of action on a grand scale was Ralph Nader's "Campaign GM" project on corporate social responsibility in the late sixties and early seventies. Nader and his activists attempted to force the company, through shareholders, to take more action regarding pollution cleanup and auto safety. Specific proposals of Campaign GM included adding public representatives to the corporate board, creating a corporate-responsibility committee, and amending the company's charter to include public-interest requirements.

The battlefield was the company's annual meetings, and while most of the proposals failed, the movement did meet with some success, prompting other organizations with other causes to use the same techniques elsewhere on such issues as overseas investments and marketing of infant formula. The Nader efforts did put a company on the defense in front of its stockholders and forced some necessary discussion of a corporation's role in the political and social marketplace.

Whatever the means of communicating with shareholders—whether an annual report, a questionnaire, notes on quarterly activities, a report on the annual meeting—*all financial communications should build toward a dominant impression that management has a clear vision of the future and that it will lead shareholders there.*

ANALYSTS

Analysts' demands for information greatly exceed those of the small investor. Their opinions are what they're paid for, and their credibility is dependent on how much information they can obtain and how well they analyze that information. "We have no interest in a corporation other than its track record and future performance," declares Thomas Rosencrants, an analyst who specializes in the insurance industry.[15] Analysts don't like sweeping statements based on little fact. But they do want projections; they want details; they want to know what senior management is thinking. Describing the nitty-gritty of what an analyst does, an experienced PR counselor observed, "You look the guy in the eyes, hear what he has to say, look at the numbers, and then decide whether you believe him or not."[16]

Corporate communications and finance people usually cooperate on financial relations. Normal techniques for communication include regular open meetings in key cities featuring top corporate officials as spokespersons. One-on-one luncheons, briefings on an annual or semiannual basis, and plant tours are also popular. Most often, however, there is the day-to-day contact accomplished through use of the telephone.

Analysts think one of the most important elements in a financial relations program is the person who manages the function. Analysts want to deal with an investor relations specialist who responds quickly to inquiries for information, has enough influence in the company to arrange meetings and get management attention, is knowledgeable about the company and the ways of Wall Street, is candid and can give both the good news and the bad, can define the limits of subjects covered, and can walk the line between what can be discussed and what cannot. This individual is friendly and, finally, attentive to detail. That is a tall order, but there are many investor relations specialists who measure up to it. Some of them have come up through corporate ranks, others are former journalists. Some have been brokers, others came from financial positions within the company. A financial relations person's attributes best come through when the going gets tough. A profile of Jean Shanaphy of J. C. Penney in the March 1980 issue of *Institutional Investor* describes her ability to keep a sense of humor during some dark days for the company when it was suffering earnings declines in the late seventies. "Jean didn't try to sugarcoat anything," said one analyst, "and she was cordial, no matter what we wrote about Penney."[17] This approach earned her top grades among analysts. Shanaphy had previously been an analyst herself, and she was understanding and sensitive to their needs.

THE MEDIA

Dealing with financial reporters is very much like dealing with analysts. The difference is that most reporters are not financially sophisticated and will not need or want the level of detail that financial analysts require. This does not mean that they are less knowledgeable, only that they have to cover more industries than analysts do. When they need in-depth information they will often go to analysts themselves as well as to corporate sources.

The key message a financial relations specialist wants to communicate to reporters is that nothing is being hidden.

Reporters are always willing to give financial people advice on how to do a good PR job. William Kreger, national editor of the *Wall Street Journal*, urges communicators to get to know who covers their company for a national news organization—which bureau, which reporter at the bureau. Go to them first, he urges. He also suggests that if a communications specialist wants to propose a feature story, it should be about the industry the company is in, with emphasis on the company, but it shouldn't be just about the company. Dorothea Brooks, business editor of UPI, suggests that general readers are not very sophisticated about business and get most of their business information from the daily press. UPI's interests, she says, are personal-finance stories and articles of human interest. Dero Saunders, *Forbes* executive editor, says his audience is the corporate manager and the investor and that he's interested in "how-to" stories and company stories—the bigger the company the better. An associate editor at *Fortune* suggests writing a letter to propose a story instead of calling, including in that letter as much material as possible. He warns not to talk off the record and not to give him stories that have run elsewhere. These snippets of advice should express a couple of key points to a manager—first, the financial press is very much like the regular press in its needs; second, each news organization has some peculiarities, and it helps to be aware of them when selling a story.[18]

When a manager meets with a financial reporter for an interview, it is wise to have at least one associate present in case the answer is muddled. Also the interviewee should be colorful with a quantity of anecdotes and quotes so his thoughts won't end up just as background. It is important to be quoted. If the manager gets into an argument with a reporter, he or she might want to suggest some other source for the reporter to try, including sources that might even disagree. Some executives recommend that interviews be conducted in the manager's office, where file material is accessible. Some suggest that the interview be taped so as to have a record of what has been said. A problem regarding quotes frequently arises. If possible, get an agreement from the reporter to read the quotes back before going with the story. If he or she is on a tight deadline, don't expect that. If the story appears and the manager feels wronged, the best approach is to write a letter to the editor, which usually will be published. It is important to be calm and set the record straight, especially by citing specifics.[19]

TAKEOVER DEFENSE

There was a fascinating story circulating a while back about how one company, faced with a takeover attempt by a Canadian firm, found a former congressman who had a buddy running a key congressional subcommittee. The subcommittee chairman was prevailed upon to hold a one-day hearing on the need for new legislation to prevent foreign takeovers. The hearing was beamed directly across the border into Toronto with lots of attendant hype. The takeover attempt was quietly scuttled.

Takeover stories have been a hot business-news topic in the last few years. While unfortunately takeovers do nothing to create new wealth for society, they can and do have a traumatic impact on a vulnerable and unwilling target company. The apparent suicide of Alvin Feldman, chairman and chief executive of Continental Air Lines in 1981 was attributed in part to news that the way had been cleared for a takeover of Continental by another airline.

In 1981 there was a flurry of giant mergers—in the multibillion-dollar range. Despite record high interest rates, two major takeovers took place in the space of just one midsummer week: E. I. Du Pont put down $6.9 billion in an offer for Conoco, Inc., in a famous three-way bidding battle with Mobil Oil and Seagram's; and Elf-Aquitaine offered $2.8 billion for Texasgulf, Inc.

An investment banker told the *Chicago Tribune*, "I thought with a 20 percent prime (rate) you'd see us putting our feet up, coming in at ten, going home at four. But we're never been busier."

It used to be that a billion-dollar merger was a big deal, said that same investment banker. "Now it's almost pedestrian." That meant that many large companies were no longer safe from takeover attempts.[20]

One of the more incredible corporate takeover battles in American history climaxed on September 24, 1982, when the Bendix Corporation announced it had given up its efforts to take over Martin Marietta Corporation and had agreed to merge with Allied Corporation. Known on Wall Street as the "Thirty Day War," the battle involved four corporate giants: Bendix, Marietta, Allied, and United Technologies. It started when Bendix's CEO William Agee attempted an unfriendly takeover of Martin Marietta. He met fierce, unexpected resistance that included a counterattempt by Marietta to buy up Bendix shares. This strategy was dubbed a "pac-man" strategy, after the popular electronic game where you try to gobble up your opponent before he does it to you. Marietta also enlisted the giant United Technologies, which agreed to join Marietta in buying up Bendix shares, with a dividing up of the company's assets to come later. It all proved too much for Bendix, which sold out to Allied. Despite claims by Bendix's Agee that shareholder value had been maximized, general opinion was that this whole episode had given takeovers an even more odious reputation than they had previously labored under. Commentator after commentator asked the $64 question: "How much new wealth, how many new jobs, how much real growth do such shenanigans produce?"

In 1982 there was also an escalation in attempts by dissident shareholders to take over firms through proxy fights. Attempts to take over companies like Marshall Field, Dan River, and others by breakup and liquidation specialists increased concerns about proxy battles. Observed Joseph R. Perella, a managing director of First Boston Corporation, "The proxy phenomenon is nothing more than somebody trying to get the benefits of the takeover—that is, unlock the values in the company—without having to put the money up to buy the whole company." Staggering boards of directors was one suggestion for handling the problem. Such "shark repellants," as these moves have been labeled, rarely seem to work, however.[21]

Companies should have a takeover *offense* as well as a takeover *defense* though defense is emphasized here. A good offense would consist of a sound corporate strategy for acquisition, a group of top-flight legal, communication, and financial counselors on retainer and, from a communications perspective, well thought-out print communications that will make a convincing case to stockholders. Also, communicators should think through the potential defensive tactics that might be used and develop options for handling them. When the action starts is not the time for brainstorming. It should all be done ahead of time.

Defensively, there are two major ways a company can fight a takeover bid: *strategically* and *tactically*; and a company must be willing to use both. Strategic responses are necessary because in today's economic environment the attractiveness of the dollars offered for the stockholders' shares often are simply overwhelming. Brokers will push stockholders to sell because of the extra commissions involved. Arbitrageurs move in early and tie up as much stock as they can. By then it may be all over.

The very reasons a company is successful—low debt leverage, big growth and return, high cash reserves, and good management—all work against it, making it attractive to both good quality suitors and fast-buck artists alike.

In this kind of environment, development of a long-term strategic defense that emphasizes positive communication of vision and proper valuation is paramount. If nothing else, it will help even up the odds when the takeover fight begins. There are many things that can be done, such as getting employees and pension funds to buy blocks of stock, staggering elections of boards of directors, full valuing of the books, monitoring stock buys, and increasing dividends and stock repurchases.

It should also be understood that there are "levels of the game." The kind of defense you use for a legitimate offer from a serious firm is quite different from the defense you use against a fast-buck artist or liquidator. Also, your defense will depend on timing. To take too many defenses early on might be cause later for a stockholder's suit, or might be seen as the waving of sharkbait by arbitrageurs. Once your company is in play, the game is usually over: either the suitor will get you or a white knight will have to step in.

Richard Cheney, vice chairman of Hill & Knowlton and the leading PR counselor in takeovers, chides companies that have what he calls a Maginot Line mentality about stock takeovers and think that a little black book full of phone numbers for their defense team, boiler-plate ads, letters to stockholders, and detailed schedules of who calls whom after an offer is announced are all that is needed to head off disaster.[22]

Morris Lee of Manning, Selvage & Lee also sees little benefit in this kind of advance planning. "No precautionary plan, no matter how comprehensive or professionally drawn, can substitute for continuing communications that pay attention to the shareholders' interests and convince the Street of the management's credibility, strength, and integrity," he says.[23] Cheney admonishes many firms for not taking the time to learn who their shareholders are and what they think.

"We also urge clients to survey shareowners to learn what their investment goals are, if they have a price objective, whether they read the annual report, what they like and don't like about management, and so on," says Cheney. He admits this is costly, but points out that it is much better than communicating in the dark.[24]

Other ways of communicating include attempting to get in touch with owners whose stock is held in street names. By including a return card with the quarterly report, a company is able to get many street holders to send in their names and address. This practice can sometimes cause duplication when brokers require that a company send such inquiries to all stockholders, including those with stock in their own names. In a takeover, however, it speeds up direct communication with the shareholder. Rules proposed by the SEC at the end of 1982 would make it much easier to communicate with all stock owners, getting past the "street name" problem.

Cheney recommends that firms also use new technology to address letters personally to stockholders. A company having problems might occasionally write a letter to stockholders about how a problem was solved. If stockholders help out in a proxy fight, they ought to get a thank-you as well. While a company obviously cannot ignore its institutional investors, it should realize that the individual stockholder is the best prospect for new business and is an important force for good public opinion concerning the firm. A company, says Cheney, should also make efforts to meet directly with stockholders. Retirees are used in some companies to phone stockholders, to insure a good turnout at a company meeting.

Employees are a public that should be actively solicited. They are predisposed toward the stock. Their efforts should be cultivated. They should be given shares and offered reduced prices on purchases. Suppliers, customers, people in communities where plants are located, and influentials are also important audiences that need to be cultivated over the long haul. This kind of *strategic* planning emulates the biblical story of the servant who set aside friends for the day he might be cast out by his employer.

HARDBALL

There are those who think that public relations arrangements during a takeover might be akin to arranging deck chairs on the Titanic—making sure enough envelopes are on hand, having printers ready, developing checklists, and more. Some takeover experts emphasize the use of outside public relations counsel, with the in-house staff playing secondary roles. In real life, however, this depends on the quality of the in-house staff. At least one recent example was not encouraging. In the famed struggle between Seagram, Mobil, and duPont for Conoco, public relations and tactical blunders were cited as a major reason for Mobil's loss, even though its bid was $1.28 billion higher.

The communications problems in corporate takeovers have also been compounded in recent years because of the high cash premiums over the market price that are involved, the large institutional holdings and the depressed prices of many stocks, and the eager arbitragers who want to step in. "The market is now a lottery," says Dick Cheney, "Every broker and stockholder is waiting for their number to come up."[25]

One of the most important functions that the communications people can perform is assisting in the development of material for use in defense communications that factually and convincingly defines the company's strengths, its past record, its prospects, its planning, and the values the aggressor company obviously sees in it.

"Takeovers are like judo," says Cheney, "You use what [your opponent] presents." The tactical battle is the main game, he maintains, especially in the eighties.

> As a target, being ready should mean first, having at hand an advisory team you can trust, and second, keeping a close watch on your stockholder list and daily trading. If a hostile offerer embarks on an open-market purchase plan, for example, being able to identify him even before he reaches the 5 percent mark, which requires filing with the SEC, may enable you to undertake any number of actions—such as planning effective litigation to discourage him from going any further."[26]

A Goldman, Sachs survey, looking at the final disposition of 114 takeover attempts showed that 72 percent of the companies were eventually taken over, and defense tactics helped delay the process long enough for 39 percent of those to find a "white knight" for a friendly rescue.

One of the most famous bare-knuckles public relations approaches to a takeover was the defense used by McGraw-Hill to thwart a bid by American Express in 1979.[27] The successful defense in that bid was the angry reaction by Harold W. McGraw, Jr. McGraw, convinced by consultants that his personal anger was the strongest defense, wrote a blistering attack citing the conflict-of-interest potential of a major corporate buyout of the ownership of *Business*

Week. That letter was released at a news conference and in full-page newspaper advertisements. It accused American Express of lacking integrity and corporate morality. McGraw-Hill sued and Amex countersued. McGraw-Hill then complained to the FCC, the FTC, and Congress. Realizing that the company it would obtain might be in shambles, American Express bowed out.

Another famous PR defense took place when Northwest Industries attempted to acquire B. F. Goodrich in 1969. The defense strategy included unearthing information that the chairman of Northwest had attributed several quarters of poor earnings to bad weather. An advertisement with press releases on the weather excuses pasted up was run under the headline "It only snows on Northwest." Northwest has mostly stuck to friendly mergers ever since.

The key to a good public relations counterattack in a takeover bid is solid information that effectively raises serious questions about the bid. This is a team effort between lawyers, who have to make sure the defense is not protecting management and hurting stockholders; the financial people, who can provide the best arguments on why not to accept the offer; and the public relations person who can find the appeals and the buttons to push that will convince key audiences of the defense position.

For example, in the takeover attempt of Foremost-McKesson in 1977 by Victor Posner the major defense, contained in an ad headlined "Why should *you* lend Sharon Steel the money to take over *your* company?", was the result of an intensive investigation into both Posner and his steel company, which concluded among other things that Sharon had a high debt-to-equity ratio and the tender would not be for cash. (See Figure 7-2.) Posner's credibility would also be on the line, and he was already being sued by several stockholders and the SEC for allegedly using pension assets for his own benefits. Early on Foremost had sued, and Posner countersued. Finally a bid was made by Posner for a stock exchange. The ad that was developed was loaded with facts and gone over dozens of times by lawyers and others. It attacked the offer. It attacked Posner personally, including his lifestyle. It attacked the attractiveness of the offer, and finally it attacked the investment banker who was handling the deal. Shareholders were urged to ask Dean Witter brokers if Witter would underwrite paper of this quality. This was an unusual attack on a broker who was only a dealer-manager in this case. Another question in the ad asked whether Sharon's credit could stand another $378 million of debt. Posner sued again, but Foremost kept up the attack, finding out more information about how a banker had overridden the regular loan officer to allow Sharon to up its debt. This information was sent on to the press. An SEC announcement of an investigation into Sharon financial statements halted the takeover attempt, and the tender eventually was dropped.[28]

Following that takeover bid, Foremost decided to upgrade its relations with institutional investors and began to schedule meetings and briefings.

FIGURE 7-2   Hard-hitting—and Successful—Ad Devised to Fend Off Takeover of Sharon Steel

SOURCE: Courtesy of Foremost-McKesson, Inc., San Francisco, CA.

POSTMERGER STRATEGY

Mergers have been described as arranged marriages. But the problems of two new companies living together are difficult and require a heavy dose of communications at the beginning. An acrimonious battle can leave a company rudderless as top management bails out and is replaced. Morale is depressed. People leave for other jobs. The press begins to notice. Business begins to suffer. It is important that before the merger is accomplished key managers be identified on each side and given special attention and motivation. These key managers should include opinion leaders within the company—managers who have the respect of other employees. Their attitude will be observed and can directly affect morale. If there is panic, people will start to run. When cuts have to be made, many companies have learned it's important to establish outplacement services, to give people time to get new jobs. The company's publics need to be reassured also: the press, affected communities, customers, suppliers, shareholders, unions, and governmental officials.

Issues that have to be dealt with in making the match work include unionization—if one company is unionized and the other is not—seniority, community impact, benefit plans, and the like. It is incumbent that a top spokesperson provide communication and leadership during this period to set the tone for the new organization. Special emphasis must be put on internal communications activities. For example, when Matsushita Electric of Japan obtained Motorola's TV manufacturing operations in 1974, it began holding ten-minute meetings twice a day between foremen and workers to talk about production, quality control, and other problems. This proved very successful over time.

FRIENDLY TAKEOVERS

Not all mergers and acquisitions are unfriendly. Sometimes a firm seeks to be acquired. In this case, efforts are undertaken to develop a communications program that makes the firm both *visible* and *attractive* to a potential suitor.[29]

This kind of image cannot be created overnight, especially for the smaller firm that is not regularly followed by analysts or major investors. It can take upwards of a year to get the right press coverage and the right approach to create a desired inquiry. One recommendation in this situation is for management to stay out of the process. It is a communications and marketing problem, an attempt to position the firm in a way that reflects a potential buyer's interests, not management's feelings. It is especially difficult to handle management's role in this scenario in an entrepreneurial firm.

Selling a company is like selling a product: Understatement isn't very effective. The sales pitch must deal with potential for future growth, prospects for new products, customer development, competitiveness. Many times a seller feels this is proprietary information and should not be released. A suggestion is to take a look at the annual reports and SEC filings of publicly traded companies in the same business and then develop a strategy.

Press emphasis must be on management successes and ability to deal successfully with problems. A letter to a business editor or reporter on the company vis-à-vis its industry is an effective approach. The communications office should also get involved in keeping track of potential buyers—monitoring clips and other sources that provide data on the background and reputation of these firms, which might be helpful in choosing a suitor.

Large firms should find it easier to get attention when attempting to sell parts of their businesses. They can simply make an announcement that divisions are on the block or, more subtly, begin restating their corporate strategy or begin noting new directions in their annual report.

Buyers in the market for new properties often need to develop an image also—designed to attract possible sellers and minimize resistance to advances. Statements of acquisition policies, that they are interested, for example, only in "friendly" takeovers or in particular categories, help position them. Foreign acquisitions, especially first moves into a particular country, should also be accompanied by a communications plan that introduces the company and its background to the foreign press.

RULES OF THE GAME

The safest route regarding communications requirements for both tender offers and proxy fights is to have the company's lawyers involved in the process. SEC rules on the problem of "materiality" are involved there, and it's a judgment call that may at some point have to be defended in court. Material issues will depend on the number of people involved in discussions, the degree of certainty that a final agreement is likely to evolve, the size of the parties involved, and unusual market activity. Necessary steps include handling of confidential information, taking risks by delaying the release of information, keeping track of what the stock is doing, dealing promptly with rumors, notifying stock exchanges regarding disclosures of material information, and monitoring potential insider trading. Major PR firms involved in financial relations also can be of great help in offering guidance through this communications minefield.

SUMMARY

1. Financial relations is more than observing legal reporting requirements. It tells the world what to expect in the way of performance from the firm.

2. The proper valuation of a firm is difficult for many reasons.

3. Companies should remember that the rule regarding financial disclosure is, When in doubt, disclose any information that might materially affect the company.

4. In an era of increased takeovers, shareholder relations are becoming more important as a corporate strategy.

5. Takeover defense is more tactical than strategic.

6. Takeovers call for planning of communications programs for relevant constituencies following the takeover—be it a friendly or unfriendly takeover.

NOTES

1. James Horton, Robert Marston and Associates, in correspondence with author, August 15, 1981.

2. Michael Seely, "Emerging Technology of Valuation," *Public Relations Journal*, April 1981, pp. 10–12.

3. Ibid.

4. Jaye S. Niefeld, "Corporate Advertising and the Wall Street Payoff—Guidelines for Bottom-Line Results," *Interface*, winter 1981, pp. 11–15.

5. Ibid.

6. Peg Dardenne, "Corporate Advertising," *Public Relations Journal*, November 1982, p. 34.

7. Terry Haller, "Corporate Ads Doomed," *Advertising Age*, January 25, 1982, p. 47.

8. Bill Abrams, "How ITT Shells Out $20 million or so a Year to Polish Reputation," *Wall Street Journal*, April 2, 1982, p. 1.

9. Kevin McManus, "The Smell of The Greasepaint," *Forbes*, August 16, 1982, pp. 78–81.

10. Allen H. Center and Frank E. Walsh, "A News Release Comes A-Cropper," in *Public Relations Practices: Case Studies* (Englewood Cliffs, N.J.: Prentice-Hall, 1981), pp. 146–54.

11. Richard E. Rustin and Tim Carrington, "Bedeviled by Lawsuits and the SEC, Muir Says It May Have Had Enough," *Wall Street Journal*, August 11, 1981.

12. See Clark W. Bell, "Big Firms Begin to Focus on 'Little Guy' Shareholders," *Chicago Sun-Times*, July 14, 1981.

13. Ibid.

14. James H. Dowling, "Main Job of the Annual Report: Wooing Investors," *Dun's Review*, September 1978, pp. 127–28.

15. Thomas G. Rosencrants, "What Analysts Want to Hear," *Public Relations Journal*, April 1981, pp. 14–16.

16. Horton, cited in note 1.

17. Laurie Meisler, "Making It in Investor Relations," *Institutional Investor*, March 1980, p. 30.

18. Jeff Close, memorandum titled "Financial Media Seminar" to staff of Harshe-Rotman & Druck, New York, March 28, 1978.

19. Reba White, "Coping With the Financial Reporter," *Financial Analyst Journal*, March-April 1978, pp. 38–40.

20. Mark Potts, "Giant Mergers Burgeoning in Reagan Climate," *Chicago Tribune*, July 12, 1981.

21. Robert J. Cole, "Proxy War Tacticians," *The New York Times*, May 17, 1982, p. 30.

22. Richard E. Cheney, "Remedies for Tender-Offer Anxiety," *Financial Executive*, August 1975, p. 3.

23. Morris M. Lee, "The Role of Corporate PR in Tender-Offer Defense," *Public Relations Journal*, April 1978, p. 28.

24. Cheney, "Remedies for Tender-Offer Anxiety."

25. Cheney, in telephone conversation with the author, August 14, 1981.

26. Cheney, "Hitchcock Scenario for Takeovers Replaces Shootout at OK Corral," *New York Law Journal*, June 12, 1978.

27. Lydia Chavez, "How to Stop a Takeover," *New York Times*, August 30, 1981.

28. Pamela Archibold, "How to Foil a Raider," *Institutional Investor*, November 1977, p. 34.

29. For an excellent summary of friendly takeovers, see Robert W. Taft, "Public Relations Aspects of Mergers and Acquisitions," in Steven James Lee and Robert Douglas Colman, eds., *Handbook of Mergers, Acquisitions, and Buyouts* (Englewood Cliffs, N.J.: Prentice-Hall, 1981), pp. 25–59.

The Manager and the New Media

8

OUR WIRED SOCIETY

When they see new technology, adults approach it cautiously and stand back, afraid to touch it; kids, on the other hand, run up and right away start handling it.

—Anonymous Media Consultant

No manager or communicator will escape the effects of the communication revolution now underway in America. The oftenheard prediction that we are becoming an information-based economy where knowledge is both "capital" and "power" is fast becoming reality.

The information (electronics) business in the U.S. jumped from $30.5 billion in 1980 to $74 billion in 1981 for products ranging from main-frame computers to video games to cable wire. The total world market is estimated to be about $500 billion with $235 billion of that in the U.S. alone. It has already been estimated that the value added of information-based producer services alone—financial, legal, accounting, marketing, management consulting, and communications—equals the value added of all manufacturing output. By 1990, between 40 and 50 percent of all American workers will be making daily use of electronic terminal equipment. By 1985, the volume of information is expected to reach somewhere between four and seven times what it was only a few years earlier.[1]

When *Time* magazine named a computer its "Man of the Year" in 1982, it was in recognition of the incredible growth of interest by American society in high-technology electronics and the birth of a new, highly competitive marketplace where computers, satellites, telephones, and TV sets were being configured like so many electronic tinkertoys to build new telecommunications designs that would provide the information highways to interconnect office, home, and market in amazing new networking configurations.

At the office, where information/communication is more quickly becoming a reality, the management of information resources and the introduction of new telecommunications services are being spurred by hundreds of high-tech firms attempting to capture a share of an exploding marketplace. In just one decade, the emphasis has moved from centralized, computer-based data processing to a "brave new world" in which communications and information processing are being interwoven in a way that will decentralize American society. This change is bringing enormous opportunities to re-work the financial services industry, international business, manufacturing, and general office management; the full impact of the process for the future can only be guessed at, especially as we attempt to evaluate strategic communications issues, policies, and practices for management.

TECHNOLOGICAL ISSUES

Numerous issues relating to the communications/information revolution were under close scrutiny by the various branches of government and the marketplace in the early eighties. Equipment standardization, opportunities for competition, and introduction of technology refinements were all being filtered through the marketplace, the courts, legislative bodies, and regulatory agencies. Competitive issues, such as the impact of the AT&T settlement and subsequent congressional action, were considered crucial to how telecommunications would develop both in the U.S. and abroad. Technical issues relating to the allocation of satellite space, transmission methodologies (digital or computer, bit versus analog or wave length frequency), and the control of international data flow, among others, were being sorted out in a new, more deregulated marketplace.

The scramble to settle these issues was aimed at clearing up how the marketplace would be organized to handle expanded opportunities for providing business, government, and consumers with the myriad of new information/communication hybrids.

ENVIRONMENTAL FACTORS

A variety of environmental forces and technological advances fueled the development of the information/communications revolution in the eighties.

ADVANCES IN SATELLITE COMMUNICATIONS.   A rapid growth in the number of communications satellites for domestic purposes has been underway since the late seventies. By 1986 eighteen new satellites will to be added to sixteen domestic communications "birds" already in space, bringing transponder capacity to well over two hundred. (Transponders are the bounce points on a satellite which relay TV-size signals up and down from earth. They give users the ability to bypass use of expensive land lines when sending voice, data, or video signals from point to point.)

GROWTH OF MICROCOMPUTERS. The rapid growth of microcomputers, made possible by the silicone computer chip, is making data processing inexpensive and thus accessible not only to business but to the home user as well. By 1990, a new generation of "smart" computers that require little user expertise and with the ability to talk are expected to be in widespread use.

LIMITED AVAILABILITY OF SPECTRUM SPACE. The new satellites and advanced microwave and cable systems are relieving some of the pressures that have built in the past on the already restricted radio spectrum. The crowding of that spectrum spurred a change in Federal policy that permitted opening of formerly restricted technologies such as cable television, low-power television, microwave, and direct broadcast from satellite to home for home and business use.

PROFITABLE EXPERIENCES IN CABLE TELEVISION. The economic success story that began in 1975 when the Time Inc. subsidiary, Home Box Office, used RCA's Satcom I satellite to begin delivering a pay television movie service, opened up an electronic "gold rush" to not only provide similar services, but also to wire American cities for a larger audience.

PERCEPTIONS OF OPPORTUNITIES. In a new, deregulated environment, many industries besides entertainment have perceived that the new technologies can provide opportunities for improving office productivity and managerial efficiency, as well as opening up exciting possibilities in financial services, retailing, advertising, and business communications.

TECHNOLOGY AND DEREGULATION

While not sure just what the long-term implications are, American policy makers, business managers, and entrepreneurs have rushed headlong to exploit a bewildering new technological garden:

- Satellite transmission around the world using efficient digital-based systems that can move words, numbers, pictures, and sounds on the same line.
- Fiber-optic strands of glass that use tiny lasers to pulse rivers of digits.
- Coaxial cable lines that can bring into the home simultaneously over one hundred channels of video or data services.
- Office of the future technologies that bring computing and video networking to users, wherever they might be.

At the same time, the charter that once gave one company, American Telephone and Telegraph, a monopoly in telecommunications has been rescinded in a national mood of deregulation, thereby opening up a significant amount of elbow room in the marketplace for competition. Starting with the Carterfone decision in 1968, which for the first time permitted non-Bell equipment to be hooked up to the Bell system, and climaxing on January 8, 1982, when the U.S.

Department of Justice announced a historic settlement of a seven-year old antitrust case that would break AT&T up into regulated and unregulated businesses, an inexorable march had begun toward a new, open marketplace, where freedom from competition was no longer the rule.

The gist of the AT&T settlement was that basic telephone service would remain regulated, but new competitors like MCI, which were already in the marketplace underselling AT&T's traditional long-distance telephone market along high volume, low cost routes, would now have to go head-to-head with a new, unregulated AT&T. Other companies, such as Satellite Business Systems, were also going into competition with Bell in the long-distance market, providing common carrier service via satellite. In late 1982, MCI announced it would conduct tests on technology allowing cable television subscribers to plug directly into its long-distance network, thus suggesting future competition for local regulated phone companies.[2]

With its strong combination of assets and know-how, the new AT&T spinoff, known as American Bell, was expected to be a formidable competitor itself in the new marketplace. Bell was perceived to be viable enough and knowledgeable enough to move into many different market segments at once, from distributed data processing to home information systems.

Overall, deregulation in the information/communications marketplace has come with the recognition that technical advances could not be exploited with or by-pass a regulated system. While Bell continued to dominate long-distance networking, competition was expected to continue escalating. In early 1983, the combined market share of the $38 billion long-distance market for MCI and other Bell challengers was a mere 2 percent, with the overall market growing at a $4 billion a year rate. Also entering the fray was a new class of smaller re-sellers, who buy up WATS and other lines and then resell usage on them at a profit. Some companies setting up their own networks, like Allstate Insurance, indicated they would sell space on their systems. It is anticipated that at some point long-distance phone service will be completely deregulated.

THE OFFICE
OF THE FUTURE

Not only are interorganizational communications technologies undergoing dramatic change, but intraorganizational communications and information systems are likewise exploding. Driving this trend forward is the incredible growth of distributed data-processing systems and the microcomputer, which are decentralizing the information processing function, putting a real live computer at any employee's desk for what used to be the cost of a fancy typewriter. What is so new is not that each manager can have a working computer at his or her own desk but rather that they can work on a common data base at the same time.

Besides the rapid growth of word processing, distributed data processing is also expanding to include reprographics (computerized storage of documents), teleconferencing, electronic mail, and other innovations. The development of "user friendly" languages will allow business sub-units to do their own data processing and even design their own applications. All this networking will eventually mean that managers at corporate headquarters will have the ability to electronically "look over the shoulders" of employees wherever they are located on a real time basis.

The rationale for installing all this new hardware is the recognition that productivity of the white collar work force is becoming a serious cost problem as the size of that labor force continues to grow. It has been estimated that the white collar work force performs at only 40–60 percent of its productive capacity and that managers spend up to a third of their time on routine tasks. Productivity gains from this group have been meagre up to now. When automated systems are introduced into the office environment, improvement takes place rapidly. Employees seem to come up continually with new and better ideas for saving time and money.

MANAGERIAL PRODUCTIVITY

There are numerous ways in which managers can utilize the office-of-the-future technologies to improve their own productivity and that of those who work for them. New analytical tools, such as electronic spreadsheets, statistical analysis and graphing, decision-support systems, and econometric modeling, improve decision making. When inquiry systems are installed and combined with electronic mail, for example, information can be pulled from a data base and inserted into a text document and be distributed immediately. A Bell Canada study in 1979, based on a pilot system that included electronic messaging, text processing, information retrieval, administrative functions, and analytical tools, showed that employees' use of time improved with such a system, as did access to information, attitudes toward office-system technology, and quality of work life. Fewer phone meetings, fewer one-to-one contacts, and fewer interruptions resulted. But the system also spurred demand for greater information by users.

What long-term effects will these new technologies have on organization? For one thing, the power structure may change. Some predict that the structure of organizations may eventually be built around the structure of the information and communication system. Telecommunications will blur the distinctions between centralized organizations. The trick will be to set up systems that do not sacrifice autonomy.

Work will be able to be done at any time and in any place, removing the eight-to-five window for working as asynchronous methods of communicating, such as electronic mail and voice messaging are introduced. Messages will be shorter, more time will be available to develop responses. Communications will be informal. The ranks of middle management will thin as computers take over staff "beancounting" and analysis jobs. Line jobs will become more performance-oriented.

The socialization of employees will be more difficult, as they may no longer be working close to each other. Working at home may cause new kinds of stress for certain personality types. And there will be managerial problems associated with motivating, controlling, and evaluating distant employees. The real problem that no one has yet addressed is related to the fact that people still like to be around other people and that the "culture" of our office-based society may be more of an impediment to decentralizing the work place than any other factor. The office, like the central city, really is an adaptation of the bazaar, a mini-marketplace full of sideshows—meetings, grapevines, typing pools, dining rooms, sales calls, and the like. The new communications technologies have yet to develop a culture that replicates the textures and hues of our contemporary business life. Videoconferencing may never replace the "look in the eyes," the handshake, and the "sizing up" that comes from a personal meeting, just as working at little green screens all day massaging data may never replace "walking the store."

On the other hand, experiments underway at Control Data Corporation in Minneapolis show that anywhere from $8 million to $27 million might be saved through a 10 percent productivity increase resulting from a telecommuting program in the next four years, involving between 1 and 3 percent of the company's work force. "Those numbers are conservative," says Ronald Manning, General Manager of CDC's office technologies. "We're actually seeing more like 20 percent productivity increases in our current experiments." From a business point of view, the benefits of telecommuting might include better retention of employees, lower office costs, and energy usage reductions. The chief *benefit* to the worker is not having to make the journey to work. The biggest *cost*, however, will be the social isolation that results.[3]

The new information/communication technologies may result also in the development of cybernetic systems in which computers make routine decisions on how to steer the corporate ship. This does not mean they will make major decisions, like where the firm is going, what its goal is, and how it is going to get where it wants to go, but computers could make the routine decisions regarding inventory management, cash reserves, ranking of options, and so on.

At Tandam Computer Company's corporate headquarters, an informal style of management prevails, but only because of the firm's rigid system of computer controls. Eight separate computer systems check on production controls, cost standards, quality controls, and management reporting systems. With the computers keeping track of company performance, managers tend to concentrate on people issues.

Research conducted at Southern Methodist University indicates that use of computers can aid in executive decision making sessions. Advantages include the ability to poll participants, rate issues based upon agreed criteria, and rank options. The idea of this approach is to interface computers with the decision making process.[4] In a book on managerial cybernetics, Stafford Beer introduces the "war-room" concept for management, a situation analysis and control room where top management evaluates and responds to various external developments affecting the organization. In this war room of the not-too-distant future, there would be:

1. Voice recognition, voice synthesis, and touch-screen input/output devices that would allow human interface with computers, telecommunications, and computer systems.
2. Greatly expanded but very filtered real-time information sources.
3. Animated holographic video projections of digital information presented graphically in three physical dimensions.
4. Enhanced televideo, television, and data communications, all digitally used.
5. Large, flat screen displays of digitized video message.
6. Increased utilization of computers that program themselves.

Communications and computer technology will tend to improve information to management, whether through a war room or a computer terminal. Better decision making may result for more complex decisions. There will need to be an emphasis on anticipatory information, for in routine decisions, real-time information will be important.

To be of value, information will have to be under the control of the user, and be timely and relevant, reliable and accurate, and inexpensive. Managerial expectations of the new communications technologies will focus on reducing workloads using understandable data accompanied by graphics. They will expect more real-time internal and external information. Senior management will want systems that filter out irrelevant data while providing facts to make crucial decisions. Will this brave new world become a reality? At some firms it is already taking place. The number of CEOs on the learning curve will grow geometrically in the next few years, as a new generation takes over.

MOVING TOWARD
INFORMATION
MANAGEMENT

With microcomputers proliferating in offices everywhere, some feel that a "band-aid" approach to information management is taking place. Says a senior VP with Booz, Allen & Hamilton, "There are guys who run off to get their own computer and create information and a model with no perspective as to the needs of the corporation as a whole." One survey reported that in 1982 there were 213,000 personal computers being used in daily work activities by white collar employees. By 1985 this number is expected to jump 85 percent to 394,000. One of the main concerns is that employees begin working off common data banks, so an electronic "Tower of Babel" does not ensue.[6]

Writing in the *Harvard Business Review*, data processing expert Richard Nolan stresses that companies must make strategic decisions about the new technologies. For example, a heavy equipment manufacturer may have to redirect priorities and make use of robotics to meet a competitive threat surrounding product quality, while a high technology company might decide to invest in computer-aided design, and a financial institution might choose to invest in automated tellers to gain market share, while a grocery business might choose to go to warehouse automation for inventory management.

"The information required to make such strategic choices effectively must come from managers who can maintain a high-level perspective," he says.[7]

To help executives who have to cope with the more traditional data-processing centers of many companies, some firms are setting up information centers where executives can get help in finding facts they need and tools for analyzing them quickly. Most of the centers are run as adjuncts to existing data-processing departments, but function differently. Instead of funneling requests through a team of programmers, the centers let managers retrieve and manipulate information on their own. For example, Travelers Insurance Company has twenty consultants who field 4,000 calls a month. The key to success here is quick response time[8], so it is to Travelers' advantage to have these consultants do their own computer work rather than wait for responses from programmers.

The process of introducing these new information and communications systems should emphasize involvement of employees who will be using these technologies. The initial attempt by many companies to introduce remote word processing systems in the seventies was an institutional disaster in many cases because the system was imposed by ambitious manufacturers and gullible management. The lesson for managers is that the introduction of any kind of new office technology, be it word processing, distributed data processing, or videoconferencing, should involve employees who are going to use it. They should participate in the decision making process and be told regularly what is going on. Technically, we're dealing with a revolution, but institutionally we must manage it so it is evolutionary.

NEW TOOLS FOR THE OFFICE

Almost one-half of the ads in the December 1982 issues of *BusinessWeek* dealt with office automation. The message was clear: Managers now have available to them a rapidly expanding tool box of high tech devices to increase productivity. Some of these new tools include:

ELECTRONIC MAIL.   Intramurally, electronic mail is a sophisticated version of passing notes in the classroom, except that it is accomplished on a video screen with a typewriter keyboard. Externally, the system uses telecommunications networks to permit the users to communicate with customers, suppliers, or the media via a format similar to Western Union's Mailgram service. The U.S. Post Office provides a similar service, called "E-COM" in which a computer generated messages and mailing lists can be routed to major cities where they are then printed and sent via mail to the designated location.

TELECONFERENCING.   In its simplest form, the plain old phone call is a form of teleconferencing. Teleconferencing refers to a technology in which people in different locations can communicate via voice or video. Teleconferences can range all the way from an audio conference call to slow-scan television to full color, full motion videoconferencing. Corporations such as ARCO Oil Co. and Allstate have spent millions of dollars in the past few years setting up elaborate videoconferencing centers to connect their various locations. AT&T has developed a national videoconferencing network with conference room facilities available in many cities for rental by the hour. The cost of teleconferencing is dependent upon the amount of bandwidth necessary. Full video with color uses a substantial amount, while slow-scan, in which a slide-like frame of video is sent via regular telephone lines every four seconds, uses a regular pair of telephone wires. The "electronic blackboard" that is often used to make a point during televised football games is also growing as a teleconferencing technology. A refinement of that technology allows users to add writing capabilities to slow-scan that permit simultaneous use by many persons in different locations. GM has invested in this technology which will permit engineers in different locations to see a broken part and recommend solutions. The idea behind teleconferencing is that it saves time and money spent on travel to and from meetings. But it appears that the real long-term advantage of teleconferencing, especially videoconferencing, is the ability to bring live video and audio to play in bringing together many individuals in an organization at one time.

In 1979, an agricultural company, attempting to grab high visibility for introduction of a new herbicide in the soybean market, sponsored a live, one-hour television simulcast at the annual American Soybean Association meeting. Soybean experts in two major producing countries—the U.S. and Brazil—were linked via satellite to counterparts in two major importing countries—Japan and the European economic community. Reportedly this was the first time that four areas of the world had been interconnected live via video.[9]

Companies throughout the U.S. have begun using satellite hookups more frequently for large-scale national and regional videoconferences. Besides savings in time and travel costs, videoconference allows more people to attend an event. In the spring of 1981, Allied Van Lines, from its Chicago headquarters, conducted an all day videoconference for fifteen hundred agents and employees in twenty-eight cities. This hookup replaced the usual round of six regional meetings. Shortly thereafter, the National Association of Realtors used videoconferencing to teach new mortgage-financing techniques to five thousand realtors viewing the live presentation in ninety-five locations. Datapoint, a manufacturer of advanced computer products in San Antonio, ran an all-day program to twenty-six cities on a new switching device. The live videoconference was employed after the company had been criticized in the past year by its customers for not being fast enough with product rollout information. On hand were management staff, communication managers, and even some sales prospects.

New production companies have been formed to arrange and produce such video teleconferences. Holiday Inn, through its HI-NET service, provided the sites for both the realtors' and the movers' videoconferences. Over three hundred Holiday Inns have earth station downlinks (originally installed to receive cable movies). In addition to fixed sites, portable downlinks are available from a number of vendors.

The total market for teleconferencing, including equipment and transmission service, is expected to expand from $16 million in 1981 to about $380 million by 1985. Costs for video teleconferencing have been dropping dramatically. A five-site full video hookup with audio return (for questions) cost about $100,000 in 1981. In less than a year the cost had dropped to around $35,000. By the summer of 1983, Satellite Business Systems was to begin marketing an international videoconferencing service that would cost less than $5,000 an hour.[10] Bell charges for use of its U.S. service in major cities was running less than $500 per half hour in late 1982. (See Figure 8-1.)

A study of hands-on users of videoconferencing noted that of the respondents, from large Fortune 500 companies who had participated in an average of twenty videoconferences over a month to three years, indicated that the videoconferencing had had a significant impact on both meeting time and nonproductive time; that is, it reduced the length of meetings, decreased time away from home and office, and provided easier access to information. Three-fourths of these frequent users reported an increase in their personal productivity. The study concluded that that "there is a clear perception of videoconferencing as having the ability to increase communication within the organization, to heighten the visibility of top management, and to improve employee morale."[11]

Taking exception to the trend towards videoconferencing, John Naisbitt in his future-predicting book, *Megatrends*, suggests that increased teleconferencing is "another trend that will not happen, talking with people via television cannot begin to substitute for the high touch of a meeting, no matter how rational it is in saving fuel and overhead."[12]

VOICE MESSAGING.   This is a computerized method of storing telephone messages and playing them at the receiver's convenience. With the telephone so omnipresent in the office and because this is a fairly simple technology, it is becoming very popular. An antecedent of this technology was the answering machine. Some managers claim the new voice messaging systems are responsible for increases as high as 80 percent in productivity, since four out of five attempts to reach people by phone are reportedly unsuccessful.

Voice messaging can also be used to send dictation to a secretarial pool (the old word processing approach), send a message repeatedly to a number of receivers, check on messages that have not been received, and even as an audio notepad. Users say the system works best for short messages.

FIGURE 8-1   Bell Picturephone Designed for Long-Distance Videoconferencing

SOURCE: Courtesy AT&T Long Lines, Bedminster, NJ.

COMPUTERIZED PHONE SYSTEMS.   Instead of making a telephone connection immediately, a data bank would be consulted on where to send the call and this would, among other things, allow companies with many outlets to have a single nationwide phone number. Also, in a computerized phone system, all voice (analog) transmissions are translated into computer bits (digital). This will mean that phone lines can become more efficient and able to send, for example, pages of data in two to four seconds, as opposed to twenty seconds with the current analog system. Bell is expected to begin going to this service in the near future.[13]

DISTRIBUTED DATA PROCESSING.   Today's status symbol is the lowly type-writer keyboard (hooked, of course, to a computer and screen). Managers check the latest information on production schedules, economists do modeling, attorneys research cases, engineers design components, all using advanced, decentralized (distributed) data processing. The hit of the 1982 U.S. COMDEX computer fair was the introduction of a new generation of smart computer software that allows multiple displays and manipulations of data on a single screen via a movable cursor or "mouse" that permits the user to move visually between data bases.

A fast growing area has been development of data bases to serve business users who have their own computers. These data bases, which number close to a thousand, include *The New York Times* Information Bank, the Dow Jones

News/Retrieval Service, and McGraw-Hill's Data Resources, which provides economic forecasts. The Dow Jones News/Retrieval Service provides many distinct services including news of competitors, financial news, economic news, government regulatory decisions, foreign news, and the well-known Dow Jones Business Wire. Available through other data bases are such topics as an index of foundation grants, science abstracts, agricultural reports, and the like. New data bases are being created all the time. One of the more interesting is one in New Jersey which interconnects junk yards for inventory and pricing information concerning auto parts on a statewide basis.

VIDEO STORAGE AND ACCESS. Use of computer-based microfilm access systems or interactive videodisc technology (a computer-driven video system that allows access via "menu" to different bits of video on a disc) is becoming more widespread for use in training and point-of-purchase. For example, if vacationers want to travel to Hawaii, they might go to a videodisc terminal, select Hawaii by pushing a touch-sensitive screen, then select their island from the menu, and further select information about that island: tourist sights, hotels, entertainment, airline connection, and so on.

CABLE TELEVISION. Cable companies, anxious to find new revenue sources for their capital-intensive enterprises, have begun looking to the business customer. They are trying to sell business on systems that can link headquarters offices with nearby branches and carry everything from voices to pictures to computer data at higher speeds and lower costs than local telephone companies. *BusinessWeek* reported that analysts predict cable's share of business telecommunications could reach $11 billion by 1990. By the end of 1983, American Telecommunications Company's Denver system will not only allow corporations access to computer data bases, but also feature its own information bank for selected business sectors such as advertising, energy, and tourism. In Boston, Cablevision, the city's franchisee, was installing a twenty-three mile loop to carry voice, data, text, and video and electronic mail. Manhattan Cable in New York City has added twenty new miles of business cable, claiming a 40 percent price advantage over New York Telephone for similar service.[14]

TELECOMMUNICATIONS AND TRAINING

Advanced communications and information systems will change the nature of training and education in corporate settings.

The economics of moving people great distances via airplane, lodging and feeding them for the purpose of exposing them to a speaker or group of speakers in a conference or workshop makes less and less sense as new technologies offer electronic convening of such meetings. Even the sending of one person to various locations to give the same message to several different groups makes little sense with teleconferencing devices such as the "electronic blackboard," which provides instant transmission of voice and graphics anywhere where phone lines are. A teacher showing accounting fundamentals could work easily with such a device. Other teleconferencing technologies have already been covered.

Using computers with advanced interactive software such as Control Data Corporation's widely touted training program PLATO, companies can quickly introduce computer aided instruction. There are four elements to such systems: course information, questions on the information, analysis of the student responses, and routing instructions that determine what the student should see next.

Interactive video disc technology is another training technology. It is being used quite heavily by Ford Motor Company to train dealers and mechanics. The system marries a computer to a videodisc unit, allowing "branching" or "routing" as much as the computer instruction allows. Ford, in order to make this technology user friendly, reportedly spent $250,000 devising a golf course game to be played via interactive disc to get dealers, salesmen, and mechanics to use the technology. The benefit of interactive disc extends to providing sight and sound, which computer-aided instruction cannot.

MANAGEMENT STRATEGIES

Unfortunately, as a society, we do not always match our abilities in technology and engineering with effective utilization. Many times we build the machine before we know what to do with it. The late CBS newsman Edward R. Murrow once said that unless we used it wisely, television would become merely "lights and wires in a box." The same might be said of the new technology. The medium is *not* the message. We're past McLuhan. The medium is only a medium, the hardware. The challenge now is the software, the message.

The manager must learn first of all how the new technology works. He or she should get the feel of it and understand the basics, including costs. More important, the manager should attempt to develop a capacity to creatively apply the technology to organizational challenges. A lot of vendors sell technology, but the most valuable and important thing one can buy is the software—the *creative application*. A two-hundred-thousand-dollar videotape system is great to have, but the real question the manager needs to ask is, "What are we doing with it?" How does the system fit into the firm's human-resources development program? How does it interface with the communications strategy? How does it help achieve productivity goals?

A commitment to developing an annual report to run on cable television's free public-access channels is a good idea, but who is going to watch it? How is the show going to be promoted? What "message" about the firm is the show going to convey? Some of these questions are technical, some are managerial, and some are both.

Responsibilities need to be established for looking at the new telecommunications possibilities and applying them. Should the ideas come up from a staff office or down from the executive committee? Should the firm look into slow-scan teleconferencing as a substitute for the "day trip" to the field? Should there be a mix of the two? In what proportion? Who should make the decision?

Should some employees be allowed to work at home at data terminals? Should the firm experiment, or wait until the results are in from other companies trying this? What impact will this have on our employer-employee relationships?

To prepare for an age in which information and the ability to communicate are the principal strategic resources, the manager must analyze his or her business's competitive position, set goals for the future, and apply the new technologies whenever they will provide a competitive advantage.

Adaptability is the key management posture in this period of rapid change. A strategic plan that includes regular analysis of these new technologies in the company's environment, internal structures, and resource availability will allow quick response to opportunities and threats that arise.

The diversity of media created by the new channels of communication is confusing and changing almost daily. New technologies and hybrids have to be evaluated in the light of the industry a company is in, its size, and its predicted growth rate, as well as the compatibility of the new technology with existing information systems and the relative costs.

Cost is a tradeoff variable in most strategic decisions of this type because improved engineering, competition, and the learning-curve effect will lower the price of the good or service over time. The decision for the manager may become one between the immediate competitive advantage and the potential to improve product quality and service for the customer, and long-term cost savings and a more refined technology.

MAJOR QUESTIONS TO ASK REGARDING THE NEW TECHNOLOGIES

1. Is it cost-effective?
   Can in-house staff provide same service for less?
   Will it increase productivity substantially?
2. Have I researched the technology sufficiently?
3. Should I wait for the improved model coming out in three months?
4. What can I accomplish with it that I can't without it?
5. Can I use the technology to generate revenues?
6. Will it *really* improve information dissemination?—communications (intra, inter)?
7. Can I afford to *not* have the new technologies?

POINTS TO REMEMBER

1. *Software* isn't everything, it's the only thing.
2. Narrowcasting will require greater promotion, marketing.
3. Having the new technologies in place now is a sign of good management. Promote it.
4. Don't be afraid of it (it's dumber than you are).
5. Nothing beats a smiling, human face. 😊

HOME INFORMATION SYSTEMS

The office revolution in communications may be overshadowed in the next decade by developments now underway in home information systems. The telephone, cable wire, and a small computer, along with a TV screen, will provide the hardware base for the new system. People will be able to "interact" electronically with school, business, and bank; be able to play the stock market internationally, on a real-time basis; obtain fire and burglar protection; and actively participate in government via feedback programs, in addition to receiving entertainment. (See Figure 8-2.).

Home information systems (HIS) is a generic term that refers to a broad range of services that can be delivered to the home. Potential vendors will include publishers and information providers, bankers, brokers, advertisers, data-base holders, the Yellow Pages, retailers, and mail-order companies. One-way delivery mechanisms are known as *teletext*, and two-way systems are referred to as *videotex*.) Home feedback terminals range from simple ten-key pads to full computers.

In mid-1982, New York's Chemical Bank became the first financial institution in the U.S. to provide at-home banking service, *PRONTO*, via phone lines and Atari computers.

HIS will provide a large market for business that will arise from equipment purchases, transaction fees, basic subscriptions, and advertising. According to a study by Booz, Allen & Hamilton, potential stakeholders in the home information system market will include:

- Electronic vendors
- Publishers and information providers
- Retailers/direct-sales outfits
- Banks, brokers, and insurance companies
- Advertisers and agencies
- Voice, data, and video communication firms

Markets that will be challenged to hold on to their position will include:

- Publishing

FIGURE 8-2 Sample Frames of Teletext from KEYCOM Electronic Publishing

SOURCE: © KEYCOM Electronic Publishing, 1982.

- Telephone and mail
- Retail/wholesale
- Travel and entertainment
- Transportation equipment
- Education[15]

Yet to be determined, however, is just how great consumer acceptance will be for the new technological services.

The QUBE system, a primitive, interactive ten-key device developed by Warner-Amex, is a forerunner of more sophisticated home-information systems to be developed and tested during the coming decade. Users will be able to call up and interact with alphanumeric and graphic displays for many types of transactions:

- Electronic mail
- Electronic banking
  account balances
  loan and bill payment
  credit card accounts

- Utility payments
- Classified ad listings
- Real estate listings
- Community announcements
- Airline information and reservations
- Electronic merchandising
- Catalog shopping
- Library access
- Educational services
- Stock reports
- Weather reports[16]

There are four basic types of home information systems:

1. *Teletext (A)*—One-way broadcasting. These systems transmit only graphics or text within the "gaps" on the television signal. One-way means the user can call up specific information but cannot interact with it. Requires signal decoder in TV receiver.
2. *Teletext (B)*—A broadband signal using a full broadcast channel (over air or cable) to transmit teletext. It is already used on some cable systems for community "bulletin boards," consumer tips, and so on. It should expand rapidly. Also requires decoder.
3. *Videotex (A)*—A narrowband system that uses telephone lines for data transmission and interaction. Slower than cable or fiber-optics systems, but since the telephone is already "in place," AT&T has a jump on competitors in establishing a massive information network.
4. *Videotex (B)*—A broadband system like QUBE that allows full interaction. Most promising technology for videotex development.

Hardware for videotex home information systems, is available, though expensive. Foreign-originated systems, such as the British *Prestel*, French *Antiope*, and Canadian *Telidon* systems, are in limited use and are being used in numerous experiments. The FCC has not adopted a standard, and England, France, and Canada would all like to see their system designated as the standard one. One American attempt, Home Information System, has been produced by MIT for Booz, Allen & Hamilton. The HIS hardware includes a 48-K Apple microcomputer, a laser-disc video player, and a regular TV screen. This combination allows HIS users to mix data and audiovisual presentations. Rather than gaining access through a keyboard, HIS users simply touch their circuit sensitized screen to activate any portion of the service "menu." HIS experiments by Booz show a strong market with a potential for 17 million to 30 million homes having videotex by 1993.

While generally staying out of hardware development, American businesses—especially retailers, financial institutions, and newspaper publishers—have been using the existing hardware to develop consumer services. Though they consider the potential consumer-demand level very unclear, many feel it is necessary to be prepared if and when the market explodes.

Two graphically sophisticated home information systems have been tested in the U.S. AT&T and Knight-Ridder combined to testmarket *Viewdata* for six months in 150 homes in Coral Cables, Florida. Information from the *Miami Herald*, banking and payment of utility bills through the Southeast Banking Corporation, and shopping from Jordan-Marsh and Sears were offered.[17]

Also, CompuServe and Warner Amex's QUBE in Columbus, Ohio, offered Atari terminals to access 100 subscribers with newspaper information from the *Columbus Post Dispatch* and banking services from Bank One Corporation.

These investors all have independent as well as interwoven stakes and benefits in their projects' success. For bankers the number of branch officers and tellers could be drastically reduced as customers read bank statements, paid utility bills, and filled out loan applications on home television sets. They would enjoy lower check-clearing costs and larger cash reserves, as customers would need less on-hand cash to pay bills. For department stores, the costs of postage and printing of catalogues could be lowered, and labor costs of large stores might be reduced.

Newspapers could place classified ads, births, deaths, and stock market figures on the system to free costly page space. And although it seems that newspapers are competing directly against themselves by providing videotex news, they may actually be attempting to protect their advertising revenues as stores increasingly use videotex ads to sell goods.

CONSUMER RETICENCE

One of the first priorities for new technology proponents will be to educate consumers about the benefits of the system and remove their fear of the hardware. A first step is to develop "user-friendly" technology with easy-to-understand software that gives the consumer confidence in his or her ability to handle the system, while providing a feeling of security.

Experience shows that people enjoy using interactive systems but perceive them as a novelty rather than a serious tool for everyday use. Gradual introduction of the capabilities, beginning with the least threatening and demanding, is the key to full consumer acceptance. Existing cable systems, such as QUBE, began by offering nonthreatening forms of interaction through video games and participatory programming that provided sampling of topical issues.

Another step was introduction of electronic financial services. People are becoming accustomed to automatic-teller machines, bill payment by phone, and other innovations that familiarize them with "computerized" banking. It is hoped by those in the industry that videotex offerings will at first be only a slight extension of this concept. Industry experts believe that financial services are crucial to the profitable development of videotex since theirs are among the industries most heavily involved in experimentation.[18] Experts believe that unless financial services are accepted, more elaborate services will also be rejected.

At present there are consumer fears that transactions via videotex are not "economically controllable." For example, QUBE's interactive system often produced unexpectedly large bills due to user misunderstanding of the charges. This resulted in consumer anger and confusion as well as derogatory press for Warner. When *qualitative* elements are brought in, the price/benefit relationship is even more complicated. People are buying not only a concrete service or product, they are buying convenience and time. In the early stages of videotex's introduction they also are buying status.[19]

By 1990, experts say, possibly 20 percent of consumer buying will involve some form of electronic marketing. This will mean smaller warehousing costs for retailers. Videotex experts believe further that the new at-home shopping systems will generate $10 billion a year in revenues by 1990. Over 100 major advertisers, including Chevrolet and Procter & Gamble have started advertising over teletext systems. CBS and AT&T were conducting tests in early 1983 in two hundred homes in Ridgewood, New Jersey, providing users with access to the Associated Press wires, Merrill Lynch wire, *The New York Times*, and on-line shopping.

Similarly the costs of using the interactive system go beyond mere dollars. They include potential loss of privacy, social contact, and the sensory satisfaction of the experience. For example, shopping for many is a form of recreation and social contact. Will consumers be willing to regularly punch up choices on a screen? Or will they use videotext only when the weather is inclement? How important to the purchase is personal contact with the merchandise and sales personnel?

All of these influences must be considered in the pricing decision. Developers are experimenting with a variety of plans to find the most effective cost structure. In December 1982 the *Times-Mirror* Co. completed tests in Southern California of an elaborate videotex system in which a variety of customer charges were levied. One aspect of the test was designed to determine if customers preferred to be charged by the hour, by the page, or by the month.[20] Among those pricing methods under consideration in other tests are a per use charge, a flat fee, a percentage of transaction value, tiered charges, and various combinations.

Although information is strongly desired by cable consumers, it appears they are not willing to pay for information alone. Experts believe that for videotex to grow, a whole range of services will have to be offered at a blanket price of less than fifty dollars a month. Also the cost of the hardware package for the home will have to drop below five hundred dollars for adoption to take place. Many feel that straight text transmission via cable is the most viable possibility at present.

Parallel to the pricing issue is that of service offerings. In studies on consumer interest in interactive services, response has been strong for information services. Financial transactions are the most popular interactive services because they require less user involvement. Issues facing business interested in this burgeoning market include:

1. What facet and/or level of the market to go into

a. Provide the mode of information transmission
b. Manufacture and sell technological components
c. Develop and sell services
d. Run the central computer system
2. When to enter the market
3. What the cost of market entry will be
4. Who the consumers will be

NEW MARKETING TOOLS

The market researcher will be a major beneficiary of the new information and communications technologies. Cable television will allow the researcher to control the transmission of programming, commercials, and concepts to selected groups of viewers. Responses of those viewers will be measured through interactive systems. Viewership may also be measured through households linked to universal product code (UPC) scanner systems. Purchases would be recorded automatically in some stores. Data from such information systems will be much more accurate, timely, and complete than traditional methods of survey and diary recording.

A system called TELLUS includes a portable unit that automatically displays questions, usually with multiple-choice answers, and passers-by record their answers by pressing buttons.

Telephones and TV sets used together allow companies to conduct live and recorded videoconferences. Interviews are conducted without any physical intrusion into a subject's home, and the system even allows for a focus-group study without being limited to any particular region.

Data-collection technologies, such as in-store scanners, CRT interviewing devices, and telephone networks, can be used in combination with telecommunications systems to measure consumer response as never before. For example, if a marketing firm wishes to monitor the effects of ads or promotions, it is much easier to isolate retail movements to very specific time periods. A. C. Nielsen reports have been speeded from sixty to ten days using UPC systems instead of shelf audits. A real concern for the future, however, is that interactive systems will open the door to greater eavesdropping on consumers and become a threat to privacy.

THE CHANGING MASS MEDIA

The new communications technologies are dramatically widening the number of potential sources for dissemination of information and entertainment video programming to the public. Innovative uses of new and old communications technologies are expanding rapidly in a new era of communications deregulation. In city after city new cable television wires are giving people forty channels for video viewing rather than the traditional three or four.

Cable is the most rapidly growing of these new technologies, but others loom in the wings, such as subscription television, low-power television, direct broadcast from satellite to home, and multipoint distribution services. In the area of audio broadcast, pressures have been growing for increasing the number of signals on the AM radio frequency.

Originally a technology for bringing improved television reception to out-lying areas, cable antenna television (CATV, or Cable,) has experienced phe-nomenal growth since Time, Inc.'s Home Box Office movie service was launched in 1975 and it became apparent that a lot of people were willing to pay upwards of $25 per month for first-run movies at home. Since then numerous companies have bought up cable firms and bid vast sums to wire large cities, becoming in the process "multiple system operators" (MSOs), who hope their heavy investments will be quickly rewarded by viewers tired of commercial TV.

With all those new channels available, advertisers believe that over the long-term the television industry will go the way of the magazine industry— from a time when a few majors predominated to today's situation in which many specialized publications have carved out niches. (The television equiv-alent of this is called narrowcasting.) As major communications conglomerates have moved into cable to protect their position, concern has been raised that diversity could be thwarted.

Subscription Television (STV) has already proven successful in many cities, where authorized TV stations have been allowed to sell scrambled signals to homes that have purchased special decoders. A monthly fee is charged for the service, which consists mostly of movies or sports.

Low Power Television (LPTV) was adapted from a repeater system that boosted a TV signal in areas of difficult terrain. Now low power has been given independent status. It was originally conceived for use in small communities, to allow local programming via broadcast signal and also to provide extra channels for minorities in medium-sized markets.

Direct-Broadcast from Satellite (DBS) allows homes, business and other receiving points to obtain signal reception of television or other video services directly from satellite. While the cost of receiving dishes (downlinks) has dropped to as low as $250, regulatory and copyright issues defining which signals can be freely "plucked" from the sky are not yet solved.

In 1982, the FCC gave permission to Satellite Television Corporation, a subsidiary of COMSAT, to launch a two-satellite system for the eastern third of the U.S. by 1986. The full system is expected to cost $1 billion and be in operation shortly thereafter. United Satellite Television and General Instrument Corporation planned to launch in 1983 what they called "the world's first direct satellite-to-home pay TV broadcast service." The venture intended to provide four channels of programming for $15 per month plus special pay-per-view options to 30 million homes located in markets where low density makes cable service uneconomical.[21]

Multipoint Distribution Services (MDS) are systems where frequency space from the radio spectrum is used to relay TV, voice, or data signals from building to building in a specific geographic area via microwave. A typical example is the local TV station that broadcasts live via its minicam unit. Such systems have business applications and are already in use by schools and TV stations for live remote broadcast. Also banks are beginning to use MDS to communicate with branches. Signal range is about twenty-five miles.

Cellular Telephone Systems are a series of low-power radio transmitters serving an eight-mile hexagonal cell, which handle telephone calls to and from moving vehicles and automatically switch the calls between transmitters as a vehicle moves out of range. The technology is allowing thousands of drivers in major cities to enjoy a once-restricted status symbol—the car telephone.

THE ROLE OF
TRADITIONAL MEDIA

The new technologies are expected to have significant impact on traditional mass media—commercial television, radio, newspapers, and magazines.

People are abandoning commercial TV for some of the new technologies. Erosion is taking place as people buy home video recording and playback devices, but the real impact is coming from cable television. Advertisers on commercial television networks were seen to be most affected. Consider:

AUDIENCE DECLINES.   According to Jayne Zenaty, manager of media research for Leo Burnett Advertising, there has been an erosion in TV market share of three points per season nationally since 1981. "I expect that trend to continue at least through 1986," she says. "The reason is not only cable, but the rise of independent stations brought into communities via cable, stations such as Chicago's WGN and Atlanta's WTBS." In some markets, the share erosion (percentage decline of people with sets tuned to network television) is higher than others, but the national television networks are still delivering sizeable audiences and raising their rates.

"ZAPPING."   A 1979 study by A. C. Nielsen Company found that 31 percent of viewers whose video cassette recorders have a fastforward switch used it to skip over commercials on playback.

AD RULES.   A 1982 consent decree announced by the government and the broadcasting industry signaled an end to self-regulation by television stations through the National Association of Broadcasters and elimination of all restraints on the duration of TV commercials. Still left standing, however, is an FCC rule prohibiting more than sixteen minutes of commercial time per hour.[22]

A 1981 report by Ogilvy & Mather, the advertising agency, estimated that overall share of audience in prime time held by the three major networks would decline to 71 percent by 1985 and 59 percent by 1990. To buttress its forecast, Ogilvy & Mather pointed to San Francisco, where viewers have a choice of seven broadcast stations and 40 percent of the homes are wired for cable. In that city the overall share of the three major networks in 1982 was only 70 percent.

The *newspaper industry* over the past three decades has been consolidated into several large companies, with some stalwart independents remaining. The afternoon newspaper has continued to disappear because of distribution problems and the growth of television as the primary news medium for the general public. Newspapers have adapted, however, by developing new feature sections and by segmenting the market. Also newspaper production has evolved into a computerized operation—from drafting stories on a cathode-ray-tube (CRT) display screen to cutting and folding and bundling at the press.

Since they are primary generators of information on current and public events and their information services support most radio and TV operations, the papers appear to be well positioned for the coming new technology, especially videotext and teletext services.

Additionally it is hard to imagine a time when there will be no strong markets for local, state, or regional news. Newspapers like the *Wall Street Journal, USA Today* and the *New York Times* are already using satellites to transmit facsimile pages to regional printing plants. Newspapers in the future will not be limited to the physical form of the newsprint page but may go video.

It is predicted that ultimately some newspaper sections, such as classified and display advertising, will be pulled away from newspapers by competitive television cable systems. Like other media companies, newspaper companies are branching out, seeking new avenues in communications to support their publishing operations. Cable TV is frequently a secondary enterprise for them because of a compatible programming need for local information. Additionally newspapers tend to have strong community roots, which are advantageous in winning cable contracts from municipal governments. Some newspaper companies own radio stations, periodicals, and book-publishing divisions as well, and clearly newspapers are poised for the eventual merger of media.

Magazines, after conceding the mass market to television, have begun to carve out special-interest niches in the communications marketplace. Today magazines are proliferating and, for the most part, thriving. As a group magazine publishers are looking for joint ventures in cable television. Programming-starved cable companies, trying to figure out how they are going to fill fifty or even a hundred channels, are allying themselves with the authority and consumer loyalty magazines enjoy. Magazines in turn see electronic publishing as their means of survival. A spokesman for the Meredith Corporation, publisher of *Better Homes and Gardens* and several other magazines, said his company's commitment to cable programming was viewed as a way to boost circulation and advertising pages by presenting on TV material that reinforces articles and subjects used in the magazine.[23]

An offshoot being explored by publishers includes Demand Electronic Publishing (DEP), where the viewer/reader selects text, images, and even the audio component and then receives a homemade magazine printed on a high-quality printer located in his or her home. This is not to say that magazines will soon be passé, but they may have to look toward smaller and smaller market shares as the new media cause the entertainment and information industries to segment further. Publishers are now selling information as a product instead of as a particular physical package called a magazine, book, or newspaper.

Radio receives less attention than other media because its potential is limited to using the allocated spectrum band more thoroughly and efficiently. Radio stations over the years have proliferated along with other communications vehicles, increasing from nine hundred full-time AM stations in 1945 to two thousand stations in the same microwave band in 1980. Present technological developments include the introduction of stereo broadcasting for AM stations, networking via satellite, and proposals to decrease band width to all stations (vetoed by the FCC in 1982).[24]

National Public Radio, in an attempt to increase revenues, has come up with a new service that will allow customers to tape a preselected radio program for a subscription fee. The process is pegged to a patented automatic recording technique that works through a computer to link a consumer's radio and tape recorder to a signal that will be sent overnight via satellite. Called "Codart," it will sell for $5 to $15 monthly.[25]

CABLE TELEVISION

In the early 1980s cable television was the hottest of the new telecommunications technologies. In city after city multimillion-dollar franchises were let by municipal governments to construct, operate, and maintain cable systems that would bring dozens of new television channels into the home for a few dollars a month.

Spurred on by the success of the Home Box Office, dozens of media conglomerates began developing similar programming services, hoping to establish an early presence and position themselves for the future. The experience of HBO showed there is a significant audience willing to pay twenty-five dollars or more per month, in addition to the basic cable service charge for movies. While dozens of experiments in both home-information systems and in the entertainment areas being developed by cable continue, hard data on the cable market remain elusive. As an executive of one company told *BusinessWeek*: "It's wonderful—all these people spending millions and not a dollar of profit in sight yet."[26] The marketing director of a cable company cautioned, "All we really know about the new technologies *is* that there are people willing to pay twenty-five dollars a month for movies. That's all we know. Everything else is a crap shoot."

CBS, after spending $30 million on a cable cultural network, pulled out of the project in 1982, attributing the venture's downfall to low audiences and ad revenues. The action scared high-flying cable executives everywhere. Industry sources predicted that by 1983 there would be losses by cable programmers of hundreds of millions of dollars and a shakeout among cable program services, particularly those national cable networks supported by advertising revenues rather than cable subscribers' fees. Overcompetition for advertising dollars and for slots on cable systems would combine with high programming and other operating costs, it was suggested, and doom many of the struggling networks. Cable advertising revenues were expected to rise about $1.6 billion annually by 1987, a 600 percent increase over 1982.

By the end of 1982, all fifty of the top U.S. advertisers were in cable, and probably 85 percent of the top two hundred. According to TV veteran Mike Dann of ABC, the crisis for cable television is in the "areas of marketing (getting people to buy it) and advertising (getting advertisers to support it)." Dann says that cable TV is like a Cuisinart, where you have to tell people what it can do. He predicts that cable's ability to sell in depth "will revolutionize selling techniques far more than the supermarket did in the retail business." He predicts that "once the marketing and advertising legs of the cable television explosion are completed, the present rapid growth of cable will seem like a snail's pace compared to what will happen in the next five to seven years."[27]

With the wiring of America approaching 30 percent of U.S. homes by the mid-1980s, advertisers have jumped aboard the bandwagon, hoping to establish an early presence, find a new medium that can deliver a more segmented video market, and offer an opportunity to develop commercial messages longer than the expensive thirty-second format of network television.

Skeptics maintain, however, that cable television offers little other than "more of the same" as commercial TV. They contend that programming that was traditionally free—movies, live sports, the arts—is now being segmented out for cable and will have to be paid for by the viewer. For example major sporting events such as title fights, certain college football games, and tennis matches now are going to new networks such as Getty Oil's Entertainment and Sports Programming Network (ESPN), for cable only showing.

To date, however, most programming has followed the HBO lead, with a heavy orientation toward satellite-delivered cable programming emphasizing Hollywood reruns. Showtime, The Movie Channel, and other services have concentrated on this market.

Other major services have included the twenty-four-hour-a-day all-news channel, Cable News Network, developed by the Ted Turner organization in Atlanta, and a host of smaller offerings emphasizing children's programming ("Nickelodeon," "Pinwheel"); minorities programming ("Black Entertainment Television," "Spanish International Network," and "Gala Vision"); religious programming; R-rated movies ("Escapade"); and rock concerts.

In 1982, 23 percent of the 77.8 million homes in the U.S. received cable. That figure is expected to double by 1990. In 1981 alone, more than forty-nine thousands street miles of cable were laid at a cost of more than one billion dollars.

CABLE ADVERTISING
POTENTIAL

As major markets are wired and the methodology for sampling viewership was established, the cable technology was expected to become a major factor in advertising. While cable revenues from advertising in 1981 reached close to $50 million, this was still a small figure when compared with commercial television's $12.7 billion in annual revenues.

One of the attractions drawing advertisers to cable programming as opposed to commercial TV is that costs are less, and target markets can be segmented. Concerning costs, a network TV spot can cost more than $150,000 for thirty seconds in prime time. A thirty-second spot on the Cable News Network, for example, was selling for as low as $315 in 1981.

The medium is also perfectly suited for *selective marketing*. ESPN viewers one Sunday in 1981 saw a commercial for a Norman Rockwell original painting that had a lowest acceptable offer of $120,000. Fifty bids were received based on the ad, and the painting sold for $125,000.[28] If a company sells specialized products such as golf clubs or BMWs, a mass market is not efficient. Cable television is an alternative medium to magazines and newspapers.

Advertising experts believe that when market penetration by cable TV reaches 30 percent, it will truly become a viable medium for national marketing. Aiming toward that target already is the Cable News Network, which broadcasts news to 5.7 million homes with paid commercials.

From an advertiser's point of view, the most promising aspect of the new cable technology is the freedom it affords to experiment with the commercial message format. New commercial lengths—ten minutes, thirty minutes—whole programs that combine commercials with information (called informercials) are being tried out. Companies could also experiment with product categories banned on commercial television, such as liquor, and cigarettes, and ladies in frilly lingerie.

Already beyond the stage of experimentation is the Shopping Channel, a satellite cable venture of the Times-Mirror Cable Company, and Comp-U-Card, a private shopping service beamed daily to 150,000 cable subscribers in six *Times-Mirror* markets. The program runs sixteen hours per day, seven days a week, with each half-hour product program repeated five times a month. After paying an initial $18 in dues, the viewer can order merchandise by calling a toll-free number, and he or she is entitled to discounts ranging up to 40 percent. Merchandise comes from Federated Department Stores, which owns part of Comp-U-Card.[29]

A regulatory analysis of potential problems in cable conducted by the staff of the Federal Trade Commission has raised concerns about advertising policy.

The study emphasized that in the short run cable advertisers will be able to target income, lifestyle, demographics, and expenditure characteristics of their audience much more accurately with cable than with radio or TV and that while the cost per exposure may be higher, the probability of affecting sales will be higher as well.

The FTC predicted that instead of passively receiving a thirty-second TV spot, the viewer "will be asked to enter into a dynamic interactive process." This new technology, the FTC added, will mean longer marketing messages and new creative approaches to the design of these spots as well. Also, the FTC suggested, the viewer will have to be more stimulated to watch a twenty-minute "informercial." The agency expressed concern over the possible "blurring" of lines between *information* and *commercial message.*

For example, a program segment on how to decrease gas consumption sponsored by an auto maker might *appear* to be consumer information while in reality it is merely an extended advertisement. The FTC also worried that an "information gap" might be created with more information available to those who can pay for the new services.

From its institutional perspective, the FTC suggested that two-way, interactive cable systems could pretest the effectiveness of disclosure remedies that the government might be considering in an ad claim inquiry case. Finally the report concluded that the new technology would benefit the small advertiser, who would now have more access to the media as price and space barriers dropped.[30]

PUBLIC ACCESS

One of the most promising aspects of cable wiring of American cities in the early 1980s has been the potential for public access to programming.

In city after city the franchise battle included offers and bids that promised designation of public-access channels, studios, mobile equipment, staffing, and training for individuals and groups. The model success story, often retold, is that of Reading, Pennsylvania.

Reading, a community of ninety thousand, has had a public-access center since 1971. It is a quiet little town with good schools, responsive government, traditionally low unemployment, and a large over-sixty-five population (20 percent). When American Television & Communications Corporation (ATC) bought the franchise in 1969 it installed new "return" lines for interactive television. Special research using federal grant monies was done on how to make the system helpful to the older population. By the use of split-screen interactive techniques, people at each of many access points interact live on cable. This has allowed the city to conduct local public hearings, for example, and many other innovative ideas have become reality as various open and closed loops are patched together:

• An operatic baritone sings, discusses his career, and chats informally in the same hour with hundreds of different people in many locations.

- Three attorneys in one small room answer questions and talk with people scattered in widely separated parts of the city.
- Without leaving his workbench, a wood carver shows the art of making fine gunstocks and answers questions from people all over town.
- An expert in emergency psychiatric care talks to the staff of one hospital, while staffs of two other hospitals participate from their own locations.
- A weekly singalong is held among two senior centers and a state hospital for the elderly. Many participants unable to travel have made friends with each other over the years, as well as with home viewers.

This type of programming runs in Reading about four hours a day, Monday through Friday, and centers on many issues involving senior citizens. Once a month a producers' committee meeting is held, which is open to public involvement and brainstorming. Seven public-school districts, two parochial high schools, four area colleges and universities, and the Berks County Intermediate Unit have an interconnected schoolcasting system, which is also linked to hospitals, neighborhood citizen centers, and ultimately all cable subscribers, allowing all manner of interchange. Students produce weekly football or basketball coverage, plays, and news program, focusing on school events.

Local government experience with the system has inspired increasing citizen participation, with the facilitation of such activities as polling on local issues. One cable company brochure states: "It seems ironic that the medium most responsible for the predominance of one-way passive consumption of information is also the medium by which people can realize just the opposite." The Reading story is based on ten years of experience in a medium-sized city. It is a most hopeful sign of the potential of cable television on the public and not-for-profit sectors.[31] The most exciting aspect of the new technology and citizen access is that many thousands of people in the society may some day soon be able to get involved in a medium that has been restricted since its beginning. The opportunity for new ideas to be expressed in this medium will be enormous.

MUNICIPAL REGULATION

There is another side, however, to the municipal cable picture. Unless there are responsible public officials, active and concerned public-interest organizations, and honest vendors, there cannot be other Reading stories. Expectations and promises are not always realized without persistent public involvement.

Michael Langley, a senior policy analyst on the Atlanta City Council staff, described what happens when promises are not enforced, in an essay in *Community Television Review*. The proposal that won the Atlanta cable franchise promised six government-access channels—two for internal, closed-loop communication; one shared by the city government and the U.S. House of Representatives; one for police and fire departments; and two for the city library. The proposal stated nothing about the number of personnel needed to run these stations or the time needed to put together programming for them. It did say the company's central studio and remote facilities would be available for government use. Also alphanumeric information capacity (text on a screen produced by a character generator) was promised for publicizing city council agendas. Other promises were made, but fifteen months into the franchise period, wrote Langley, "the state of Atlanta's municipal-access channels is greatly diminished from what was portrayed in the company's promise in the request for proposal."

The only government programming now being done is the alphanumeric. Two of the city's channels were removed by the FCC because of possible conflict with airport communications. Langley points to five lessons learned from this experience:

1. The cable company's franchise proposal is a marketing tool, and only the franchise agreement is enforceable in court.
2. The franchise agreement is the only legal source for insuring the development of municipal service channels.
3. Local governments need the expertise of consultants during the franchise-granting period and all the way through to the end.
4. Fewer channels that are backed up with equipment and personnel are better than a lot of channels no one can use.
5. Two-year renewals of the franchise agreement are the only hope of fixing a situation like Atlanta's.[32]

Cable company promises for public access can be significant and can give the companies a competitive edge. During the negotiations period for Boston, for example, commitments for studios, equipment, and training ran all the way from $1.1 million to $1.8 million. Warner Amex's proposal called for a $3.5 million Center for Interactive Programming that would be intended for local programming and also as a "cornerstone" for national video production. Also, annual operating funds of up to 5 percent of Warner Amex's local revenues, to be administered by a not-for-profit corporation, were promised to support public access.

Those involved in community access to cable see it as a basic urban utility. The Miami Valley Cable TV Council in Dayton, for example, has trained hundreds of persons in handling portable TV recording equipment. In Madison, Wisconsin, which has a twelve-channel system, original programming is managed through the local library, which turns out thirty to fifty hours a month with community input. Programs include health department information, educational movies, fire department training programs, and programming for the disabled and handicapped.

Some of the more interesting programming being produced through local access pertains to social change. At the 1981 conference of the National Federation of Local Cable Programmers social-change programs on subjects such as breastfeeding, productivity problems in the post office, municipal boat races and their community impact in Austin, Texas, and oil drilling in the Canadian Maritime Provinces were viewed.

The experiment at Reading, the programming in Madison, and the training in Dayton create great expectations for the public use of the new technology. At the very least, government units will be able to develop closed loops for municipal agencies such as police and fire, provide schools with the ability to share resources, and give city government a way of measuring public opinion quickly.

SUMMARY   1. The communications revolution is underway and is having significant impact on the office environment. It will have important impact on the home and the marketplace also in the decade of the eighties.

2. The technological revolution underway is fueled by advances in satellites, computer technology, and governmental deregulation of the communications industry in addition to some market success with showing movies over cable television.

3. Information management in the office is becoming more important in the search for improved productivity.

4. New office technology includes electronic and voice mail, teleconferencing, data-base creation, video storage/access, and computer conferencing.

5. Home information systems may have great impact in areas such as banking and retailing, as well as information services. But there is no market at present.

6. The great strength of traditional media like newspapers, television and movies is their access to information, data, and other software bases.

7. Cable television appears to have great potential, but nobody knows for sure.

NOTES

1. See Eli Ginzberg, "The Mechanization of Work," *Scientific American*, September 1982, pp. 67–68. Also, Martin L. Ernst, "The Mechanization of Commerce," *Scientific American*, September 1982, p. 152.

2. "MCI Plans Test of New Cable Tie," *The New York Times*, November 19, 1982, p. 34.

3. Frank Corrado, "Working in the Electronic City," *Chicago Tribune*, November 23, 1982, p. 17.

4. See David J. Kull, "Group Decisions: Can Computers Help?" *Computer Decisions*, May 1982, pp. 70–160. Also, John Naisbitt, *Megatrends* (New York, Warner Books, 1982), p. 201.

5. See Stafford Beer, *Brains of the Firm: The Managerial Cybernetics of Organization*, 2nd ed. (New York: John Wiley & Sons, 1981); and "The Shorter Catechism of Stafford Beer," *Datamation*, February 1982, p. 148.

6. "How Personal Computers Can Backfire," *BusinessWeek*, July 12, 1982, p. 56.

7. Richard L. Nolan, "Managing Information Systems by Committee," *Harvard Business Review*, July-August 1982, pp. 73–75.

8. "Helping Decision Makers Get at Data," *BusinessWeek*, September 13, 1982, p. 118.

9. "Ciba-Geigy Corp. and American Soybean Assn. with Dorn," in *1980 Silver Anvil Winners* (New York: Public Relations Society of America, 1981), p. 51.

10. Jerry C. Davis, "Satellite Firm to Market Worldwide Video System," *Chicago Sun Times*, October 22, 1982, p. 82.

11. Neesa Sweet, "Should There Be a Teleconference in Your Future?" *Crain's Chicago Business*, August 30, 1982, p. T8.

12. Naisbitt, *Megatrends*, p. 46.

13. Andrew Pollack, "Computerized Phone Systems," *The New York Times*, November 11, 1982, p. 30.

14. "Cable Gets Ready for Business," *BusinessWeek*, November 22, 1982, pp. 119–21.

15. Booz, Allen & Hamilton, "A Special Booz, Allen Study of the Home Information Systems Market," 1981.

16. Jennifer Lau and Amy Truitt, "The Data Wave: Home Information Systems," unpublished paper, November 15, 1981.

17. "Information Services: Reading Between the Lines," *Cablevision*, August 10, 1981, p. 32.

18. See "The Home Information Revolution," *BusinessWeek*, June 29, 1981, p. 74.

19. See Eric Pace, "Videotex: Luring Advertisers," *The New York Times*, October 14, 1982, p. 33.

20. "*Times-Mirror* to Start Videotext Test in California," *Broadcasting*, October 26, 1981, p. 52.

21. See Susan Spillman, "Head Start for dbs Claimed," *Advertising Age*, August 16, 1982, p. 70; also, Ernest Holsendolph, "TV Satellite Launching by Comsat Unit Backed," *The New York Times*, September 24, 1982, p. 36.

22. Dr. Jayne Zenaty in conversation with the author, December 29, 1982; also see Sandra Salmans, "If TV Ads Get Zapped by Viewers," *The New York Times*, November 24, 1982, p. D17; and Ernest Holsendolph, "Rules on TV Ads' Time Dropped, All Restraints Could Be Nullified," *The New York Times*, November 24, 1982, p. 1.

23. Jacques Neher, "Meredith Taking Its Franchise to Cable," *Advertising Age*, February 2, 1981, p. 70.

24. Charles Jackson, "The Allocation of the Radio Spectrum," *Scientific American*, February 1980, pp. 34–38.

25. Morrie Gelman, "NPR Adopts Pay Radio for Revenue," *Electronic Media*, September 23, 1982, p. 3.

26. See Philip H. Dougherty, "Planning for Cable's Acceptance," *The New York Times*, November 22, 1982, p. 39; "Talking Business, with Dann of ABC, Cable TV's Prospects," *The New York Times*, October 26, 1982, p. 34; and Charles Storch, "Most Cable Networks Will Fold, Study Predicts," *Chicago Tribune*, September 3, 1982, Sec. 4, p. 11.

27. "Home Information Revolution," *BusinessWeek*, op. cit.

28. John E. Cooney, "Cable Television is Attracting More Ads, Sharply Focused Programs Are One Lure," *Wall Street Journal*, March 31, 1981, p. 48.

29. John E. Cooney, "With Video Shopping Services, Goods You See on the Screen Can be Delivered to Your Door," *Wall Street Journal*, July 14, 1981, p. 48.

30. "FTC Sees Murky Waters in New Video Technology," *Advertising Age*, May 5, 1981, p. 34.

31. "The Reading Dialogue," American Television and Communications Corp., 1981.

32. Michael Langley, "Expectations vs. Reality in Atlanta," *Community Television Review*, July 1981, pp. 28–29.

The Manager
As Communicator

9

A gruff but personable sort who speaks his mind, Mr. Garvin is nonetheless a consummate pragmatist. Narrowly defined, his goal is clear, to see that Exxon makes money, but in a broader sense, he must also see to it that the organization keeps adapting to the changing environments in which it operates. In pursuit of that long-range objective, he has assumed an unusually visible profile for an oil executive, going so far as to appear on radio and television talk shows. . . .

Given the traditional public distrust of big business, and the all-but-universal suspicion of big oil, the sandy-haired executive has his hands full.

—Anthony J. Parisi,
in *The New York Times Magazine*

A NEW AGE

American business people have not gone out of their way to embrace the principles of communications management, nor do they particularly enjoy learning how to practice them. But, if nothing else, they are, like Mr. Garvin, pragmatists.

They realize the cold facts of the current environment:

- The urgent need to reorient the American business culture to compete in an international business marketplace has put new emphasis on improving worker productivity and effectiveness.
- Deregulation is changing the business environment for financial institutions, communications, hospitals, and other sectors of the economy.
- American society is changing. People are becoming less heirarchical, more interested in "contributing" than just "working," more entrepreneurial, less corporate, more media savvy.
- Society's expectations for business have increased in the past decade, and the lines between what is "private" and what is "public" have blurred. Also solutions to social and economic problems developed by the public sector have become discredited.

- The general level of public understanding of business issues has increased with concern over the economy.
- Major developments are underway in telecommunications, which will soon improve business communications, at the same time making business leadership more visible and involved in field operations.

Managerial adaptation to communications problems has been to a great extent reactive. Change is effected only following a crisis. It wasn't until business came under attack on various consumer, environmental, and social-justice fronts that it began to understand the importance of public affairs.

It wasn't until the oil embargo and the negative public outcry that followed that the oil industry began upgrading communications strategies.

Even when companies have anticipated communications problems they have not always fared well. Mobil Oil, which has organized itself strategically and spent lavishly on public affairs, still has not learned how to meld *what it says* with *what it does*. It sends mixed messages, too often communicating with its heart and not its head.

Yet it is not easy to judge communications management. Often its practice is more an art than a science, as delivering lines with good timing always has been. And the stage of public events is more theater in these days of mass media than many have realized.

IN SUMMARY

This book has endeavored to lay out a framework for understanding the principles and practices of effective communications management. First and foremost, it has emphasized that *the basis of all effective communications is the believability of the person or organization speaking.*

Without credibility a company's words will sound, to quote St. Paul, like "tinkling brass." But the problem of credibility is generic to the institution of business in America as well. The mass media, especially pulp novels and Hollywood movies, dwell on the negative in portraying American business.

Once the precept of credibility is understood, the board of directors should develop a strategic vision, a vision that relates not only to the economic future of the firm but to its societal role as well. It is from this strategic vision that the chief executive and his or her staff will establish policies upon which an effective communications program can be built.

Aspiring managers must understand this theoretical model and apply it to their own business organizations, evaluating the weaknesses and strengths of their firms in the areas of credibility, vision, and policy. A certain check on the success of the communications programs is to take a reading of that firm, its *credibility* and *image* in the marketplace, to look from the outside in.

The nuts-and-bolts fundamentals of communications management take place at the staff level where programs are developed to implement corporate policy. That policy should be directed at both *internal* and *external* communications activities. Internal relates to the economic mission of the firm; external, to the noneconomic issues. The thesis here is that attention to external issues—government relations, issues management, advocacy advertising and the like—can also affect the economic mission of the firm, at least at the margin. A firm that attempts to be active in the marketplace of ideas can only benefit in the long run in the new public environment.

In looking at the practice of communications management, we have described reasons for the cat-and-mouse relationship that has developed between the press and business. At the same time, if there is one area of communications where there are some hopeful signs, it is with this relationship. The major stumbling block remaining is the problem of dealing with the electronic medium, specifically television news. Evidence shows, however, that business people are learning how to handle themselves in front of a camera, which is fortunate, since the coming telecommunications revolution will put more and more business leaders in front of more and more television cameras.

We have also attempted to deal with two particularly difficult communications issues that affect the firm: *financial* communication and *crisis* communication. Until adequate research explains how the firm is properly valued, it will be necessary, especially in the current takeover environment, to diligently work to communicate a corporate vision and to nurture stockholders.

Crisis management is another serious problem. The sudden death of a chief executive, a plant explosion, a surprise lawsuit by the government, all are examples of unexpected calamity that can befall any firm. A key strategy here is for management to sit down and "imagine" many possible types of disasters and establish specific methods and lines of communication for dealing with them.

In a brief overview of the new technologies and some of their potential effects, we have shown that awareness will be required of all managers as we enter the final years of this century. The new technologies will dramatically change the nature of international business as markets and field operations become interconnected by satellites. The coming "global village" and "electronic cottage" will alter management principles dramatically. It is not too early for managers to begin developing scenarios that address these new worlds.

Our overall message is that managers must master communications principles and techniques. It is clear that recent events have *pushed* communications into the forefront and that the future is *pulling* it to an even more prominent role in corporate management. Consequently greater emphasis should be placed on evaluating how communications management can support corporate operations in the future.

Below is a series of questions developed by Hay Associates to help managers assess their communications programs:

		YES	NO
A.	**Policy**		
	1. Is there a written policy supporting sound communications, known to your organization?	☒	☐
	2. Does the policy provide for two-way communication in fact?	☒	☐
	3. Does the policy have management's active support?	☒	☐
	4. Does the policy commit the organization to sincerity, honesty, and frankness?	☒	☐
	5. Are the objectives stated clearly?	☒	☐
	6. Does *one* individual have the overall responsibility for administering the policy?	☐	☒
B.	**Program**		
	1. Is there a written procedure to implement the policy?	☐	☒
	2. Do all communication activities and media conform to the policy and are they coordinated?	☒	☐
	3. Are the policy and program reviewed regularly for correctness and effectiveness?	☒	☐
	4. Does top management take an active part in the program?	☒	☐
C.	**Delegation of Authority**		
	1. Is there a published organization chart so that channels are understood?	☒	☐
	2. Are accountabilities defined?	☒	☐
	3. Do supervisors know their accountabilities for relaying information up and down the line?	☐	☒ – *Varies*
D.	**Keeping the Supervisory Organization Informed**		
	1. Are supervisors given advance information about the organization's plans and progress?	☒	☐
	2. Are supervisors given the "why" of all matters transmitted directly or through them to employees so that they can discuss the subjects intelligently and answer questions?	☒	☐
	3. Is there a specific method for keeping top management regularly informed about employee thinking and rumors?	☐	☒ *various methods*
	4. Do supervisors meet regularly with employees for discussions?	☒	☐
	5. Is there a clear understanding between the employment department, the training department, and the supervisor as to what the new employee is told and who is responsible for telling him or her?	☒	☐
	6. Is there a check list of items to be covered with new employees?	☒	☐
	7. Are employees encouraged to seek information from their supervisors?	☒	☐
	8. Are supervisors trained to transmit information to employees and answer their questions?	☒	☐
	9. Are bulletins given to supervisors before they are placed on bulletin boards?	☐	☒ *not always*
	10. Are there regular management meetings?	☒	☐

11. Do supervisors meet with each of their subordinate supervisors on a regular schedule? ☑ ☐

12. Is there a procedure for getting supervisors' ideas on labor contract improvements? ☑ ☐

13. Are supervisors advised immediately of important grievance settlements and contract interpretations? ☑ ☐

14. Is there a supervisor's manual for ready reference on all important problems? ☐ ☑ *seven manual*

15. Is there a manual of policies and procedures which is kept up-to-date, and is it available to all supervisors? ☑ ☐

E. The Personnel Department's Accountability

1. Is the Personnel Department's accountability for communications defined? ☑ ☐

2. Are communications duties delegated clearly within the Personnel Department? ☑ ☐

3. Does the Personnel Department function in such a way that it facilitates communication through the line, rather than causing short circuits? ☑ ☐

4. Does the Personnel Department keep the management organization informed on important activities and trends in personnel and labor relations matters? ☑ ☐

5. Is the Personnel Officer a party to major policy decisions? ☑ ☐

F. Appealing to Employees' Interests

1. Are employees' basic wants and interests (security, recognition, fair wages, opportunities to advance) considered in determining what information to present to the organization? ☑ ☐

2. Are employees given information about:
   —total compensation (base salary, benefits, incentive compensation)? ☑ ☐
   —opportunities for advancement? ☑ ☐
   —internal or external training opportunities? ☑ ☐

G. Information about the Business

1. Are employees given information about:
   —background and philosophy of the organization? ☑ ☐
   —the use of services or products—where, by whom, and for what? ☑ ☐ *Sometime*
   —the way pay is determined? ☑ ☐ *to some level*
   —the way individual performance is measured? ☑ ☐

2. Are production plans and schedules projected for the organization? ☑ ☐

3. Do employees know the employment plans for the months ahead? ☑ ☐

4. Are organization changes reported to employees before being released to the public press? ☑ ☐

5. Is the standing of the organization in its industry made known to employees? ☑ ☐

6. Are employees told about:
   —organization goals? ☑ ☐
   —building plans? ☑ ☐
   —new products or services in advance? ☑ ☐

—research projects and developments? ☒ ☐ *at time*
—important customers? ☐ ☒
—product or service successes? ☒ ☐
—advertising plans and campaigns, in advance? ☐ ☒

7. Do employees hear frequently about:
   —operating problems? ☒ ☐
   —material shortages, if any? ☒ ☐
   —customer complaints? ☐ ☒
   —the "break-even" point? ☐ ☒
   —sales outlook? ☐ ☒
   —the role of stockholders? ☐ ☐ NA
   —value of advertising? ☐ ☒
   —costs of doing business? ☐ ☒
   —the organization's financial situation? ☒ ☐
   —the significance of productivity? ☒ ☐
   —the organization's competition? ☐ ☒
   —the significance of government regulations? ☒ ☐

8. Do employees understand:
   —the company's philosophy of employee relations? ☒ ☐
   —problems of financing the business? ☐ ☒
   —the importance of profits? ☐ ☒
   —the value of their individual jobs? ☒ ☐

H. Information about Employer–Employee Relations

1. Are the benefits and advantages of employment with the organization often highlighted for employees? ☒ ☐

2. Are new laws, regulations, and interpretations affecting employees explained to the organization? ☒ ☐

3. Are employees aware of efforts to stabilize employment and progress in that direction? ☐ ☒

4. If there is a union, has its place in the communications program been determined? For example, has consideration been given to:
   —giving the union copies and advance notice of communications distributed to employees? ☒ ☐
   —educating union spokespeople on basic economics and company problems in day-to-day discussions and contacts? ☐ ☒

I. General Economics and Business Conditions

1. Are broader issues of our economic system discussed with employees? ☐ ☐

	REGULARLY	OCCASIONALLY	NEVER
—the burden of taxes	☐	☐	☒
—government spending	☐	☒	☐
—our essential freedoms	☐	☐	☒
—the interdependence of big and small business	☒	☐	☐
—machines make jobs	☐	☒	☐
—national labor policy	☐	☒	☐
—the reasons for high standard of living	☐	☒	☐
—the causes of inflation	☐	☒	☐

173

		YES	NO

2. If you use "canned" material, is it supplemented with information regarding its application to your organization? — YES ☒ NO ☐

3. Do you keep employees informed on general business conditions and forecasts? — YES ☐ NO ☒

J. Individual Employee Progress

1. Do employees have written data regarding their job responsibilities? — YES ☒ NO ☐

2. Do employees know what their advancement opportunities are? — YES ☒ NO ☐

3. Is there a periodic performance review of each employee? — YES ☒ NO ☐

4. Is the employee told how he or she stands, what his or her good points are, and in what respects he or she needs to improve? — YES ☒ NO ☐

K. Does the Top Officer of the Organization:

	REGULARLY	OCCASIONALLY	NEVER
—talk with employees in a group?	☒	☐	☐
—meet socially with employees?	☒	☐	☐
—visit informally with employees at their work station?	☐	☒	☐

SOURCE: Hay Associates, 1982.

STRATEGIC QUESTIONS

The strategic issues that corporate planners and aspiring managers should address cut across the spectrum:

1. WHAT IS THE CORPORATE VISION?

• Has the board of directors articulated a mission statement for the firm that commits it to an economic role that benefits society?

• Does the mission statement establish a clear vision of where the company is going?

• Does the mission show that the firm has positioned itself in a way that will allow it to prosper as new communications technologies are introduced?

• How does the corporate vision interface with society's changing expectations for business?

2. WHAT IS THE CORPORATE COMMUNICATIONS POLICY?

• Is senior management committed to implementing effective policies that put the corporate vision to work?

• Through what mechanisms (formal and informal) does senior management establish communications policy?

- What expectations have been established by senior management for communications performance?
- Is senior management anticipating technological innovation in communications or reacting to it?
- Is senior management aware of the firm's constituencies—the financial community, employees, the local community, shareholders, and the general public—and what messages are being sent to each?
- How are those messages being received? How does the corporation "look" from the outside perspective of these groups?

3. What Is the Role of the Communications Manager in the Firm?

- Are the products and activities of the communications staff an accurate reflection of the corporate communications policy?
- What is the status of the senior communications manager?
- What quantifiable performance goals have been established for the communications program and its subelements?
- What improvements could be made in the various components of the communications function—product publicity, financial communications, crisis management, employee relations, and so on?
- Is the function being monitored and evaluated regularly and objectively? What quantitative measures are used?

4. How Does Communications Affect Other Staff and Line Operations?

- Is there a strategy to communicate information that will lead to a correct valuation of the firm's stock?
- Is there a cost-effective marketing/publicity mix for the firm's products?
- Does employee communications take into account the media sophistication of employees?
- Has adequate crisis planning been done for the corporation?
- Is there a central point for intelligence gathering within the firm that cuts across organizational lines?

5. What Impact Will the New Technology Have on the Company?

- What new business opportunities/threats are being created for the firm by the new technology?
- How can new technologies be introduced in a way that minimizes impact on the traditional structure of the organization?
- Can the new technologies be used to cut costs? Improve decision making? Strengthen marketing channels?
- What new business ventures can be tied to the new technologies in communication?

6. What Changes Should the Firm Be Making In Its Communications Department?

- Should the communications function be reorganized?
- Should some new hybrid be developed that melds the communications function (software) with telecommunications (hardware) of the firm?
- Should intelligence gathering be integrated into the communications function?

NEW APPROACHES TO COMMUNICATIONS

In 1983, the Ford Motor Company established a new "Public Affairs Electronic Communications Office" with 20 employees. The time is ripe for companies to begin experimenting with reorganization of the communications function.

It is not too early for corporate planners, academics, and others who are interested in development of the art of management to begin exploring for efficient models that comprehensively address the strategic issues of communications management—from teleconferencing to intelligence collection, from quantitative evaluation to press relations, from takeover defense to issues management.

The management discipline has not yet addressed communications issues in any systematic or comprehensive way. Public relations has been left to practitioners (staff people), and it is only recently that senior management has become involved with "public affairs." The major business schools for the most part have failed to encourage research in communications management, with the exception of interpersonal communications issues handled by organizational-behavior departments.

The problem to be sure is neglect, and it is most easily seen in the haphazard and casual way in which communications has been integrated into corporate activities. In small to mid-sized firms the function is often delegated to managers as part of other duties as assigned: PR to the legal department, financial communications to the treasurer. Yet an enormous amount of corporate resources is spent on communicating with the numerous corporate constituencies. With all the new electronic "toys" telecommunications will make available, it is more crucial than ever for senior management to find comprehensive, logical frameworks for communications that optimize the right *messages* with the right *media* and impose rational management upon the entire process.

Communications is not getting easier. It is getting harder because there are more means available both to send and to receive messages. The packaging and prioritizing of messages for and from the media is becoming a more intricate process that will evolve through trial and error as new technologies are introduced.

MEDIA FOR MANAGERS

Today's managers, as the Chinese curse goes, live in "interesting times." They realize that the road to the top requires the ability to play with a new set of rules—those of an interconnected world, a vast stage upon which they must strut and fret in front of a growing audience.

What strategy for acquiring competence in managerial communications must managers set for themselves in this brave new world?

Here are some suggestions:

1. *Develop interpersonal skills.* If you have trouble expressing yourself orally and/or in writing, work on acquiring that skill. Read books, take courses, and join speaking clubs. Work one on one with a colleague. Learn especially how to handle yourself in front of nonbusiness groups. When the chance arises to communicate under pressure, grab it for the experience. Some firms offer courses that provide just such opportunities.

2. *Become active in community affairs.* The aspiring manager should become involved in community affairs early in his or her career. Usually the young manager spends the first half dozen years or more totally involved in learning the business and climbing the ladder. Time should be set aside for experience in the nonprofit sector, as a volunteer in organizations that are involved in public issues. This type of activity will provide experience in dealing with nonbusiness issues.

3. *Read the papers and watch TV.* This does not mean just the business papers, but general-circulation papers, and if possible the *New York Times.* Every day there are instructive lessons from the stage of public and private life. Watch how people get caught in falsehoods, how politicians posture, how business people act and are portrayed. Also watch television interview shows and dramatizations to understand how business is portrayed. This will aid you in developing the "outside" perspective any really good communicator must have—the ability to stand off and look objectively at what his company does.

4. *Imagine the future.* Learning how to scan the environment for signs about the future is especially important in communications not only regarding technologies on the horizon but also for evaluating public issues that might have an impact on the firm.

5. *Think "credibility."* If information will be the capital of the future, the value of that information will depend on its believability. A personal commitment to sincerity, honesty, and candor—integrity—is fundamental.

At different times, the emphasis in management has been on accounting, finance, marketing, and administration. In the very near future, communications and media will be in the spotlight.

SUMMARY   1. Business people, being pragmatists, are learning the principles of communications management because of changing societal expectations.

2. A manager interested in communications management must ask a number of strategic questions regarding the firm's corporate vision, its communications policies, the role of the communications manager, the impact of new technologies, and the importance of communications to management.

3. The media-oriented manager must learn to develop strong interpersonal skills, become active in the community, keep up with the media, visualize the future, and think in terms of credibility.

Credibility and Propaganda

Below are excerpts from a lecture delivered in 1953 by the former head of Britain's renowned World War II psychological warfare unit, R. H. S. Crossman. The late citizen-activist David Dinsmore Comey, who for many years was a thorn in the side of the nuclear power industry as a consumer advocate, included the notes in an exceptional speech delivered at the Atomic Industrial Forum in Los Angeles in 1975. In that speech, Mr. Comey cited seven rules on effective propaganda developed by Mr. Crossman in a lecture at Oxford. The comments are Crossman's; the headings are Comey's.

1. THE BASIS FOR ALL SUCCESSFUL PROPAGANDA IS THE TRUTH.

It is complete delusion to think of the brilliant propagandist as being a professional liar. The brilliant propagandist is the man who tells the truth, and tells it in such a way that the recipient does not think that he is receiving any propaganda. The art of the propagandist is never to be thought a propagandist, but seem to be a bluff, simple, honourable enemy who would never think of descending to the level of propaganda.

2. THE KEY TO SUCCESSFUL PROPAGANDA IS ACCURATE INFORMATION.

If you give a man the correct information for seven years, he may believe the incorrect information on the first day of the eighth year when it is necessary, from your point of view, that he should do so. Your first job is to build the credibility and authenticity of your propaganda, and persuade the enemy to trust you although you are his enemy.

3. THE MOST SUCCESSFUL PROPAGANDIST IS THE PERSON WHO CARES ABOUT EDUCATION.

The job of propaganda is not merely to enter into some arid debate with the Government of the other side; it is to stimulate in people of the country thought for themselves, to make them begin to be, not cogs in a machine or

179

units of a collective organization, but individuals. Individualism is the first act of disloyalty to a totalitarian government, and every individual who begins to feel he has a right to have a view is already committing an act of disloyalty.

4. TO DO PROPAGANDA WELL, ONE MUST NOT FALL IN LOVE WITH IT.

In the last war the British did better propaganda than any other nation in the world. We British were ashamed of our propaganda and therefore took more trouble to conceal what we were doing. The Russians undoubtedly did the *worst* propaganda during the War, and the Americans in many ways had the failings of the Russians in the propaganda field. The Germans, because they *loved* propaganda, could not do it. Lord Haw-Haw was a disaster to the Germans because he was obviously a propagandist.

5. A SUCCESSFUL PROPAGANDIST CANNOT AFFORD TO MAKE MISTAKES.

Ten good truthful news stories will be cancelled by one mistake. We found this throughout the war with Germany. If one mistake was made about something which the Germans could check, they would write off the rest of our propaganda as lies. Therefore, that which is written about what goes on in an enemy country must not only be checked and double-checked for fact, but it must be written in such a way that it sounds credible to the enemy and not to us.

6. THE PROPAGANDA MUST BE CREDIBLE TO THE OTHER SIDE, NOT YOUR OWN.

If I write a leaflet which members of Parliament will describe as good propaganda, it will probably read as such crude 'propaganda' that it raises the morale of the enemy. In order to make it really credible to the enemy it must sound a long way off from what most members of Parliament regard as the 'good tough stuff' to tell the enemy. All British leaflets were classified as 'secret'. Members of Parliament, if they could have discussed in Parliament what we were saying to the Germans, would have complained that the propaganda organization was 'appeasing' the Germans. It was essential to make the leaflets credible *to a German*—not to the House of Commons.

7. IT IS THE UNDERSTATEMENT WHICH SUCCEEDS BEST.

Our bulletins in German were the most objective sober bulletins of all that were put out by the BBC. We could not afford to be caught in any inaccuracy. The German listeners would not swallow anything, because they were on the lookout to prove us liars. We had to be 101 per cent accurate. We had to claim less than we actually did. There is nothing more effective than saying that there has been a moderately severe raid on Essen, when 2,000 people have actually been killed. That sort of thing gives the enemy cold shivers. The BBC once reported that after a certain mission to the Continent seven British planes had failed to return. The German radio had just described the same incident, stating that five planes had failed to return. In this case we were merely accurate: two planes which the Germans had seen leaving the continent were already crippled and failed to get to England. The psychological effect on the German public, however, was far greater than mere apparent accuracy would ever have achieved. It demonstrated dramatically our capacity to go beyond what was necessary in the direction of candor.

Communications Issues in Public and Not-for-Profit Sectors

More than one-third of the United States GNP is spent by government—federal, state, and local. If expenditures on private education, nongovernmental health-care delivery, and a broad assortment of not-for-profit activities are added to this figure, it turns out that one-half of the nation's expenditures for goods and services flow from public-service institutions.

This appendix explores some of the particular communications issues faced by managers in government and not-for-profit organizations.

GOVERNMENT COMMUNICATIONS POLICY

Communications functions in governmental settings usually are referred to as public-information or public-affairs activities. The history and development of this function are an embarrassment from a professional viewpoint. The reasons for this embarrassment are both laudable and unfortunate. They are laudable in the sense that there is no "ministry of information" in the U.S. and that the Constitutional guarantee of freedom of the press separates the press from government. They are unfortunate because the press on its own does not adequately cover the institution of government, thereby leaving a gap in public knowledge, and politicians and appointed officials jealously vie for the public spotlight, making the information function in government a natural squabbling point. The history of the development of public information at the governmental level in the U.S. reflects a continuing battle between executive agencies and legislators over whether communications activities are a form of bureaucratic enhancement for an appointed official or serve an important function of providing information overlooked by the press.

The battle was first waged publicly in 1908 with the Mondell Amendment when then Secretary of the Interior Gifford Pinchot was attempting to awaken Americans to the need for conservation. Western commercial interests led by Congressman Franklin Mondell pushed through an amendment to a Department of Agriculture appropriation prohibiting use of funds for public relations activities. In 1913 Massachusetts Representative Frank Gillette got an amendment passed that prohibited use of publicity experts in government. That amendment is still on the books today. (The number of public-information people in the federal government today is around twenty thousand.) Public information grew during the two world wars when it became propaganda oriented and its value to government became apparent.[1] During World War II the importance of film in propaganda and information activities was also recognized. (To this day the Defense Department has the government's largest film-making facilities.)

To date, members of Congress and legislators, who use communications techniques to the hilt in getting and staying elected, and news media people, who rely heavily on government public-information activities, regularly attack those government information activities as a waste of tax money. Yet one analysis of twenty-two newspapers has shown that "one-fifth of the stories published in both the foreign affairs and health, education, and welfare fields are traceable in whole or in part to formal releases or statements issued by executive agencies involved."[2]

It is important to divide the activities of government information programs into components. Ray Eldon Heibert has defined four basic activities: *withholding* of information for national security, legal, policy, and other reasons; *releasing* information to communicate information about governmental activities; *staging* of events and announcements to emphasize activities of government; and *persuading* through paid and unpaid advertisements for causes such as army service, prevention of forest fires, and encouraging education.[3]

All but *persuading* are concerned with day-to-day coverage of the affairs of government. *Staging* especially has become more important in the last two decades owing to the increasing public reliance on television, which is very dependent on picture stories. That has resulted in the growth of communications-management activities from the White House on down. There are specialists who develop "opportunities" for media coverage and exposure, others who plan step-by-step "advancing" of public appearances. Make-up people, diction consultants, and advertising experts are all necessary.

Stephen Hess in his 1981 book, *The Washington Reporters*, observes that reporters "resist assignments they think are dull (the departments of agriculture, commerce, and treasury and the regulatory agencies)." He implies that the reporters seem bored easily, especially TV reporters, and that government agencies seem to "repel" reporters. Reporters, he notes, tend to connect with the constantly changing political types and agency heads who come and go every few years, not the permanent government of civil servants. "By not connecting with the permanent government, reporters reinforce the lack of a historical memory in news gathering," he observes, and he quotes the conclusion of former Carter speech writer, James Fallow, that both politicians and reporters "imagine that the world of public life is created anew each day, or at most every four years."[4]

Persuasion more correctly falls into the area of a government propaganda activity. The restraint on advocacy is a general public view that government should not get too involved in regulating the day-to-day life of citizens. So while it is acceptable for the government to campaign against smoking, people still want to be able to buy cigarettes. The government can advocate energy conservation, but people balk at the fifty-five-mile-per-hour limit and rebel against "gas guzzler" taxes on autos.

Journalist Edward Cowan has raised reporters' concerns that advocacy should be kept out of certain information activities—that government tampering with such things as employment statistics or energy forecasts for political purposes is wrong.[5]

INFORMATION AND
ADVOCACY: AN EXAMPLE

In the first two years of its existence as a government agency at the start of the 1970s, the U.S. Environmental Protection Agency allocated to its public-information function a yearly budget of nearly $5 million. This budget reflected the need of Congress and the executive branch to get aboard an issue that had swelled rapidly in public support in just a few years and had necessitated quick institutional response in American society.

The information staff of the new agency had been thrown together from five programs that had been located in various federal agencies. New people were brought in, including a top GOP polling expert, to get the program moving. It was a fascinating mix of nearly 125 people—bureaucrats, outdoors enthusiasts, ex-newspaper people, campaign workers, and corporate PR people. An exceptional press staff, complete with advancemen and speech writers, was formed. On the first anniversary of the agency, an agencywide teleconference was held with audio feedback from each of ten regional offices. Later hundreds of thousands of dollars would also be spent on "citizen-participation" programs, an effort spurred by activists to get a supportive but generally apathetic public charged up about such technical issues as regional water-quality planning, building of sewage-treatment plants, and industrial permit challenges. It was a period of great experimentation in communication between people and government. Much of the environmental legislation of the seventies can probably be traced to the strong relationship between government policy-makers, public information officials, and citizen activists and an attractive public issue. And yet, throughout this entire period, and even now, there is still no clear national legislation regarding the extent to which government should get involved in advocacy. (Witness the still schizophrenic federal policy regarding cigarettes—with one branch of government involved in encouraging people not to smoke while another branch is involved in encouraging the growth and production of tobacco.)

EPA's efforts, mostly in the area of persuasion or advocacy, reached well beyond what most people might have expected. One of the problems in advocacy, at EPA as well as most other public agencies, is that the efforts were never correlated quantitatively with needs ascertained through opinion sampling. As a matter of fact, public opinion throughout the seventies and into the eighties, consistently showed strong public support for environmental protection by the government. Whether or not EPA ever engaged in advocacy may not have mattered. Information activities during much of the early to mid-seventies resulted in strong and at times unquestioning press coverage. Strong credibility achieved early on by high quality appointees sustained that coverage. But advocacy needs for program goals (auto tuneups, water planning, strong state programs) were never really evaluated.

POLITICAL AND
PROGRAM PEOPLE

Most governmental communications people at the federal, state, and local level are divided into two distinct classes: (1) political and (2) program.

Political communications people are usually key aides, many times ex-reporters, who served in a campaign or were at the official's last place of employment. They become press contacts, speech writers, political advisers. They usually come and go with an administration. They contrast with program types, who are involved in career positions and often work in more routine public information activities, such as advocacy, producing leaflets and brochures, answering the mail, producing public-service spots, and publishing newsletters. In business terms, the program people are much like product publicity specialists who support marketing efforts; the political communications people function like corporate policy officials. The line public information people in government are involved in supporting the legally mandated responsibilities of the organization, while the political communications people are concerned about the political survival and enhancement of the elected or appointed person they work for. The problem here is that "the line between the need to inform as a public service and the desire to gain popular support for political objectives has never been satisfactorily delineated."[6]

For example, on assuming office, the Reagan administration immediately attempted to impose strong political control over government information activities as a means of cost cutting but also, some suspect, as a way to centralize as much as possible all government information activities. This is typical of all new administrations.

On the program side, Deputy Budget Director Edwin Harper asked taxpayers in early 1981 "who receive [examples] in the mail or otherwise learn about the wasteful activities by federal public relations departments to mail samples to him care of "Flics & Flacs," Office of Management and Budget, Washington, D.C. "Flics" referred to wasteful government movies and "flac[k]s" a negative reference to PR people. In addition, a moratorium was slapped on the production of new audiovisual materials. Previous abuses he cited included two Defense Department films, one costing $70,000, the other $100,000, both on the same subject of spotting spies. He noted that there were already twenty-two other films on the same topic. Another example was dissemination of fifty thousand copies of a pamphlet on "Dried Flower Arranging," plus others on mulching, auto rust, and new-car purchasing. Harper's program was backed up by a presidential statement that declared that "controlling spending on public relations, publicity, and advertising is an important contribution to our overall goal of cutting out waste in the federal government."[7] Unfortunately, many worthwhile information activities including consumer information on topics such as energy savings were reduced during this period as well.

While information activities were being trimmed, the new administration also moved quickly to install its appointees into top public-affairs positions. In addition, a special media-coordination unit was installed at the White House to plan news management for both the president and all cabinet members. Emphasis was placed on plugging press leaks and preventing "multiple voices" from speaking out on issues. The new administration installed a specific issues-management operation to track voter concerns and weave them into speeches, appearances, and campaign strategy for all administration officials. Utilizing grassroots mobilization machinery developed during the campaign, the administration could generate a letter blitz with the flick of a computer key to bring aboard a reluctant member of Congress in support of legislative proposals. This machinery worked superbly during the first round of budget cuts in the summer of 1981.[8]

LACK OF PROFESSIONALISM

The political attitude that dominates senior management of most public bodies in the U.S. tends to undermine professionalism among communications personnel. One explanation for this is that the rapid turnover in organizational management results in an infusion every two or four years of senior managers who are new to government and either have only private-sector backgrounds or come from a political arena where PR has been associated solely with election activities. In both cases it is hard to understand the need for public-information activities in support of program goals.

At the federal level this problem is compounded by an amazing lack of understanding of the public-information function in the government's own human resources management agency, the Office of Personnel Management (OPM). The personnel standards used to decide the grade of public-information officers were last revised in 1961. A 1980 attempt by OPM to update the standards resulted in a torrent of criticism because it was perceived as a ploy to downgrade the function to a series of mechanical skills. The standards, as they exist, do not take into account the changes in society that have influenced both public and private sectors in the last twenty years. While staying away from serious evaluation of positions in engineering or law, the OPM, like Congress and the press, finds it easier to go after public-information personnel. As one writer notes, "Government public-information work is no more socially acceptable as a legitimate function of government than it was forty years ago."[9]

Besides these problems, a public-information professional must often face hostile fellow bureaucrats in attempting to carry out his or her duty. A public agency is visible by its very status. But bureaucrats by nature are usually just the opposite.

Having suffered through endless reorganizations and changes in leadership and priorities, they abhor visibility. They have learned to keep their heads low. Getting these people to cooperate in public-information activities is difficult, if not impossible.

Other problems facing public-information officials include red-tape procedures that can impede creative efforts. A film bid that is the low bid, for example, is accepted, no matter what the quality of the vendor. Also government information programs, unlike marketing or advertising operations, often must generally rely on public-service time for advocacy. This situation may deteriorate over time as deregulation of broadcast media eliminates public affairs and public-service programming requirements. In addition, unless approved by the OMB, agencies are generally prohibited from doing public-opinion sampling or market research. Compounding these problems is the fact that despite millions annually spent on public information nobody, at least at the federal level, has ever established any evaluation standards relating to public affairs or information activities. The General Accounting Office has stated:

> Evaluating public affairs activities has been, and still is, difficult because Government agencies do not uniformly define 'public affairs' and are not consistent in reporting and evaluating their public affairs costs. Campaigns—those promotional efforts which emphasize specific issues over a specific period—also are not uniformly defined and evaluated.[10]

PRESS COVERAGE

A sustaining interest by the fourth estate in the affairs of government has kept the "sunshine" of public exposure coming through the windows of government in this country. The affairs of local, state, and federal government have been covered with increasing sophistication throughout the years. Government is a traditional hunting ground for investigative reporters, and the Pulitzer Prize frequently is given for a series of stories on government corruption.

Press coverage of governmental affairs often makes up for the crippled public-information operations of many departments. The coverage given to governmental affairs is substantial, though it tends to concentrate on politics. The type of credible coverage afforded public bodies cannot be bought by the private sector. On the other hand, a governmental body or agency that tries to bar the press at the door or is generally uncooperative and unresponsive will find itself with little public sympathy when changes occur. Also, an agency that is not responsive to public scrutiny is perceived as trying to hide something and such a "red flag" is an invitation for an enterprising reporter. As in business, credibility is the key to organizational survival, although it is a lesson that public officials continue to forget.

There are those who maintain that there will always be a certain suspicion of governmental officials among reporters. Hunter Thompson, the political writer for *Rolling Stone*, summed it up crudely but accurately when he once noted that all politicians consider reporters "swine" and all reporters consider politicians "crooks." The verve of reporters for real investigative reporting seems to have waned since Watergate, but the long view is that the healthy disrespect of press for politician and vice versa is beneficial to the public.

The real difference between business and government press coverage is however that *the public has a fundamental right to know what government is up to*. This is forgotten time and time again by both bureaucrats and elected or appointed individuals.

GOVERNMENT MEDIA GAMES

The election process in the United States is based on ability to dominate the media through advertising and press coverage. Once a politician attains office, the need and desire for press coverage to sustain image and name recognition becomes easier by virtue of control of that office. One of the classic portraits on this subject was captured by Joseph Nocera of the *Washington Monthly* in a 1978 article titled "How to Make the Front Page,"[11] Nocera described an aging senator who suddenly found himself in a tough reelection fight because he had spent too much time during his career "being a nice guy and doing good things" for his constituents and not enough on his image. This was the wrong approach, said Nocera. "You've got to be out front, hopping on the issues, demanding investigations, railing at recalcitrant witnesses, declaring, observing, challenging, contending, emphasizing."

It was Nocera's contention that the political ability to make news and grab headlines is instinctive. He noted how some senators grabbed headlines by letting word get around that they answered their own phones, by tearing off doors to their offices, and by telling reporters they despaired of the institution they had just been elected to and were thinking of resigning, just after arriving in Washington. "That kind of shameless, get-press-at-any-cost attitude can't be taught," said Nocera. But he went on to note that there are certain techniques that can be learned.

One rule, he said, is to forget about standards, which means not to worry about getting one's name in a national publication so long as there is some coverage. This public official wants his name in the paper, no matter which one. Some years back, a memo went up on the bulletin board of one of the Chicago newspapers warning reporters to check with the editing desk before calling a certain congressman for a quote on weekend stories. This memo was issued after the congressman ended up being quoted in three stories on different topics one Saturday. He knew weekend papers were "light" on news.

Another suggestion from Nocera is to go to the White House—where the press corps hangs out—often and elbow into such events as bill signings. "Lifestyle" coverage is another way to get in the press. Taking up jogging or building a big kitchen was the approach of the seventies. In the eighties it is living lavishly and throwing big parties.

One of the best ways to get headlines is to run a committee or a subcommittee, says Nocera, or to establish a policy organization when leaving office. It's a good base for grabbing headlines. In conducting hearings, Nocera suggests a "curtain-raiser," that is, releasing an opening statement early Sunday evening, which details the reason for Monday morning's hearing.

Another Nocera suggestion is, "Go to the scene of the crime." In early 1981 Labor Secretary Raymond Donovan joined federal investigators closing in on sweatshops around the country, in order to garner headlines. A press release from his office described the "event":

> The drunk on the trash-strewn sidewalk barely lifted his head as the unmarked van pulled up in front of a loft in Manhattan's Chinatown.
> Crouched inside the van, Secretary of Labor Raymond J. Donovan and a team of his wage-and-compliance officers were about to investigate sweatshop conditions in the garment factories above. . . . Donovan, the compliance officers, and their Chinese-speaking interpreter bypassed the broken elevator and raced up the stairs. They fanned out to two separate floors of the building. It was time to go to work.[12]

Still another technique—a very effective one—is to provide news pegs. Nocera mentions one congressman who keeps his staff busy going through various government reports to find information, especially statistics, that would make a good story. And, says Nocera, "use the electronics"—such as telecopiers, radio-tape machines that feed voice automatically to stations for use on the news.

For television, he says, feed the right questions to reporters, use snappy quotes, personalize the story for each station, say it all in thirty seconds, and know station deadlines. Finally, Nocera suggests, "Be a leaker." According to Nocera's strategy, if one leaks regularly to a paper, the paper won't be so inclined to investigate its source later. One of the best techniques, he suggests, is to cultivate a source for leaks in an agency and then leak the information personally, which wins chits and helps get the reporter an "investigative" story.

Some reporters who might pooh-pooh press releases relish leaks. Nocera sees leaks as just another way of releasing information.

Nocera's tongue-in-cheek rules for getting press coverage are often bizarre but are all based on real-life examples. Some are applicable only to elected officials.

The cardinal rule for managing public-information activities in government is the same as for business: Tell the truth. Says Eileen Shanahan, an old Washington pro, who ran public affairs at HEW and worked at the *New York Times* and the *Washington Star*: "It's perfectly okay to put your best foot forward . . . to accentuate the positive and maybe not to tell the negative unless asked. That's within the rules. But to lie or misrepresent is unacceptable." She suggests that inevitably public relations people in government serve as "advocates" for their agencies. "I am not personally concerned about an army of government public-affairs people," she says, "There may be some short-term manipulation. If the press is lazy, it gives the PR advocate an advantage." She cautions government officials against taking cold calls from the press. She thinks the public-information officer ought first to find out what the reporter wants to know.[13]

ADVOCACY

A major question about government programs advocating behavior changes in the population is simply, do they work?

According to the General Accounting Office,[14] the following questions are not answered in even the best evaluated government public-affairs programs:

1. How does each funding request relate to past and future efforts?
2. How is the amount of promotion to be used determined?
3. What management structures have been considered to best achieve program objectives?

For example, from 1972 through 1977, the Department of Health, Education and Welfare spent $5.8 million on a national effort to increase public awareness of high blood pressure and to reduce the number of people who have it. Statistics showed that between 1970 and 1975 the stroke death rate in the U.S. decreased by 18 percent, twice the rate of decrease of the previous five-year period. In addition, a 50 percent increase was observed between 1971 and 1976 in the number of visits to physicians for hypertension-related reasons. There *seems* to have been a correlation between the public-information program and the reduction in strokes and visits to doctors, but an accurate evaluation has never been done. Luckily, there were measurable indicators in this instance.

National advocacy programs to get people to stop smoking, prevent forest fires, stay in school, or buy cars that get good gas mileage are more difficult to assess. Would infusion of more federal funds have made a difference in the hypertension campaign? If the agency had been able to advertise rather than having to rely on public-service announcements, would the statistics have been different? Was the amount of perceived impact of the program related to the cost? Was the program cost effective? Against what standard?

These kinds of questions have never really been tackled in government. Yet millions of dollars are spent each year by government agencies for advocacy efforts. Some have wondered, for example, about the millions of dollars in free television time allocated by the networks to the Advertising Council to urge urban residents to prevent forest fires, while cities were losing population to suburbs because of bad housing policies, high disease rates, crime, and poor schools. General Accounting Office studies of government information and advocacy programs have found repeatedly that agencies generally are not required to establish goals for their information programs. Also agencies tend to be less than candid about their expenditures in the public-information area because of the traditional hostility of Congress. For example, in a 1975 study of the Agriculture Department, the GAO noted that the department differentiated between offices involved in "public information" and "public affairs." The rationale given by the department was that public-information offices explained agriculture programs to the public and therefore were not included in public-affairs expenses. What then was public affairs?

Another hazy area is the definition of *advertising*. The Office of Management and Budget regards advertising as *paid* time or space in the print and broadcast media to promote government activities and services ("Join the People Who Joined the Army," for example.) GAO, on the other hand, puts public-service announcements into this category.

The blood pressure awareness program mentioned earlier got higher marks from the GAO than the antismoking campaign did. The blood pressure program had been managed by a private contractor who was responsible for (1) managing an information center and (2) assisting in the development of several other program components such as professional education and media activities.

The cost of that program in 1978 was $1.8 million. Public-service messages were developed by the Advertising Council and cost about $200,000 per year. The program also coordinated special projects like the National High Blood Pressure Month and a program for federal employees. The blood pressure program's strength was that it did have a *primary measurable objective*—to reduce the number of people having high blood pressure from 4.8 million to 2.4 million. Planning and evaluation studies to develop strategies were formulated according to such parameters as general knowledge about hypertension, physician attitudes, life insurance costs, and hiring practices.

When data indicated that *awareness* did not necessarily result in effective hypertension control, the program increased emphasis on public, patient, and professional education. From this study GAO concluded that information and education campaigns need four key elements to succeed:

1. *Objectives.* Information campaigns should have clear objectives that can be achieved at a reasonable cost. Meaningful objectives are also important in determining program success.

DEVELOPING PUBLIC INFORMATION CAMPAIGNS

I. **Establishing Objectives**
   A. *Legitimacy*. Does the organization have the authority to pursue the objectives?
      1. Is the campaign related to the organization's mission? If so, how?
      2. Is the campaign mandated by law?
   B. *Specificity*. Are objectives adequately described so that progress toward and achievement of the objectives can be determined?
      1. Are the objectives quantitative?
      2. Are the objectives qualitative?
   C. Relationship with cost and other program objectives
      1. Have the objectives been developed with adequate knowledge and consideration of program cost and costs associated with the problem?
      2. Have the objectives been developed with adequate knowledge and consideration of other program objectives?
   D. What are the objectives?
      1. Agency recruiting.
      2. To educate and/or modify behavior such as high blood pressure and smoking.
      3. Promotion of government objectives such as pollution control and sale of savings bonds.
      4. To inform or advise such as those eligible for Federal assistance.

II. **Planning the Campaign**
   A. Targeting
      1. The more precisely the intended audiences are identified, the better will be the specific messages based on audience knowledge, attitudes and behavior, and media habits. Has the intended audience been adequately determined?
         a. Should the audience be general?
         b. Should the audience be a narrow segment of the population?
         c. Can selected audiences be prioritized?
      2. How was the target audience established?
         a. How was the prevalence of the problem determined?
   B. Timing
      1. What should the lifespan be?
         a. Should the campaign be finite or continuous?
         b. If continuous, at what level of effort?
      2. Have incremental steps or milestones been established?
   C. Budgeting
      1. What is the basis of resource estimates?
         a. Based on budget constraints?
         b. Based on amount of effort needed?
   D. Campaign methods
      1. Is there a strategy developed which specifies a coordinated approach for each segment of the target audience?
      2. Will alternative strategies, concepts, and approaches be pretested in the planning stages? If so, how?
      3. What media will be used?

        a.   What products will be used for each media?

        b.   How has it been determined that the selected media and product will be successful?

    4.   What other communication efforts will be used?

        a.   Intermediary channels such as community and professional organizations.

        b.   Education channels.

    5.   Will other interpersonal approaches, such as workshops and seminars, be used?

    6.   Have the potential barriers to effectiveness been identified and countermeasures planned?

    7.   Is an outside contractor being used to support the campaign? If so, why?

        a.   What is the nature and cost of contractor support?

  E.   Availability of similar information

    1.   Has there been an effort to determine if materials and products are already in existence?

        a.   At the National Audio Visual Center?

        b.   At the Government Printing Office?

        c.   At the Consumer Information Center?

        d.   At private organizations?

III. **Monitoring and controlling campaigns**

  A.   Is there in-process feedback on the campaign?

  B.   Where does control reside?

    1.   Public affairs management?

    2.   Program management?

IV. **Campaign effectiveness evaluation**

  A.   Is there a planned evaluation effort?

    1.   What is the nature and extent of the evaluation of goal achievement and adequacy of campaign strategies?

    2.   Are any forms of product testing planned?

  B.   What are the major external influences and how have they been accounted for?

  C.   How is effectiveness evaluation tied into feedback information for campaign control?

SOURCE: Government Accounting Office, 1979.

2. *Audience targeting.* The more precisely the intended audience is identified, the more closely the specific messages will be based on audience knowledge, attitudes, and behavior and media habits.

3. *Information channels.* To deal with complex issues that may require a change in attitude or behavior (carpooling, littering, smoking) often requires a mix of information channels including media, community elements, professional organizations, and interpersonal contact.

4. *Evaluation.* Evaluating the effectiveness of information dissemination can be difficult, especially when such factors as economics, personal attitudes, and behavior are involved. Nevertheless it is important from the outset to establish clearly how information dissemination can be evaluated. Such evaluations can take many forms, from measuring distribution of informational materials to conducting complex studies of behavior changes.

THE PARKS IN HOUSTON/
THE BRIDGES IN MISSOURI

The need for advocacy programs at the state and local levels becomes more apparent as cutbacks in federal support programs, increases in the cost of financing local government, and the tightness of money affect delivery of services. School financing, park acquisition and maintenance, upgrading of a community's capital plant, for example, require a strong advocacy component.

In 1979 the Houston Park Board and other Houston residents realized that the city was growing dramatically, that acreage needed to be created for parks, and that a constituency needed to be created to support these efforts. Obstacles included apathy, lack of public awareness, government emphasis on economic development, and invisibility for the parks board.

The strategy adopted included naming an information and development officer for the board, building visibility with local media, and creating a public identity for the board by emphasizing the background, reputation, and civic involvement of its members.

Speeches to such groups as the Chamber of Commerce, the Junior League, and garden clubs were arranged. Accomplishments of a small low-cost neighborhood park were emphasized. A documentary television show on the history of the parks system and the problems facing it was financed by the board and shown on the local public TV station. In addition, a lobby group of citizens was formed. Local officials up for reelection, including the mayor, were made aware of the issues and solicited for support of an upcoming bond issue.

A brochure aimed at bank trust officers, lawyers involved in wills and trusts, CPAs, and other special groups who might have influence on donations was developed. Enough public interest was created to ensure passage of the bond issue. It also contributed to an improved political climate, as mayoral and council candidates jumped on a now popular bandwagon. 1980 was set aside as "Give a Park to Houston Year," and a major benefit was held. Donations increased as well.[15]

In St. Louis, Fleishman-Hillard Public Relations was asked to get involved in helping pass a statewide bond issue needed to repair unsafe bridges throughout the state. Revenue funds from gas taxes had fallen as consumption of gasoline decreased, and repair costs had escalated. Additionally a proposal for a high-gloss ad campaign one year earlier had been defeated by an eight-to-one margin because of citizen suspicion that road builders were pouring money into the campaign.

Fleishman-Hillard first conducted a statewide poll to see if voters would support the bond issue. Seventy-eight percent said they would, but when voters were asked if the money might be better spent on education, the numbers turned around. It was a vulnerable issue.

The agency elected to launch a low-key, low-profile campaign. *Local* benefits of the program would be stressed. The purpose was to minimize opposition. In order to raise funds for the campaign, Fleishman-Hillard suggested combining the road issue with a water bond amendment also being proposed. Both campaigns would share a budget of $100,000.

Within a two-week period every editor and news director in the state was visited by proponents, who emphasized local benefits. All state legislators were contacted and supplied with poll information showing the 78 percent support figure. Opposition from a number of sources, including the mayor of St. Louis and twenty-three legislators, did arise. But the home-town emphasis continued, with special efforts to persuade local officials to take the lead.

Just before the election, state highway officials made two hundred public appearances. Every city of thirty thousand or more population was visited at least five times, and the professional PR staff concentrated on the two major cities: St. Louis and Kansas City. During the final two weeks stories were placed emphasizing school-bus detours to avoid bridges, potential loss of federal funds if the amendment did not pass, impact on tourism, and the poll results. The issue passed with support from 73 percent of those voting. Most important, the state legislature read the results as a mandate for future appropriations.[16]

PUBLIC OPPOSITION

The Missouri bridge program emphasized the importance of picking the right strategy in dealing with a public issue. One problem that has vexed officials at all governmental levels in the past two decades has been how to achieve effective community consensus to implement public policy.

Proposition "2½" in Massachusetts, Proposition 13 in California, and similar campaigns have been among the more recent efforts by small groups that have achieved amazing success in stopping government dead in its tracks. The City of Chicago was stopped in efforts to build a crosstown expressway; highways in San Francisco, Milwaukee, and other cities were left dangling in the air after citizens dug their heels in and said no to governmentally supported projects. Nuclear power plants, highways, mass transit, sewage-treatment plants—major public-works projects—have been stopped or delayed because of public opposition. In the coming years such opposition may extend to the siting of hazardous waste disposal areas, urban redevelopment efforts, and energy conversion facilities.

The contentious nature of public feelings regarding such projects are the result of years of governmental abuse by "visionary" urban planners, engineers, and elected officials who tore down neighborhoods, put up expressways and housing projects, and otherwise chewed at the urban fabric without regard for public opinion or community well-being. Increasing sophistication by community groups and individuals in dealing with these nightmares bred a generation of sophisticated citizens who learned how to manipulate the political and legal process in order to halt proposed projects.

The general economic downturn of the past few years plus the worn condition of the physical plant of many cities and drastic cuts in public-works projects have somewhat abated public resistance to capital projects, but the lessons learned in the recent past are not easily forgotten.

Part of the trouble comes from the realization that legislative bodies have delegated an enormous amount of decision-making authority to government agencies and bureaucrats in the implementation of programs and projects. Highway improvements, regional shopping centers, downtown revitalization, and water-quality planning are left to government officials, allowing them wide latitude in such areas as site selection and condemnation. Officials try to concentrate on implementation but find themselves spending hours, days, and months dealing with citizen groups, neighborhood groups, and dissident politicians instead of planning, engineering, and supervision.

A group of civic-minded persons in Colorado in the mid-sixties attempted to bid on the 1976 Winter Olympics. But the plans came to a halt when a coalition of community groups banded together and got out a *no* vote on a referendum to finance the project. Their issue: environmental impact. Officials have learned that while it is often difficult to get a project approved and going, it is easy— sometimes amazingly so—for a small group to come in and veto that project. And many times that veto is not exercised until late in the game.

A number of behavioral scientists have developed strategies that can help agencies to move ahead with their projects and deal effectively with citizen complaints and problems at the same time. Such efforts are lumped under the umbrella term *citizen participation* or *public participation*. Techniques that have evolved range from organizing coopted advisory committees, printing slick publications, and running public hearings to more sophisticated approaches such as setting up field offices identifying all potentially affected interests, monitoring media, and hiring advocates to represent the negative viewpoint in the development process. It is very difficult for professionals—in any work situation—to let the public watch over their shoulders while they work.

Developing alternatives for public consideration, holding community meetings, and anticipating possible problems are all distasteful tasks. However, the potential "veto" that groups or individuals can use to stop a project mandates just that sort of approach.[17] The private sector is not totally immune from this process either. U.S. Steel, in developing a site near Conneaut, Ohio, for a possible new major steel-making facility, spent three years and more than $3 million laying the groundwork for the mill, eventually scrapped for economic reasons. Most of the site location work dealt with potential environmental impact, and great care was taken to involve as many parties as possible as early as possible so that when the approval came the plant could proceed without interruptions.

Behavioral scientists involved in public-participation strategies believe that the key factor involved is, once again, credibility—that an agency that undertakes reasonable efforts to deal with all potentially affected parties in a fair and just manner can be successful, even if some parties are more adversely affected than others. If a person feels a decision is being imposed without an opportunity for involvement in that decision-making process, then he or she is likely to react negatively.

An agency that chooses the best course of action from a list of alternatives essentially has made a *political* decision. The extent to which the decision has been politically achieved will determine whether there has been a good public-participation process or not. Part of the background problem is citizen apathy. Most people won't get involved until they see surveyers setting down little sticks with yellow ribbon in front of their homes. Only at that point will they realize the significance of the issue. That's when citizen action starts.

Public officials who understand these facts of life can at least attempt to neutralize them. But they have to be flexible and willing to seek out those potentially affected, listen to them, and if necessary, modify plans.

Some suggestions for managing public-participation issues include avoiding confrontation, training the staff to deal with the public, minimizing public relations ploys, dealing with truly affected people. (Don't think the mayor necessarily represents every interest in the community.) Defining issues too narrowly and being insensitive to the power needs of organizational leaders are frequent pitfalls.

These tactics are not easily accomplished. They are time consuming and often expensive (the Corps of Engineers used to allocate up to 10 percent of a project's cost to citizen-participation efforts), difficult to relate to a technical process, and hard to impose in a bureaucracy.

MARKETING IN GOVERNMENTAL AGENCIES

Many governmental agencies have dabbled in marketing activities.[18] Some prominent federal examples include efforts of the Defense Department to build an all-volunteer army, post office programs to encourage consumers to use certain priority mail programs and zip codes, and the ill-fated effort of the Treasury Department to gain acceptance for the Susan B. Anthony dollar.

At the local level, many municipalities have used sample surveys to obtain information regarding voter priorities for delivery of services. In other cases, marketing has been used to sell the citizenry on programs, such as new bond issues. In some instances, de-marketing has been used to reduce demands for services, such as welfare.

Generally, however, government managers shy away from "marketing." They see it as a business-oriented process. Government managers try to formulate policy that avoids risk rather than searching out opportunities—that is, they pursue reactive rather than proactive policies. At the same time many governmental agencies are concerned with the need to economize in provision of services and to face shifting "client" groups. These situations can benefit from marketing. Activities such as cutting programs, targeting problems more effectively, shifting programs to other agencies, and forecasting of future needs and responses can be aided by use of marketing research.

An example: A fire department in the Midwest was faced with budget problems. It lacked sufficient equipment and manpower to serve its level of demand. Using market segmentation and planning, the department developed fire-prevention and safety programs tailored to user segments: increased fire-prevention programs in high-risk buildings and industrial areas. It was thus able to reduce demand for services.

Not all government agencies benefit from marketing. The ones that do are those that can effectively use the private sector for delivery of services, those that provide different services to different market segments, those in fluid environments with rapidly changing client needs, those that have unpopular programs or high amounts of discretionary resources, and those that are well managed and can integrate marketing into the budget and planning processes.

One of the major impediments to marketing in government is that much of what agencies do is legally mandated and externally imposed. Economic logic and political expediency don't always mesh in such a system. Governmental units normally cannot promote or advertise in the commercial marketplace. They are limited to public-information activities. They cannot experiment with the marketing mix of pricing, delivery systems, promotion, or product development.

Marketing researchers, however, believe that government officials have relied too long on economists, lawyers, and journalists rather than on legitimate research techniques for information. Most politicians feel they know what the public wants, but studies have shown government officials tend to underestimate citizen support for taxes or their level of satisfaction for services by as much as 20 percent.

IMPROVING
NOT-FOR-PROFIT
MANAGEMENT

The big budget cuts in the not-for-profit sector in the early eighties renewed interest in improving management of this area. Business people who previously had spent anywhere from 1 percent to 10 percent of their pretax dollars in support of this sector have been deluged with requests to fill the gaps left by government spending cuts. That has increased business's concern for upgrading the general management of not-for-profit activity.

James Beré, chairman and chief executive of Borg-Warner Corporation, said that during this period it was important for business to "better define" its own philanthropic goals as well. Beré noted that even with cutbacks by government, business would continue to pour billions into social activities. In 1980, for example, $45 billion was claimed on tax returns as "contributions." The problem, said Beré, "is to determine what is being done with [the] money. . . . Perhaps we need to concentrate our resources to assure measurable results." He noted that while organizations continued to bemoan cutbacks, few cited methods they hoped to use to compensate for cutbacks. "More and more of us feel that if our donations are to mean anything, they must be subject to efficiency tests similar to those we demand of our own operations," he warned. He added, "Most grant-seeking organizations offer audited statements but these simply certify that the money was spent and somebody said it was spent."[19]

In the past the not-for-profit sector has not considered management skills important. There's the story of the manager of a symphony orchestra who was contacted by a business-school professor and asked if one of the students could work there on a summer internship. "What instrument does he play?" was the response. This thinking is readily apparent in the poor salaries offered to MBA students who seek to work in this sector. Salaries of up to ten thousand dollars a year less than those offered in the private sector are common. In many instances this speaks more to the priorities of the organization than to its financial well-being.

MARKETING NONPROFIT
ORGANIZATIONS

In a pioneering article published in 1969, Kotler and Levy suggested that the concept of marketing should be broadened to include the activities of public and nonprofit sectors.[20]

In recent years, nonprofits and government agencies have moved cautiously yet steadily in this direction. In the educational field, universities faced with rising costs and a dwindling student population have incorporated marketing into their communications programs. Nonprofit hospitals, realizing that more patients are becoming health-care decision makers when it comes to choosing hospitals, are developing programs and services from a marketing viewpoint. Arts organizations such as symphonies, theaters, and prominent museums are embracing marketing strategies to cope with increased competition from other groups, cutbacks in federal funds, and the growing demands for people's time.

In the nonprofit sector, communications has expanded beyond a perceived need for publicity and public relations to a realization that the delivery of a product or service must be integrated into a comprehensive communications program that aims to influence behavior of consumers. Organizations have realized that high visibility obtained through effective public relations must be attached to direct-mail solicitations, fund-raising campaigns, and other marketing efforts. It is in the focusing of communications efforts to marketing that the nonprofit organization reaches a wide range of constituencies: members, funding sources, clients, boards of directors, and more. Also, a nonprofit usually relies on a number of different funding sources, ranging from community leaders to foundation executives to service consumers, and must tailor market- ing efforts in many directions. One of marketing's greatest strengths is its ability to *organize* communications activities into a strategy that seeks to affect behavior.

The accent more than ever is on identifying these key publics, establishing goals for each group, and developing strategies for achieving those goals with effective consumer research.

For example, there is the concept of "belonging" that has been identified as a strategy for bringing in certain groups to support an organization financially. One "belongs" to the museum or symphony "family" and receives special privileges—first place in line at a new exhibit, an opportunity to meet the orchestra at a gala night, an invitation to a private summer picnic at the zoo. Exclusivity, membership, belonging, all for $25 per year.

Colleges have developed this approach extensively. Clubs are established for donors at various contribution levels, football tickets are allocated on the basis of donations, alumni receive regular news about members of their class and what's going on at the alma mater. Invitations are sent out for annual alumni days, where professors are trotted out to titillate the mind on topics ranging from voices in outer space to how to balance a checkbook. Important public figures are given honorary degrees, and the institution basks in the afterglow.

Activist organizations must also be sensitive to their giving constituency. "Stirring things up" with the "system" is important to gain visibility, maintain organizational credibility, and garner financial support from members and foundations. This can mean challenges in the courts, the legislature, and the bureaucracy, but especially in the press. Good press coverage of a crusader leading a charge is a sure sign to contributors that "things are happening."

Labor unions have always been one of the biggest and most important categories of not-for-profits. The traditional strength of labor has been in organizing large numbers of workers to achieve economic and social goals. In the last two decades labor has been a force behind consumer, environmental, and health and safety issues, and at times leaders have been even more commit- ted than the membership. The first attempts at using political action committees to support congressional candidates came out of the labor movement. Labor learned how to use its grassroots strength to lobby Congress. It sent organizers back out into the field to use that grassroots support for social and environmen- tal legislation.

COMMUNICATIONS AND
MARKETING

One of the major needs of not-for-profits is to enhance their PR activities with marketing. A community theater group once decided to expand in a suburb that appeared to have a substantial potential audience.

Enormous publicity was generated to encourage season subscriptions and to get people to attend opening night. The first play, however, was a very highbrow, intellectual duel of words that nobody understood or could get excited about. The theater closed and reopened later with a new name.

The theater group did a fantastic job of PR, but it had not done its marketing homework or researched community preferences. An analogous situation was that of the restaurateur who came into the same community and opened up a "ritzy" restaurant that failed because the community could not support the price level nor provide the number of patrons needed to make it successful. Again, it was essentially a marketing problem that research could have prevented. Philip Kotler in his book on not-for-profit marketing, emphasizes that marketing exists "to sense, serve, and satisfy customer needs. PR exists to produce goodwill in the company's various publics so that these publics do not interfere in the organization's drive to satisfy its customers."[21]

Marketers in not-for-profits, says Kotler, will analyze markets for the organization's services in terms of the public's needs, perceptions, and preferences. They will advise on appropriate services while PR people will handle the problem of communicating with various publics.

In the not-for-profit sector these functions—communications and marketing—are really closely tied since communications provides the tools for marketing, especially free communications.

The publics that an organization must deal with should be identified, then prioritized. Their perceptions of the organization should be measured, and goals should then be established to achieve those goals.

A combination of marketing and public relations efforts was used effectively in the late seventies by little-known Lesley College, which "stands within the shadow" of Harvard University in Cambridge, Massachusetts. Lesley is a complex professional teachers college with many programs, centers, and lab schools. It specializes in pre-elementary- and elementary-teacher training. Administrators of the college felt that if it was to survive in a period of general difficulties for higher education, it must be more visible. A program was developed whose objectives included: (1) providing a public identity, (2) increasing enrollments in a period of teacher-need decline, (3) attracting more funding from public and private sources, (4) increasing placement opportunities for graduates, and (5) boosting innovative programs to maintain its reputation. These objectives were both marketing and PR oriented.

The plan focused on positioning the college as a major spear carrier for improving "economic literacy" in the U.S. The college brought in a special college-oriented PR firm, then sought cooperation of figures such as the president (Jimmy Carter), and prominent Bostonians (Tip O'Neill, Henry Cabot Lodge, Joan Kennedy) to help get national exposure for the issue of economic literacy, an issue that was quite visible at the time. Next a blue-ribbon national advisory board of economists, educators, and industrialists was put together to aid the new program at Lesley: the National Center for Economic Education for

Children. This was all heavily publicized. At the same time market research was employed to determine ways to boost enrollment and retain students and to select the most productive mass media for promoting evening and continuing education programs. A coordinated graphics program was undertaken as well to give the school a cohesive image.

First results of the program included a public launching of the new center by President Carter, with advisory board members in attendance. Major national news coverage followed. The new center provided opportunities to bring many prominent persons to the college to look at its programs. In one year 1,221 press releases went out, 47 ads were placed, and 133 radio spots were aired. The national press covered a Young Writers Conference, a kindergarten conference, and Joan Kennedy's attendance at the graduate school. As a result of this attention, placements jumped to 95 percent, the highest in the nation; new undergraduate enrollment jumped 24 percent; retention was boosted 16 percent. And finally, private gifts and grants went up 287 percent in one year. Also an endowed chair in economics in elementary grades was established—a first.[22] The Lesley program proved that a combination of PR and marketing works well. Almost the whole effort was accomplished under or below a regular budget. The evaluation of the Lesley program was quick and clear. It also shows the importance of a *good idea*. The move from communications to marketing in the nonprofit sector has been pervasive. Organizations are realizing the fact that they have to define their products, determine niches, understand their "customers," and promote accordingly.

This change in the nonprofit sector results from a reorienting of national priorities. A number of trends have been identified as a result of these changes:

- increased public concern over both the credibility and accountability of nonprofits. Does the organization do what it says it does? Are its programs beneficial? Is it believable?
- greater demands on nonprofits in light of cutbacks
- more difficulty in raising funds
- heavier emphasis on direct mail, television, advertising and image
- greater pressures for good management
- increased competition from other groups with similar goals
- increased emphasis on marketing and goal setting.[23]

University of Illinois Marketing Professor Alan R. Andreasen emphasizes that too many nonprofits use a selling orientation that equates marketing efforts with persuading an audience they ought to accept the offering because it is better than any others, rather than using a product orientation which, according to Andreasen, "involves focusing on an organization's basic offering and a belief that the best marketing strategy for increasing sales is to improve this offering's quality." He comes down on groups that think they know best what the public wants, or who think that if consumers just knew more about the product they would want it, or who are sure that there is just one marketing strategy that works ("you always use a brochure for marketing a university") or who, worst of all, cannot look at their offering from the customer's perspective.[24]

For a long time, the Cincinnati Ballet had that "selling" orientation, running one money-maker each year, "The Nutcracker," and hoping it would offset losses from its "art" offerings. A group of enthusiastic volunteers helped turn the situation around. Said the marketing committee chairman, "When the folks who had been underwriting us so generously over the years said, 'We can't write these checks forever, guys,' we realized we had to go to marketing. We weren't building sufficient audience, pricing, or marketing support to get away from our addiction to 'The Nutcracker.'"

The first step in turning things around was research. The staff and volunteers first developed a list of adjectives from previous reviews that they could use in advertising. They then hired a top-notch designer who developed some highly attractive, unorthodox posters. The posters were also sold publicly. (See Figures A-1 and A-2.) The committee researched the demographics of their audience, mailed out discount coupons to high-potential zip codes that matched those demographics, and inaugurated a series of downtown "brown bag" ballet mini-performances that provided audiences with a $1 preview of an upcoming ballet (as well as a dress rehearsal for the cast). This was a great success. Luckily, some top name national stars like Baryshnikov and Godunov decided to play Cincinnati and this gave the ballet the feel of a "winner." While not out of the woods yet, the Cincinnati Ballet has moved to a product orientation and is now really marketing.[25]

Health care organizations are also turning more and more to the notion of marketing their services. Faced with cost containment pressures, competition from store-front emergency rooms, and the need to develop new services, hospitals are learning the importance of developing a communications strategy that melds with marketing. Hospitals in the forefront of these new marketing efforts are learning how to plan and manage their image and reputation, because they know:

- Occupancy rate is a function of reputation.
- Image can influence the cost of borrowing.
- Image helps differentiate one hospital from another.
- A good reputation facilitates "certificate of needs" by local influentials.
- A reputation is an indicator of management effectiveness.
- Reputation and performance feed off one another.

The first thing a hospital must do is establish its goals and objectives. What does it want to be known for in the community: quality care? state-of-the-art facilities? professionalism? friendliness? Once the senior management and board determine those goals, quantitative research must be undertaken to determine:

FIGURE A-1   Innovative Posters Designed to Grab Audience for the Cincinnati Ballet

Source: Courtesy Cincinnati Ballet.

FIGURE A-2

1. percent of people in the community who choose the hospital as their first choice.
2. attributes that people associate with the hospital.
3. how the hospital compares with its competition.

At this point, targets can be established for name recognition, preference, and reputation. For example, "name recognition of our hospital in its core service area will be raised from 79 percent in 1983 to 85 percent by 1985" might be one target. Communications strategies would then be developed to achieve those targets. Constituencies would then be designated and communication programs targeted at them. In the above example, the community at large would be the targeted constituency. Other constituencies that could impact goals might include the medical staff, employees, patients, and even the media.

Since many hospitals have high occupancy rates, image and reputation strategies in some cases would be "protect" strategies. Also, strategies would be developed to determine new products and their likelihood of community acceptance. Examples here might include introducing a cancer care center, a sports medicine program, a fitness program for industry, even a hospice. Patients would be high on the priority list of constituencies not only because they are prime customers (via their doctors) but because more and more they are beginning to make decisions on what hospital they use for elective and outpatient care, and also because they "tell the stories" about a hospital that result in the hospital's reputation and image. Since their main interface is with hospital employees, those employees also become a key constituency in the image development process.[26]

Good research will keep the hospital from marketing services to segments of the population that are unfamiliar with the hospital, for example, or from selling the hospital as an institution to people who are regular patients. And since many hospitals refrain from advertising, good communications becomes the key to marketing.

CHEAP TRICKS: COST-EFFECTIVE COMMUNICATIONS

Usually the cost of communications activities for any organization is substantially below marketing and advertising. Communications activities have been traditionally labor intensive, with software expenses far outweighing hardware. This may be changing as the new communications technologies such as cable television, interactive video, direct satellite broadcast, and other technologies are introduced. These innovations will be expensive but in some cases will be offset by productivity increases and reduction in such areas as travel budgets.

In the not-for-profit sector especially, there are needs for cost-effective communications approaches.

The Minimal Program.　In most offices the basic public-information tools are already present—the *telephone*, for example. With a telephone you can deal with the media, and talk with constituencies. Ann Wexler, the highly regarded constituency builder in the Carter White House, had two basic tools: a telephone and a phone list. With these simple tools she put together large coalitions of disparate groups whose special interests could be addressed. The next most important tool is a *mailing list*. You can start small—with a list that can be photocopied on gummed labels. If your office has a combination word processor/microcomputer, you can store the mailing list right in the computer and spit out lists and individually typed letters by the score. Software programs are available to keep the list current. The mailing list should contain a list of key publics or constituencies: members, officers, media contacts, prospects, affiliated organizations, and so on. The next step is to develop *basic written material*: a short speech on the organization and its goals and activities and also a pamphlet with the same information. Next a *graphic symbol* for the organization should be adopted. You can employ the likes of a Raymond Loewy, as Exxon did for its logo, or you can find a class of design students and offer a small prize for the winning symbol. As you begin to grow, a *newsletter* becomes important. Many organizations have found that tremendous costs can be saved by blending good graphics and copy and using an inexpensive format of newsprint. The savings over offset paper can be substantial. Finally you might consider developing a small exhibit. You can buy table-top panels with velcro patches for a couple of hundred dollars which allow you to change the exhibit regularly, depending on audience and use.

Slide Shows.　An organization that needs to expand its outreach efforts or has a somewhat difficult-to-describe program should develop a slide show to take around. A good amateur photographer can put together a slide show that can be scripted for various publics: service clubs, clients, employees. The show should be no longer than twenty minutes—with pictures matched to words. Emphasis should be on people pictures. If you have a couple of hundred dollars to play with, a better approach might be to tell your story through taped interviews with your staff or clients. Do the interviews, then have them edited (a radio reporter in your community could do this), add narration where needed, and buy a tape synchronizer/recorder that automatically advances the slides to mesh with the tape. Good professional photographers cost anywhere from seventy-five to five hundred dollars a day plus expenses. The payoff is that you will hold your audience's attention and interest.

Special Events.　A new wing to a hospital, the arrival of an important person to speak at your organization's annual dinner, new quarters, an anniversary—all are good excuses for special-events publicity that keeps your organization visible. The Chicago Lung Association, an organization that emphasizes special events not only for publicity but for fund raising as well, has held cocktail parties in a toy store at Christmas, sponsored dances and bowl-a-thons, and involved visiting celebrities for its special events.

TOLL-FREE NUMBERS.   If your organization can afford as little as fifty to seventy-five dollars per month, it can share a toll-free number for sending out materials to interested callers. For a few hundred dollars a month it can have its own toll-free line, which gives people instant access to your organization on a regular basis. For around a hundred dollars your organization can install a phone attachment that will keep track of calls when no one is in the office, or give out a message.

SPEAKERS BUREAU.   A major urban utility that was being attacked by con-sumer and environmental organizations quite regularly decided that the best way to get its message across was to use company volunteers who would be available to speak on a number of topics to community groups. This approach can be effective; it provides the opportunity for give and take with an audience. It is a labor-intensive activity, however, and can take up many evenings for those involved. A booklet listing speakers and topics can be distributed for groups to pick and choose from.

PUBLIC-SERVICE ANNOUNCEMENTS.   Many radio and television stations reg-ularly run community calendars, which will announce your event or activity. Others will run public-service messages varying in length from ten to sixty seconds. All you have to do is provide copy that can be read by an announcer. For television a single slide with your logo or a graphic can be provided with a brief announcement. Some stations will provide free videotaping time for organizations to do public-service announcements.

PUBLIC-AFFAIRS PROGRAMMING.   Many radio and TV stations run weekly public-affairs shows, call-in shows, and the like. Find out what shows each station carries and talk with the producer of that show, attempting to interest them in your organization's activities. Relate your organization to current events or show how your organization is involved in a subject of current or continuing interest. The Federal Communications Commission has for many years re-quired stations to do a certain amount of public-affairs programming. Those restrictions are being lifted, and the future of these types of shows is unclear.

AWARDS PROGRAMS.   Awards are an excellent vehicle for developing pub-licity and goodwill. Stage annual awards programs. Set out categories and rules for nomination in a brochure. Encourage submissions that contain testimonial materials. Hold a luncheon, invite a prominent local speaker, and pass out awards. Good press coverage is possible. This is an especially effective tech-nique for organizations that are frequently involved in conflict-oriented activi-ties. It provides a chance for the group to show its more positive features.

NATIONALLY PRODUCED MATERIALS.   An organization that is part of a larger national or regional association should produce materials that complement, not duplicate, national publicity activities.

TELEVISION PROGRAMMING.   Under this topic would be such things as movies and videotapes. Movies are a good investment because they can be edited for many different formats. Movies can be used for public-service announcements or advertisements. Shorter versions can be put together for different audiences. And most places have 16 mm sound projectors available. Movies also provide a distinct credibility that videotape is now only starting to match. Videotape, however, is coming more and more into use. Also production costs can be cheaper—editing and mixing of sounds and picture are easier and special effects are dazzling. For television presentation one preferred method is to shoot the program on film and then edit and finish it on tape. The expected boom in cable television in the near future plus new and more compact equipment should make videotape the more common tool in the future. In many medium and smaller markets, it is also quite possible to show movies over local television or develop a program for public television.

SPECIAL-TOPIC BROCHURES.   Organizations have many different types of publics to deal with, so it is important to put together a standard message that can be tailored to the interests of different constituencies via separate brochures.

PRESS SUPPORT.   General information about your organization—a list of key officials and phone numbers and background on them—is very helpful to news desks at papers or radio and TV stations. An occasional visit to the news desks also puts a name with a face and can pay off down the road.

HOLLYWOOD.   If you have ever read Ben Stein's insightful book on Hollywood TV script writers, *The View from Sunset Boulevard*, you might consider at some point giving your most glib employee a bagful of money and sending him or her to Hollywood to buy drinks and chat with writers for the major TV comedy and dramatic shows. The issues your organization faces, the types of things it does, what it is trying to accomplish might be best communicated to the American public through commercial TV. Personally, I think that much about the independent sector and "values" can be transmitted to the public via the arts—theater, music, television. Offbeat ventures such as photo exhibits, dramatic radio programming, and touring musical companies carrying a message offer a field ripe for exploitation.

NOTES

1. David Herold, "Historical Perspectives on Government Communication," in *Informing the People*, Lewis M. Helm *et al.*, eds. (New York: Longman, 1981), pp. 14–21.

2. American Institute for Political Communication, *The Federal Government-Daily Press Relationship*, quoted in *Informing the People*, ed. Lewis M. Helm et al. (New York: Longman, Inc., 1981), p. 32.

3. Ray Eldon Heibert, "A Model of the Government Communications Process," in *Informing the People*, pp. 8–13.

4. Stephen Hess, *The Washington Reporters* (Washington, D.C.: Brookings Institution, 1981), p. 126.

5. Edward Cowan, "Problems with Government Advocacy: A Journalist's View," in *Informing the People*, pp. 38–50.

6. Dom Bonafede, "The Selling of the Executive Branch—Public Information or Promotion?" *National Journal*, June 27, 1981, p. 1153.

7. James Coates, "Reagan Team Hits 'Wasteful' U.S. Publicity," *Chicago Tribune*, April 21, 1981.

8. See Hedrick Smith, "Coping with Congress," *New York Times Magazine*, August 9, 1981, p. 12; and Sidney Blumenthal, "Marketing the President," *New York Times Magazine*, September 13, 1981, p. 42.

9. See Lewis M. Helm, "Public Affairs Proposal Points to Restricted Activity," *Federal Times*, November 3, 1980, p. 12; and Kenneth H. Rabin, "The Government PIO in the '80s," *Public Relations Journal*, December 1979, pp. 21–23.

10. Comptroller General's Report to the Committee on Governmental Affairs, "Difficulties in Evaluating Public Affairs Government-Wide and at the Department of Health, Education, and Welfare," LCD 79-405, January 18, 1979, p. 1.

11. See Joseph Nocera, "How to Make the Front Page," *Washington Monthly*, pp. 12–23.

12. News release, U.S. Department of Labor, Washington, D.C., USDL 81-225, May 4, 1981.

13. "Public Information in Government: Some Contrasting Views," *Management*, summer 1980, pp. 9–11.

14. See note 10.

15. See "City of Houston Parks Department" in *1980 Silver Anvil Winners, Index and Summaries* (New York: Public Relations Society of America, 1981), p. 27.

16. See "Committee for Safe Roads with Fleishman-Hillard, Inc." in *1980 Silver Anvil Winners*, p. 35.

17. See *Citizen Participation Handbook for Public Officials and Other Professionals Serving the Public*, 3rd ed. (Laramie, Wyo.: Institute for Participatory Planning, 1978).

18. See Michael P. Mokwa, "Government Marketing: An Inquiry into Theory, Process and Perspective"; Dale D. Achabal and Robert W. Backoff, "An Innovative Adoption Perspective for Marketing in the Government"; Kenneth L. Bernhardt, "Consumer Research in the Federal Government"; George Tesar, "The Role of Marketing in the Introduction of Consumer Products by Government"; and John R. Kerr et al., "Program Planning and Evaluation: A Citizen-Oriented Approach," in *Government Marketing: Theory and Practice*, by Michael P. Mokwa and Steven E. Permut, (New York: Praeger, 1981).

19. James F. Beré, "Business Must Define Its Philanthropic Goals," *Chicago Sun-Times*, August 18, 1981.

20. Philip Kotler and Sidney Levy, "Broadening the Concept of Marketing," *Journal of Marketing* 33 (1969):10–15.

21. Philip Kotler, *Marketing for Nonprofit Organizations* (Englewood Cliffs, N.J.: Prentice-Hall, 1982), pp. 381–82.

22. "Lesley College with Interpreting Institutions" in *1980 Silver Anvil Winners*, p. 13.

23. See Don Bates, "Eleven Signal Trends in Not-for-Profit Public Relations," *Public Relations Journal*, November 1982, pp. 22–23.

24. Alan R. Andreasen, "Nonprofits: Check your Attention to Customers," *Harvard Business Review*, May-June 1982, p. 105.

25. Dale Keiger, "Marketing Turns around Cincinnati Ballet," *Advertising Age*, July 5, 1982, p. 20MW.

26. I am very indebted to Terrence Rynne of Westlake Community Hospital for his insights and work in the area of hospital strategy, upon which this material is based.

Public Relations Emergency Plans

Following are two examples of emergency plans: the first prepared by National Gypsum Company of Dallas, Texas and the second from Airco, Inc., of Montvale, New Jersey.

PUBLIC RELATIONS IN AN EMERGENCY: NATIONAL GYPSUM COMPANY POLICY

It is most difficult to maintain good public and press relations when an accident or emergency occurs. In such a situation there are persistent, seemingly unrelenting inquiries from the press, the community, business associates, government agencies, friends and relatives of employees, and other interested people. Fatigue and tension can cause short tempers and lapses in efficiency. Unless great care is taken, months of good public relations work can be undone in a single day.

A delicate balance must be achieved between refusing to answer questions and giving hasty and ill-conceived responses. On the one hand the Company can be accused of withholding vital information. On the other, partial or unclear answers can result in unfavorable stories and false rumors.

However, providing good emergency services for the media can earn friends for the Company regardless of the nature and scope of the problem.

National Gypsum Company has an excellent safety record. Thorough precautions have been taken to eliminate accidents. The Company does not anticipate any serious incidents, but it must have a plan for dealing with such contingencies or it may well be considered incompetent and poorly managed.

The following Emergency Operations and Communications Policy is adaptable to any National Gypsum unit with logical modifications determined by the nature of the specific segment:

An authorized spokesperson, usually the unit's Senior Executive, should be desig-

210

nated in advance to represent management on the scene and to be responsible for the implementation of this program;

If there is a person other than the Senior Executive who is in charge of the unit's public relations program, he or she should automatically assume the responsibilities of Press Officer. If not, a Press Officer for emergencies should be designated in advance by the Senior Executive;

The Senior Executive should assure that the Division CEO, the Group Vice President and Corporate Public Relations Office are immediately informed of the nature of the emergency and that they are kept current on all developments for the duration of the problem;

Factual information on all personnel injuries should be given to the employees' families as soon as the Senior Executive has confirmed the facts;

This information should not be given to the media, if at all possible, until after the families have been notified;

The Press Officer should service the media with information as soon as facts can be verified and within the parameters of Company policy;

No Company employee should speculate on anything that has not been positively and officially verified, such as the cause of an accident;

The Company should take the initiative in informing the press and local government authorities if they are not already aware of the situation;

Reporters and photographers should be permitted access to Company property when, and only when, their safety can be absolutely guaranteed. If there is any question regarding the safety of the site, the media should be serviced with a steady stream of current information and advised that they will be permitted to visit the scene when the situation has been stabilized;

No Company employee should release any damage estimates or construction costs until they are officially assessed and issued by the Senior Executive;

The Press Officer, and all Company personnel, should emphasize to the media National Gypsum's safety record and the continuing precautions taken to avoid accidents;

The Press Officer should utilize all means of communication to provide factual information to offset rumors or misstatements;

The Company should inform, as quickly as possible, all interested publics including employees' families, shareholders, the financial community, suppliers, customers, members of the "affect community," and, of course, all media.

WHAT CONSTITUTES AN EMERGENCY?

An emergency is a situation or event that may be interpreted in a manner harmful to the Company; that is subject to coverage by the news media in a way that is not in the interests of National Gypsum Company. Such emergencies include, but are not limited to:

A plant accident involving serious injuries or fatalities;

Any event that requires the assistance of such outside agencies as police, fire or medical;

An explosion or fire;

Death of a Company executive from causes that appear to be related to his or her official duties;

A riot or civil disorder on or near Company property;

An Act of God.

In short, any incident, situation or happening that focuses unusual media and public attention on the Company, must be considered a public relations emergency.

EMERGENCY PROCEDURES

Immediately upon awareness of the emergency, the Senior Executive, who is the executive in charge, should alert the designated Press Officer. Each of these people should appoint substitutes to back them up in case they are unavailable when an emergency occurs.

The Senior Executive should confirm that the police, fire department, etc., have been properly alerted and then inform the Division CEO and the Group Vice President.

The Press Officer should contact Corporate Public Relations. If the situation warrants, a member of that department will proceed immediately to the location to assist in press relations and to provide counsel when required.

Press Headquarters.   Each unit should designate two locations to serve as central media information points in case of a serious emergency. Each location should be equipped with a number of telephones and adequate office equipment. They may, of course, be facilities that are normally used for regular business purposes.

If the emergency is centered in or near Area #1, then the alternate press location should be utilized. Employees should be informed of these plans in advance so that they are able to direct reporters.

At least two secretaries should be assigned to the Press Officer to take calls from media people whether or not a press headquarters is established. All calls should be listed if the Press Officer is unavailable to take them and he should return them as promptly as possible.

Press Relations.   Upon notification of the emergency the Press Officer should assess available information and determine if a Press Headquarters is required and, if so, at which of the pre-designated locations it should be established. The seriousness of the situation influences the need for such a facility, which can help keep media people out of the way of rescue personnel and facilitate the accurate, prompt delivery of information to the media by the Press Officer.

The Press Officer should maintain contact with all media personnel for the duration of the emergency; assure that they remain in approved, safe areas; and issue all pertinent information consistent with the Company's policy as quickly as possible.

The Press Officer should discuss the text of announcements, releases, and, whenever possible, the answers to questions with the Director of Corporate Public Relations.

When the Senior Executive determines that it is completely safe, the Press Officer should escort media people to the area in which the emergency occurred and explain the event from the Company's perspective.

Safety equipment, such as hard hats, should be readily available and provisions made in advance for distribution to members of the press as required.

The Senior Executive should be available for interviews as frequently as possible. In his absence, other Company spokespeople should substitute.

Regardless of the amount of coverage made individually by members of the press, the Press Officer should constantly obtain facts as they occur for the purpose of issuing the Company's own releases (after discussion with the Director of Corporate Public Relations).

In cases where statements relating to the emergency are made by persons outside the Company, such as government officials, the media should be invited to request the Company's comments in order to avoid incorrect estimates being made public without challenge.

The same full cooperation, within the requirements of safety, that is accorded to the print media should be given to radio and television representatives.

COMMUNICATIONS WITH OTHER PUBLICS. Depending upon the nature and duration of the emergency, special measures may be required to communicate with employees. Spot announcements on local radio stations, newspaper ads, and telephone calls on an organized basis are devices which may be used. Radio spots might be used also to reassure employees' families if the emergency occurs during the workday.

If the problem is a severe one, the Company might want to contact key community leaders by telephone as quickly as possible so that they have the facts for those who might question them. If such phone contact is necessary, the Senior Executive should assign specific personnel to make the calls.

All communication with shareholders and members of the financial community is the responsibility of Corporate Public Relations.

WHEN THE SMOKE CLEARS

A story never ends when the emergency is over. The follow-up can be of great importance to National Gypsum Company.

Stories should be developed and placed regarding the Company's effort, to aid victims; reconstruction; future safeguards; actions to thank the community for its help and other activities that demonstrate the Company's concern for its employees and the public.

A letter to employees reassuring them about future operations might be valuable.

Your list of community leaders and organizations might be sent positive follow-up material. The same or a similar mailing might go to your lists of customers and suppliers.

Material might be provided to Corporate for distribution to shareholders and members of the financial community.

It is advisable that, immediately after the emergency, the unit public relations executive discuss with Corporate Public Relations a complete, coordinated follow-up program.

AIRCO, INC.:
PURPOSE OF THIS GUIDE

This booklet is designed to help you cooperate with press representatives during emergencies, and avoid the spread of incorrect information. It does not alter any existing internal emergency plans currently established in the divisions and subsidiaries.

Uncooperative dealings with the press in an emergency situation or disaster at your plant or laboratory can be very costly to the company—in terms of reputation, credibility and employee and community relations—*for a long period of time*. It is vital that you be prepared to deal with the press in emergencies, such as on-the-job fatalities and serious injuries, explosions and fires, natural disasters (storms, floods), environmental incidents (spills, pollution) or major accidents involving company vehicles.

Here is a checklist of the most important points to remember when working with the press:

1. Establish one authorized spokesperson and, perhaps, an informed backup person.
2. Act promptly; speed is important.
3. Make the press representatives understand that you want to be helpful and cooperative in meeting their needs.
4. Do not speculate; make every effort to obtain the facts quickly, and be certain they are accurate.
5. If the press wants additional information, call corporate Communications in Montvale and your divisional Communications group. We are here to help you, and can offer advice in dealing with the press in troublesome areas. After-hours phone numbers are listed on the Emergency Procedure poster, which should be prominently displayed in your facility.
6. Notify your key plant and office personnel of all facts to keep them informed and help you dispel unfounded rumors.

Generally, the press will want—*and quickly*—answers to the following questions:

- **What Happened?** Describe the incident with as much detail as needed for understanding. Highly technical descriptions are not required, nor really wanted by the press. You should say how many explosions occurred, whether or not there was a fire, a wall or floor collapse, or if anyone was injured or killed in a fall or some other accident.
- **Who Was Involved?** *Only after notification of the victims' families* provide the press with each person's name, occupation, age and home address, and the *general nature of each injury* (burns, broken leg or back, *if known for certain*—otherwise, refer the press to medical sources). Also, supply the press with information about your people who were instrumental in rescue attempts, or who quickly reacted to emergency procedures, such as sounding an alarm, smothering a fire or closing a critical valve.

    Keep in mind that the press is helping *you* by notifying the families of all employees who were NOT injured; therefore, relieving them of their anxieties. TV and radio—because of reporting speed—can play a key role in performing this task—but, once again, *provide information on the injured or killed only after notifying the families!*
- **When Did It Happen?** Try to pinpoint the time within the nearest half-hour (shortly after 8:30 AM, or just prior to 11:00 PM). If there was a series of events, attempt to place a time on each (an explosion and fire shortly after 8:30 AM, followed by a second explosion approximately one hour later).
- **Where?** Identify the section of the plant where the accident took place (on the production line, an external pipeline, the compressor building, the shipping department). By pinpointing the area, the relatives of employees working in other sections of the plant will be relieved of concern.
- **What Was the Cause?** This is usually a difficult question to answer immediately, and *you must not speculate*. Explain to the press that you have not yet been able to determine the cause and that a thorough investigation is being made.
- **How Much Damage?** Explain that it is impossible to give a dollar estimate of the damage without careful and thorough assessment. Perhaps you can discuss the damage from the standpoint of how long you expect the facility to be shut down (only after you have had time to determine this by a thorough discussion with your engineers, suppliers and management). If appropriate, you can mention the availability of backup production from some other plant to meet the interim needs of customers.

Some questions you can expect and how to answer them:

Q. "What happened at your plant?"
A. "An oxygen line ruptured, causing the product to vent into the atmosphere. The oxygen is dissipating rapidly, and there is no danger to the surrounding neighborhood."
Q. "Was anyone injured or killed?"
A. "We have had injuries, and the plant emergency squad and local ambulance corps responded immediately. At this time we are unable to provide specific details."
Q. "Do you produce a toxic substance that could endanger the health of residents?"
A. "This is an air separation plant that takes the air we breathe and separates the major elements—nitrogen, oxygen and argon—into purified form for various applications by hospitals and by metalworking and metalproducing industries. There is nothing in these products that could be harmful to people."
Q. "How many employees do you have at this site?"
A. "Airco has 25 plant operators and some 40 distribution people at this location."

Q. "Do you know what caused the accident?"

A. "Not at this time. We have an expert team currently investigating the cause of the accident, and hope to come up with an answer soon."

CAN THE PRESS VISIT
THE SITE?

Press representatives and photographers might ask to view the damaged property. They will be insistent, and you must be patient in dealing with this request. There are certain questions and rules to help you determine your reaction:

1. Is there any personal danger; are there hot embers, escaping gas, possibility of walls or the roof collapsing, etc.

2. Could a visitor inadvertently disturb evidence that would hamper official investigations (insurance, safety, police and fire officials).

3. Assuming you can take the time, the area is safe and all investigations are completed, can you personally escort the press on a tour of the damaged facility. (Warn photographers that flash pictures cannot be taken due to concentrations of combustible materials, if this is true.)

4. Can you suggest an alternative to a tour. You might use a photographic blowup or a floor-plan sketch of the facility to explain, with a pointer, what happened where.

5. Can you assemble those people who performed heroic acts, so the press can interview them. Inform your people (prior to the interview) about the facts of the situation to avoid discrepancies between your carefully considered statements and those by people who may not be completely up to date.

Note: Keep in mind that you have no control of photographers who wish to take pictures from an airplane or from a point adjacent to Airco's property.

OTHER IMPORTANT
CONSIDERATIONS

PRESSROOM.   If possible, and a major disaster is involved, try to provide a "pressroom" for the reporters to use as a base of operations. Desks, chairs and telephones should be available. Supply coffee if a long waiting period develops.

PRESS RELEASE.   If a major disaster (having national interest) is involved, representatives of the Communications Department (corporate and/or divisional) should be at the site to assist management in working with the press and in the preparation and clearance of news releases for wide dissemination.

PLANT INFORMATION.   Have a facility fact sheet handy to avoid scurrying about for information during the emergency. Include data such as site acreage, number of employees, products made and their major uses, plant square footage, number of trucks, number of years at location, etc.

ABOUT YOUR SWITCHBOARD.   Make sure your telephone operators have a good knowledge of emergency procedures and are cooperative. They should know where to reach the authorized spokesperson *at all times*. Instruct the operators not to refer inquiries to unauthorized personnel.

IF THE SITUATION IS MISHANDLED

An example of what can happen if an emergency situation is mishandled will be helpful in guiding your actions. This is an actual case history:

Seven people were overcome, one seriously, by noxious fumes in a chemical plant. Nobody informed the press for three hours, and as the people were checked into hospitals, reporters learned of the accident and called the company. The replies were: "No comment at this time."—"When we have definite information we'll call you." The press was forced to piece together a story that was totally incorrect and very harmful to the company. The TV and radio newscasts and the daily papers included references to "blasts," "explosions," "burns"—all not true. When the company asked the media to run a correct story, the reply was "The news value no longer exists."

Some important don'ts to keep in mind:

Don't guess at the cause.
Don't guess at a person's injuries.
Don't attempt to estimate the dollar damage.
Don't say, "No comment."—"I'm not allowed to talk."—"I can't tell you anything."—"I don't have time to talk to you."—"The darn thing blew sky-high."

Remember!

If you don't know the answer, say you don't know and that you will obtain the information as soon as possible.

Keep a list of all media people who call you—their names, phone numbers and press affiliations—so that return calls can be made quickly.

Once there's a problem, a good press cannot be expected. What we aim for is tactful, honest and speedy cooperation with the media so that factual information is disseminated.

Whether you cooperate with the press or not, a story will be prepared; your responsibility is to make sure the information is accurate.

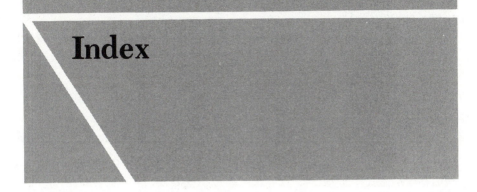

Index